DR CHRIS COWLEY

FACE TO FACE WITH EVIL

CONVERSATIONS WITH IAN BRADY

JB

JOHN BLAKE

Published by Metro Publishing
an imprint of John Blake Publishing Ltd
3 Bramber Court, 2 Bramber Road,
London W14 9PB, England

www.johnblakepublishing.co.uk

First published in paperback in 2011

ISBN: 978 1 84454 981 8

British Library Cataloguing-in-Publication Data:

A catalogue record for this book is available from the British Library.

Design by www.envydesign.co.uk

Printed in Great Britain by CPI Bookmarque, Croydon CR0 4TD

1 3 5 7 9 10 8 6 4 2

© Text copyright Dr Chris Cowley

Papers used by John Blake Publishing are natural, recyclable
products made from wood grown in sustainable forests.
The manufacturing processes conform to the environmental
regulations of the country of origin.

DEDICATION

I would like to dedicate this book to my father, Ken, who has been a constant support and supplied me with many rare resource materials; also to Michelle and the editorial team at John Blake Publishing who kept me focused, and to my friend Rich for his practical help and ongoing positive influence.

CONTENTS

Introduction   xi

PART I: THE DYNAMICS AND CONSEQUENCES OF SERIAL MURDER

Chapter 1: Killing for Kicks   3
Chapter 2: Recreational Murder Dynamics:
    Multiple Persona, Multiple Crimes   19
Chapter 3: Ashworth Hospital   79

PART II: SHATTERED LIVES: HOMICIDAL INFECTION

Chapter 4: Profiling and Victimology: Swimming
    with Sharks   93
Chapter 5: Murder and Witness Dynamics:
    See No Evil   137
Chapter 6: Communication Gulag   167
Chapter 7: Gender Profiling   193

PART III: VANISHING POINTS

Chapter 8: The 'Special' Hospitals   223
Chapter 9: Motiveless Murder   231
Chapter 10: Afterthoughts   263

Appendix A   273
Appendix B   277

References   279
Bibliography   287

AUTHOR'S NOTE: All italic quotations, unless otherwise referenced, are directly transcribed from interviews and letters exchanged with Ian Brady (dated when relevant). Quotations from published literature are acknowledged and dated in the author–date format – e.g. '(Norris 1990)' – which the reader may then follow up by referring to the reference section at the end. There is also further reading in the Bibliography.

INTRODUCTION

Criminal-profiling techniques that have been designed to identify and apprehend the perpetrators of serial homicide have almost always been based on a retrospective analysis of evidence gathered from crime scenes. In almost all cases, the development of a profile occurs during the investigation of crimes that have already been committed, after the event. Furthermore, profiles are often developed *after* the perpetrator has been apprehended. While this might offer some insight as to the factors that might need to be considered in future cases, this is obviously rather too late for the people who have already become victims.

The use of criminal profiling as a pre-emptive preventative measure has been under-researched. In cases of potential serial killers, these people need to be identified and apprehended *before* they embark on a cycle of murders. But is this actually possible?

From comprehensive analysis of case studies, various predictors have been proposed that might enable us to identify potential serial killers and rapists.

Here are some of the most common factors that have been suggested in forensic psychology and criminology research as being possible relevant predictors of serial homicide:

- neurophysiological factors, e.g. genetic brain abnormalities;
- traumatic brain injuries, especially if there is a repeated history;
- psychological factors, especially anger/retaliatory behavioural dispositions;
- history of reactive/aggressive responses to negative life events;
- posttraumatic-stress disorders;
- parental deprivation during critical stages of early psychological development;
- history of cruelty to animals;
- chronic malnutrition;
- chronic drug/alcohol abuse.

This is by no means a conclusive list. Some of these do indeed come up regularly in the case profiles of a number of serial killers, but there are a lot of people who have a significant number of these factors in their histories who do not end up committing serial homicide, and there are also a lot of serial killers who show no history of any of them.

While lecturing as a general cognitive/behaviourist psychologist, my research interests began to gravitate towards criminological history and the psychology of forensic behavioural analysis. For the purposes of this book, this research was refined in order to develop an analysis of the dynamics and consequences of serial murder. My aim was not only to study the perspectives and psychology of people who kill, why they do it and what happens to them after they are caught, but also, where possible, to gather some insight concerning the victims. Without victims, obviously, murder cycles would not and could not happen. Most victims of serial killers are strangers, randomly selected by the killer; the victim simply completes the equation. There are some rare cases, however, in which the victim plays an active part in their destruction. It was important to include research in this area if I wanted to develop an integrated picture of the full dynamics of modern serial homicide.

Understandably, but not terribly scientifically, people looking for answers in their search to identify serial killers are searching for a *single* explanatory factor. Something that absolutely guarantees that an individual is going to commit capital crimes. An 'X factor' that, if it could be identified, would allow us to say with confidence that *that* is the catalyst that will start a murder cycle. The hunt for this elusive factor, I believe, is a nonstarter. There are as many reasons for such crimes as there are people committing them. With all case histories, we can see a multitude of potential triggers, and, even if by some miracle we did manage to identify this mysterious catalyst before any murders were committed, how would we proceed then? Locking up individuals *before* they have killed because we think we *know* they are going to reeks of an Orwellian 'pre-crime' law-enforcement nightmare which I hope I will never have to bear witness to. However, I believe that it is possible to identify and examine contributing factors using a multidisciplinary approach that will allow us to say with a certain degree of confidence this it is *possible* that an individual could be heading towards a serial-murder cycle. This will enable us, hopefully, to provide appropriate intervention and, just maybe, save some lives.

Many of the contributing factors to serial murder are discussed in this book. My own opinions as to their relative strengths and weaknesses will become apparent as you read. I make no claims to offer a definitive solution but perhaps can provide a starting point towards understanding the ever-escalating rise of serial crime.

Once serial killers have been captured and convicted, we have a whole new set of problems to address, the first being: What should we do with them? Many convicted serial killers in America and the Eastern world are executed, and this will certainly stop those particular individuals from killing again (although this is not always true, as I explain later). However, by executing them, we are eliminating opportunities to develop understanding and are effectively burying our heads in the sand while more and more killers emerge to destroy innocent lives. If we 'shoot the messenger', we are unlikely to find out what the message was.

After a number of years of careful negotiations, I managed to develop the opportunity to conduct a series of interviews and interactions with Ian Stewart Brady, the infamous 'Moors Murderer'. I knew I would be unlikely to get a chance like this again, so, no matter how problematic the research might be, it seemed essential for me to try. This is the central theme of this book. What such people can tell us is, I believe, very important. How could it not be?

PART I

THE DYNAMICS
AND CONSEQUENCES OF
SERIAL MURDER

CHAPTER ONE

KILLING FOR KICKS

The multiple killing of strangers is now unfortunately something of a frequent occurrence in contemporary society. Despite some notable exceptions, this was not always the case. Other than some incidents of religious persecution and political assassinations, in previous centuries serious crime within the general population was nearly always committed for monetary gain, quite literally to put food on the table or to gain the upper hand in war scenarios. Murder, when it happened within the general population who were not involved in fighting a war, was usually a peripheral by-product of robbery in order to eliminate witnesses. Killing was simply a matter of survival. Violent sex crimes were very rare. Rape was pointless because sex could be easily and cheaply obtained.

'Blue-collar' crimes were occasionally conducted because of greed or revenge, but more often than not they were simply a matter of necessity brought on by poverty and desperation. Rarely were they the product of obsession or homicidal sexual expression. Unusual or enigmatic sex murders before the end of the nineteenth century seem to have been conducted mainly by the aristocracy and the privileged sections of society who had the time, the resources and the imagination to develop dark obsessions. It is different now.

Author and academic Joel Norris cites the 1980s as being a pivotal decade in the evolution of serial killing. In 1984, the FBI declared that serial killing had become an epidemic, at least in America (Norris 1997), with Europe following close behind. At this point in history, pretty much everyone could count on having some kind of a roof over their head and no longer had to worry too much about starving to death (in the Western world, anyway). This was when serial sex crimes/murders spread out into wider society and, unfortunately, turned into a regular feature of modern life.

The period between 1960 and 1980 appears to have been a transitional phase in criminology, which is illustrated by the emergence of a number of high-profile cases. In England, there were a number of killers who define this period in criminal history: Peter Sutcliffe, a.k.a. the 'Yorkshire Ripper', was one notable case; Dennis Nilsen's multiple murders in London are also associated with this period; but Ian Brady and Myra Hindley's Moors Murders in the 1960s are perhaps the most infamous and influential occurrences of a new type of criminality and revealed a new type of predator.

ANALYSIS BY HYPOTHESIS

Although this book is principally about Ian Brady and my interactions with him, I have also included a number of case studies, both English and American, which I believe offer reflection on Brady's motivations and beliefs, both now and at the time of his crimes. When serial killers talk about other serial killers, it affords them a way in which they can reflect on their own murders without being subject to further criminal charges or unwelcome probing by insensitive psychiatrists. Brady calls the process of projection of motivation and intent *'analysis by hypothesis'*. This is extremely painstaking and frustrating research to undertake and evaluate, but, once I started interacting with Brady and visiting him, I soon came to the conclusion that this was the best and perhaps only way to proceed. Brady had never talked in any depth about his crimes and convictions in nearly half a century, why would he start with me? So, for the first two or three years, getting him to talk to me with fluidity was almost impossible.

He sat facing me, blinking at me through his cataracts, his only interest being what I could do for him; his psyche remained firmly entrenched behind a solid defensive brick wall. Brady himself elaborated on this when he was discussing another serial killer, the infamous Ted Bundy, who made the tactical mistake of keeping all of his secrets very close to his chest, repeatedly firing or replacing his lawyers, stupidly turning down a plea bargain for life sentences rather than execution, and ending up dead as a consequence of all these mistakes. Brady comments on Bundy's psychology and his refusal to talk in detail about most of his crimes right up until the end, by which time, of course, it was too late: *'For the killer to ever reveal comprehensively his personal, psychologically deepest experiences is tantamount to psychic suicide; like blowing his brains out from the inside'* (2001).

Brady was, and is, in a similar situation: unsurprisingly,

he hardly trusts anybody at all, and initially that included me. On more than one occasion early on in my research, I wondered if perhaps I could just be wasting my time. At first, he would tell me nothing apart from very superficial comments, gossip about current affairs and how horrible life in prison is for him; and, having visited there a number of times, I can certainly vouch for that. However, little by little, letter after letter, visit after visit, he finally decided that it would do him little harm to reveal more significant information about himself, about his crimes, about his current circumstances, and that maybe this could be productive for both of us.

After exchanging a number of letters, Brady wrote to me asking me to visit him at Liverpool's Ashworth Hospital for the criminally insane, where he is currently detained. In my early visits (the details of which I describe later), both of us were very cautious, sizing each other up like rival chess players contemplating a significant match. But eventually we both realised that we had some common ground and could have an ongoing dialogue that might be useful for both of us, albeit in different ways. I wanted to research the forensic psychology of serial killing; he wanted me to understand the conditions in the hospital. So we both had different agendas at first, but quickly established an information exchange, and a *quid pro quo* dynamic emerged. I would help him out in what little ways were possible for me (basically, sending him things that might make life a little more bearable in the hospital: interesting news items, pens, music tapes and suchlike), and he would tell me things in exchange. Our dialogue went onwards from there in directions I never could have anticipated.

Brady is a convicted serial killer of several victims. He will never be released from incarceration. So what had he left to lose? Not much. This is what I believed initially, as he had made that very clear to me in his early letters, but, as it turned out later, I realised that he may indeed have rather a lot to lose. I quickly found myself walking a tightrope between compassion for the lives of the people he had destroyed and compassion for Brady himself, who had destroyed his own life in the process. I decided, early on, to adopt an objective and (hopefully) scientific approach, just to present the facts and leave it mainly up to the reader to draw their own conclusions.

Analysis by hypothesis has strengths and weaknesses. Discussing American cases with him (the, at that time, unidentified 'Green River Killer' Gary Ridgway, Ted Bundy and others we will meet along the way) was productive, in that America has the highest proportion of serial killers in the Western world, more than any other country, so there is a lot of data to work with, cases that Brady is very familiar with and occasionally identified with. Discussing British cases was more limited in terms of the information that was available in the public domain, while simultaneously being more useful because Brady had actually spent time with some of the more notorious British serial killers during his lifetime of incarceration. He had been in jail with a number of these people, so he could give me direct information from an insider's perspective.

I quickly ascertained that the main problem with discussing American cases with him, or anyone for that matter, is that the data that a researcher has access to is not terribly reliable: it is often fragmented and usually distorted either by the media – who sensationalise serial killings in an endless attempt to satisfy increasingly jaded public demands for an even more horrific case than the last one – or by the killers themselves who modify and censor the information they are prepared to reveal for a variety of reasons. One especially important reason why you have to treat conclusions based solely on American cases with caution is that they usually come from people on death row.

America is the only Western country that has not abolished capital punishment, so most of the information comes from people who have been condemned to death, and this is obviously going to influence the reliability and validity of anything that they might be prepared to reveal. While working through desperate last-ditch court appeals, the perpetrators of serial murders in America are quite literally fighting for their lives. So, for obvious reasons, they are unlikely to be especially forthcoming, and usually hang on to their secrets until – and often beyond – their execution, leaving the researcher only a limited retrospect opportunity to analyse their crimes. Why should they when faced with the following limited options?

- Lie and we will kill you;
- Tell the truth and we will kill you;
- Say nothing and we will kill you.

The odds are not exactly stacked in their favour; they are in a no-win situation. I can certainly understand this. For the most part, they have nothing to gain by talking about their crimes. With the 'Son of Sam' law – named after the 1970s Son of Sam murders committed by serial killer David Berkowitz, which states that no convicted criminal can benefit from the proceeds of any description or representation of their crimes – why on earth would they *want* to talk about them?

Ironically, in America, you have to be certified physically and mentally healthy before a death sentence will be carried out. In order to be hanged, electrocuted, gassed, poisoned or shot, depending on which state you are convicted in, you have to be healthy. Killing the healthy and sane is a confirmed legal precedent, which is why so many serial killers attempt to use insanity defences and claim all kinds of illnesses, which must be treated and cured before they can be executed. When facing such mind-boggling catch-22-style circumstances, it is no surprise that convicted perpetrators of serious crimes either do not want to talk about them or exaggerate them out of all proportion to the evidence.

On the whole, while it might be possible to get a few enigmatic comments from some American killers on death row, that is usually all you are going to get. Their ongoing appeals almost always inhibit them from talking in any useful depth, and the last people they will want to tell their secrets to are the police, hated prison officials, the press, psychologists, psychiatrists, lawyers or retired FBI agents who just want to go on TV talk shows and make a few dollars by discussing their valiant attempts to combat evil during discussion of their retrospective law-enforcement careers.

Once American 'gangplank' appeals (as they are called) have been exhausted in the federal Supreme Court, condemned serial killers might perhaps suggest that there are *other* murders that either have not been investigated or else have not been linked to them. They do this in order to tempt the authorities and orchestrate a stay of execution while an investigation can be conducted. Police want to clear their missing-persons case files or to identify bodies in the mortuary that are way past their bury-by date. The convicted serial killer on death row might state that they are able to close long-running cases by revealing new evidence. This is undoubtedly the very last chance they will get in order to save their lives, and is also perhaps the last chance that the relatives of the victims might have to achieve closure.

There are many thousands of unsolved missing-persons and murder cases. However, any advantages gained for the prisoner by adopting such a strategy are rather miserable. Once convicted and sentenced to death, prisoners may attempt to get a commutation of their death sentence to one of life without parole. Ian Brady and Myra Hindley were not sentenced to death – hanging was abolished in the United Kingdom while the Moors Murders case was being prepared – so technically Brady now has life without parole, which was the harshest sentence that could be passed at the time for crimes such as his.

Commutation of a death sentence to life without parole might appear to be a good exchange from an outside perspective, but for a condemned American prisoner this often does not seem an especially fortuitous turn of events. Many condemned prisoners in America do not even bother with their appeals after a while. They just give up. Life on 'close management' is so horrible and hopeless that many prisoners volunteer to abandon their appeals just to get the whole thing over with. 'Close management' is also known as 'source isolation'. Ian Brady is no stranger to this. I mentioned this in an early letter after I had visited him, a casual reference to the psychology of isolation. Brady shot back with:

> [Y]ou say YOU sometimes feel like Robinson Crusoe! ...
> Your world of intelligence, creativity, exams etc is on
> another planet than this. It must be quite an experience
> travelling and entering the orbit of this alternative

world of the apes. It must heighten your appreciation of the real world and sense of freedom, but also your apprehension that the species running this place are actually allowed to freely walk the streets [2003].

After visiting Brady at Ashworth and seeing what the place was like, I had to agree.

INSIDE THE CONCRETE BOX

Solitary confinement has been used historically as a punishment in prisons and most people who have experienced it are likely to agree that it is far worse than being physically assaulted. At least physical assault is over fairly quickly; a few bruises and a broken nose heal pretty fast. In most cases, solitary confinement in British prisons involves being locked in a concrete box for usually 23 hours a day with absolutely nothing to do. Symptoms from such externally imposed isolation often include anxiety, sensory illusions and time/perception distortions. Many prisoners who have experienced this for any significant length of time would simply rather be dead.

Some others, however, manage to sustain a brooding and escalating resolve to the effect that somebody *else* should be the one who ends up dead, or at the very least accountable in the end. Hope is extinguished and revenge is fermented. When many people realise that, because of their crimes, this is the best they can expect out of life, they have very little left to lose. Hope evaporates and many murderers kill again. 'If I am going to do life for two murders, I may as well do life for forty-two. Life is life, I really don't care' (Schaefer 1989). So any deterrent value goes straight out of the window and rehabilitation does not even come into the equation.

11

Ian Brady, imprisoned for life in the United Kingdom and therefore technically not having to deal with a prescribed date of execution, nevertheless might as well be on death row. His death sentence is operative just like that of any American prisoner contemplating execution. It is just taking a lot longer to be imposed. Pro-death-penalty advocates sometimes argue that, if a convicted killer is executed, we can be certain that they will not kill again; it is the 'ultimate deterrent'. This is sometimes but not always true (as I will discuss later).

Many prisoners who have active death warrants or life-without-parole sentences do, in fact, kill again, some for reasons that would seem ludicrous if they happened outside of jail. Quite often, they will continue killing even after they have been incarcerated. For example, in many American prisons, death row inmates are allowed to have a television set in their cell while they are awaiting execution, whereas in the general jail population or when under close management they are not. The matter of a TV is so serious that prisoners will murder other prisoners or guards for the sake of a television set. These are known as 'TVKs'. Mark Defriest (cited in London 1993), a Florida convict on close management (in a solitary cell without a television), reveals this:

> The matter of a TV set is so serious ... I will pause in my narrative to tell you just how serious it is. It is a killing matter ... Of all the prisoners on death row I know of 37 who are 'TVKs' ... One realizes that he must pay for his *Bugs Bunny* and *Road Runner* show with his life.

So life without parole offers very little hope. It is another

12

world altogether, a 'living' death sentence, which is what Brady essentially has. He told me: '*An execution lasting 40 years, and they want to drag it out for another 20*' (2004). This is what he is trying to deal with. He is one of the small handful of prisoners in the United Kingdom who are subject to the 'whole-life tariff'. He accepted this many years ago and has never bothered to play what would be a doomed charade by applying for parole. The death of John Straffen in 2007 (after he had spent 55 years in prison for a triple murder) now makes Brady possibly the longest-serving prisoner in the United Kingdom. Brady knows, and has accepted long ago, that he will never be released. Where would he go?

As far as American cases are concerned, for the very few who do retain hope and go for life without parole (and without a television set), this successful commutation to permanent imprisonment means that, initially at least, they are certainly not going to reveal any new information that may result in new convictions that could get them sent back to death row. In cases such as these, some prisoners suggest that they *may* have useful knowledge concerning further crimes while at the same time refusing to reveal what it is. The prosecution of serial killers is a legal minefield: one false step and the perpetrator goes free. This conundrum is a nightmare for anyone who is trying to study criminology effectively. The American penal system is a total can of worms. Nobody wins in the long run, and truth and enlightenment are almost always buried by the lethal dynamics of the situation.

The fact that Brady will never be released and therefore has pretty much nothing left to lose – and therefore no reason to cooperate or be receptive to any kind of approach – meant that my research would require a lot of patience, but it was certainly worth the effort.

LETHAL INJECTION: THE MECHANICS

I discussed the death penalty with Brady. I had been reading about lethal injection and how it is not the painless death that most people seem to assume it is. It is not like putting a sick animal to sleep, whereby the animal is simply given an overdose of anaesthetic and just drops dead in a couple of seconds. It could be as quick and 'easy' as that but this is not the case. The drugs used in American lethal-injection executions are not selected to cause a painless death. In fact, it seems to be the case that precisely the opposite is intended. The condemned are injected with a combination of industrial doses of highly acidic drugs. Each chemical has a pH value higher than six. The first, sodium thiopental, makes the person dizzy and their last words usually incoherent, if they can even remember what they intended to say. The second, pancuronium bromide (Pavulon is its proprietary name), paralyses breathing and movement, the person's lungs collapse, their last breath is expelled almost as if 'an elephant has sat on their chest' and they cannot take another (Rossi 2001).

At this point, the person cannot speak, breathe or move and appears to be dead (here, the witnesses often start leaving the execution chamber); but the person being executed remains very much alive. They are conscious and can still see, hear and feel. Next, intravenous lines are switched and they are injected with an industrial dose of potassium chloride, which induces a crunching heart attack.

The American Veterinary Association has condemned and banned the drugs that are employed to kill people for use in animal euthanasia due to the unnecessary suffering that occurs (Rossi 2001). The whole execution process takes 10–30 minutes, depending on whether or not they have to

14

do arterial cut-downs (without anaesthetic) in order to find suitable blood vessels needed for insertion of all the various needles. A sheet is then thrown over the person to save the witnesses from any unpleasantness that might occur from seeing the raw mechanics of the process.

As with all executions, there are all kinds of mistakes that can be made. They have 'blowouts', when the intravenous tubes block and have to be reinserted. It is very ugly and I cannot see how these procedures can be anything other than horribly painful and traumatic for everyone involved. Predictably, when questioned in the media, the prosecutors sidestep the issues by declaring that the possibility of regular 'execution glitches' acts as a further deterrent to capital crime. This simply is not true. Furthermore, the commonly held belief that the execution of a killer brings 'closure' for relatives of the victims is usually mistaken as well. Yes, the relatives of a victim who are mourning their death might gain a modicum of satisfaction that their killer is dead too, but by all accounts the hate and anger remain. But now they have no one to project it towards. In many cases, closure remains an elusive concept.

I discussed this with Brady. He referred to lethal injection as a *'luxury, unobtainable in this country. The mechanics of lethal injection? Whatever, it is less than forty years'* (2005). In an early exchange, he had said he might as well be *'hundreds of feet underground, buried, they can send a dumb waiter down to collect my bones'* (2003).

MAKING CONTACT

Many books on serial killers are written by retired FBI officers. Some are very well researched, others not so well (the ones that I found most useful are listed in the references). While I was researching material for a postgraduate course for law-enforcement operatives, I came across Brady's book *The Gates of Janus* (2001). This is half philosophy and half analysis of a number of cases, both British and American. While there are certainly some interesting case studies in American criminological history, the United Kingdom serial killers – some of whom Brady has met – seemed to me to be a lot more promising for research purposes. United Kingdom long-term prisoners are not living in the shadow of execution dynamics like most of their American counterparts are, and, when, like Brady, their crimes are so devastating that there is no realistic possibility *ever* of parole, they have perhaps less to lose by talking about them or analysing them, providing they can find the right person to communicate with. Writing to Brady, I had no idea what to expect; a number of people had tried to work with him before me with limited success. Among them are the respected true-crime writer Colin Wilson, a few journalists, social reformer Lord Longford and various psychiatrists at Ashworth Hospital. Brady has never told his hated psychiatrists anything useful and never will: '... *failed professionals and the private sector rejects employed for their political toadyism, I provide no material to occupy their empty hours*' (2003). None of them seemed to have got very far at all, not even remotely.

I focused on Brady's writing on the analysis of serial killing as a way of touching base. I was looking for an opportunity to research not only the dynamics and psychology of serial killing, but also the consequences for the killer, which I felt had never been thoroughly investigated in the forensics literature. I sent him a letter to enquire whether he was working on any other writing projects:

> Many academics and students have requested expansion on certain points, but I decline on the grounds that I wrote my book years ago under a progressive 'Ashwitz' [sic] regime, not the present fin de siècle penal retards, now passing through the suffocating 1950s in their regression to the 19th century. All mail now being censored [2003].

I realised that I could not just turn up at the hospital to visit him as a total stranger and expect him to talk to me, so I fired off a few letters and sent him a few news stories about various things that might interest him. I told him about my work and that I had recommended his book on serial-killing analysis to my students, although I knew better than to try to appeal to his intellectual vanity. Basically, I just wanted to see if he wished to correspond. By my actions – or (more importantly) omission of actions – he could judge my integrity and motivation for himself. I had to wait for him to invite me to the hospital and get their permission for me to visit him. I had to be very patient with the administration, who almost immediately treated me with suspicion and distrust. They read all Brady's letters and my replies and rejected lots of things on the slightest technicality. This was highly frustrating but, of course, made the research all the more intriguing.

Why were they so scared?

Why focus on Brady? A lot of people have asked me this. The answer is opportunity. It would be highly unlikely that I would ever have the chance to learn from someone like him again and, as a psychologist, I would have been insane not to explore where this might go. After almost half a century of incarceration in some of the most notorious institutions in the United Kingdom, he might, I suspected, have a unique perspective and insight, and, if he did not, then that was certainly worthy of investigation in itself. Brady also quickly ascertained through correspondence with me that he would have to be very patient with me as well in order for me to develop a clear conception of the full implications of the information he wanted me to understand.

I guess you cannot spend that long in prison without the ability to develop patience, but, for an outsider who moves freely about in the world, the stasis of vitality that you experience in the 'special' hospitals can be something of an emotional shock. Walking into Ashworth Hospital is very much like getting on to a flight when the aeroplane doors are sealed before takeoff and the cabin is pressurised. Your ears pop. It hits you physically. It is not pleasant and there is no relaxing holiday awaiting you when you land.

CHAPTER TWO

RECREATIONAL MURDER DYNAMICS: MULTIPLE PERSONA, MULTIPLE CRIMES

Serial killers often display some common behavioural patterns, but these are not as predictable as they sometimes appear in films and other media portrayals. In many cases, the 'banality of evil' obscures its very essence and, as such, this can be its most effective disguise.

The people who commit such crimes as I have explored in my research are all individuals with varying preferences and motivations that evolve over time and can be reflected in their behaviour if you look closely and clearly enough. However, with most serial killers, explanations that might shed light on their motivation can be glimpsed only *after* they have been captured. This is why profiling an UNSUB (unknown suspect/subject) while they are involved in the cycle of killing is extremely difficult, more art than science. It usually hinges on creative imagination rather than tried and tested routine and often alarmingly unreliable methods of criminal investigation.

Many will never be caught. Brady has told me many

times that we *'rub shoulders with active and potential serial killers'* on a regular basis without realising it, but when they *are* caught, or give themselves up, hindsight is often all we have to work with. Retrospective analysis is usually the only successful route we have for understanding what happened and how it might possibly be identified and prevented in the future, although, of course, at that point it is sadly too late for any of the victims. Once serial murderers have been captured, they deal with the emotional consequences of their crimes and convictions in a variety of different ways, which might give us some insight into behavioural dynamics. One thing they usually recognise and have in common is their awareness that after the first murder there is no going back. Here are some examples.

A Florida killer, Deputy Sheriff David Gore, having been convicted and sent to death row for the murder of six women, seemed understandably depressed and disturbed by his situation. He described his feelings after his first murder like this:

> All of a sudden I realized that I had just done something that separated me from the human race and it was something that could never be undone, I realized that from that point on I could never be like normal people. I must have stood there in that state for 20 minutes. I have never felt an emptiness of self like I did right then and I never will forget that feeling. It was like I crossed over into a realm I could never come back from [Gore 1983].

Another Florida serial killer, Gerard John Schaefer, convicted of two murders in 1973 while he was a serving

20

police officer (although suspected of many more), was surprised when he realised he had killed for the first time and that there was no going back: 'I wasn't struck dead by a bolt of lightning, but everything had changed' (Schaefer 1989). The utter shock that people experience when they realise that they have transgressed beyond even their own criminal confidence and capacity for ruthlessness by killing is not exactly easy for them to come to terms with. However, human beings are infinitely adaptable and, although everything has changed for ever because they have killed, and they realise they can never undo what they have done, they still try to hang on to shreds of normality and control even when they realise that this will almost certainly be impossible.

Donald Gaskins, of South Carolina, a convicted multiple murderer, rationalised his killing career rather more coldly while awaiting execution. He explained his motivation after his first kill:

> From then on, you make your own rules. You do not care any more about what anyone cares or thinks, you don't fear prison or even execution. Words don't say it, a person has to *do* what I have *done* in order to understand what I mean when I say *they can't touch me* [Gaskins 1993].

Ian Brady experienced something identical when he was caught and convicted of multiple murders, but with a very different perspective, which in his case possibly even included an element of relief. This is not unprecedented. Modern psychologists call this 'cognitive dissonance'; Freudian psychologists might label it 'repression'. Basically, our sanity depends on a narrowness of vision. This is a coping mechanism that we all use; otherwise we would all be walking around kicking ourselves repeatedly for the stupid decisions and mistakes we all make in our lives. Something dramatic happens that may or may not be your fault but that changes your whole life for ever, so you rationalise the truth into a psychologically acceptable distortion. You deal with it by convincing yourself that whatever has happened – rather than being the terrible disaster that it so obviously is – might actually be a positive turn of events. If, for example, an employment application falls through or you fail an exam, you may think, Well, it would have been a lousy career anyway; they actually did me a favour. This is a useful psychological survival mechanism for most of life's routine dilemmas, but getting caught and convicted for the systematic murder of strangers is on a completely different level.

Rationalising crimes of such magnitude involves rather more radical coping mechanisms because the murderer suddenly finds himself dealing with a life-shattering emotional storm that surpasses routine psychological balancing acts. Many people are incapable of this. They crack up and almost immediately confess because they simply cannot deal with the guilt or the fear of the inevitable consequences (with true sociopaths it is usually the latter). Serial killers usually have trouble empathising with other people, so guilt or remorse is not really of any profound relevance to them. It might cross their minds that perhaps they *should* feel guilty, they may even *pretend* to feel guilty, but this has no genuine emotional impact. Usually the only person they feel any kind of compassion for is themselves. Consequently, the emotional shock of killing is not so difficult for them to come to terms with. It is secondary. Getting away with it is the most important priority.

Additionally, while the first murder is obviously terrifying for the perpetrator, it can at the same time be something of a disappointment. *'Actions, bright and exciting in the imagination are often disappointing or farcical in practice . . . like entering a fourth dimension where the comfortable laws and rules they take for granted in normal life no longer apply; adrenaline speeds the pumping blood and distorts the faculties; immersion in the immediacy of action obviates wider appreciation'* (2001). Here, Brady is talking about another serial killer while almost transparently talking about himself. So, for most sociopathic murderers, killing for the first time turns out not to be as much 'fun' as they had anticipated or fantasised that it would be, and it may well turn out to be just an annoying and frightening mess that they resent having to try to clean up afterwards.

For serial killers, the paramount concern while committing their first murder, whether it was planned or not, is eliminating clues and avoiding getting captured, so the killing itself is usually something of an anticlimax and needs to be refined, hence more murders: *'The more times you act as supreme architect, the more you become one'* (2001). Brady discusses the murders and methods of other serial killers (in his book) almost as a wine expert might discuss various vintages. Murder as a *creative* act. This is unnerving for somebody like me, in the process of conducting research.

GUILT AND REMORSE

Of course, when they finally *are* captured, serial killers are quite capable of expressing guilt and remorse even if they do not really feel very much, and only when it suits them to do so. Myra Hindley (1942–2002), Brady's accomplice in the Moors Murders, spent decades developing an aura of deeply expressed remorse and a number of people were completely convinced that this was genuine until she attempted a bungled escape in 1974. The ridiculous plan, which included a key impression in a bar of soap, predictably failed and revealed that any remorse she felt was only for herself, a brutal slap in the face for the many people who had supported her for so long, including Brady.

Other serial killers try to convince anyone who will listen that they feel remorse, even their dead victims. The 1970s London serial killer Dennis Nilsen, desperate for company and with no one to talk to, would even drag the bodies of his victims out from under the floorboards, sit them in a chair, play them his favourite records, hold their hands and apologise to them. He described the day of his capture as 'the day that help arrived' (Masters 1985), although I would imagine he did not think that at the time, not even remotely, not for a second. Any remorse he claims to have felt at the time is almost insulting. When he was finally arrested, it seems the only thing he was genuinely sorry about was that he had been caught and locked up and could not continue killing. It seems likely that, by that time, he was getting bored with the whole thing after killing 15 men.

If you read his memoirs, it is hard to ignore the unmistakable and unpalatable conclusion that, as the murders rolled on and on and as his victims piled up, the hiding and disposing of their bodies became just an annoying routine. The dismemberment of the bodies was simply a chore as far as he was concerned: 'The victim is the dirty platter after the feast and the washing up is a clinically ordinary task' (Nilsen, quoted in Masters 1985). He even goes so far as attempting to justify many of his murders as almost as if he were doing the victims a favour, helping them out. I doubt very much they would have agreed with this sentiment while they were being strangled.

After Nilsen was finally arrested and the entire sad story of his crimes was revealed he finally, and almost immediately, told the truth and was quoted as saying, 'I did it just for me, purely selfish ... it is as simple as that.' In another interview Nilsen said, 'Well, enjoying it [killing] is as good a reason as any' (Newton 2000). However at first he desperately wanted to try to convince himself and anyone who would listen that getting caught was a good thing. What other option did he have? Spend the rest of his life regretting the irreversible consequences of his horrible crimes? Cognitive dissonance again.

AN EXERCISE IN SELF-DECEIT

Of course, serial killers can expertly deceive themselves as easily as they can deceive their victims. Well, they *try* to, but it is not always possible. Brady has been labelled the most notorious murderer since Jack the Ripper and has been voted on the Internet as being the person most people want dead. A difficult reputation to live with or try to overcome, even for someone with delusions of grandeur. He deals with it pragmatically and philosophically. Aware that there was no way his crimes would ever be genuinely forgiven by the majority of people who knew about them, he had very little to fall back on other than to cling to the belief that he had somehow surpassed the dreary lifestyles of the majority of the general population and had managed to achieve some higher plane of existence. Describing the capture of another serial killer, Brady reflected on his own situation:

' ... *the paradoxical sensation of total liberty and panache one feels when all is lost. I myself experienced it. The Nietzschean dance of laughter and delight when confronting the abyss'* (2001). 'Total liberty'? I don't think so. Liberty was permanently extinguished the moment he was arrested.

In one letter to me, Brady mentioned that a critic had remarked that his writing was 'the most dangerous to be published in fifty years'. Brady described this comment as *'unintentional flattery'* (2002). Further self-delusion.

When the Moors Murders case broke and the details were revealed to the public, the population definitely wanted someone to blame, and, when the public saw Brady's and Hindley's unrepentant and arrogant expressions on the front page of almost every newspaper, they wanted more than someone to blame: they wanted blood. Who can say what demons Brady and Hindley had to contend with while waiting on remand for trial, as their victims were being exhumed from their graves one by one on Saddleworth Moor and the death penalty was still active in British law for crimes that they had committed? Brady's and Hindley's lives were suddenly and irrecoverably thrown into the spotlight of international news and their crimes *still* make headlines, nearly half a century later.

I mentioned in a letter that I had read that someone had thrown a rock at him once when he was being moved from one institution to another. He replied that he could not remember this, and then commented, *'What kind of rock was it? Kryptonite?'* (2003).

Brady, much as he might like to think so, is no Superman. Once the details of his murders broke in the press and they were both convicted, Brady and Hindley had virtually no choices left in their lives any more. Almost all options were now eliminated and they somehow had to live with the fact that the gravity of their convictions meant there was no going back or getting out of the situation they had created together, ever.

'So many mistakes' (Brady, quoted in Harrison 1987). So what happened with Brady? Rewind to Scotland, 1938.

Ian Stewart Brady, born on 2 January, had a rather unstable but by most accounts not an abusive childhood. His father disappeared before he was born. He lived with his mother Margaret Stewart for a while and then with a couple, Mary and John Sloan. He seems to have drifted into crime at a very young age out of curiosity, just because he could, rather than specifically for monetary gain. In his first successful break-in/burglary, he did not even steal anything. He just looked around, amazed that he had done it. Nothing unusual here: it is not atypical for bored teenagers to experiment with superficial crimes. Brady's crimes did not remain superficial for long, though.

So was he 'born bad'? As far as his childhood history is concerned, there are no genetic, neurological abnormalities or head injuries on record. Other than the stigma of not having a father present, which was much more serious then than it is now, his childhood was nothing especially out of the ordinary – although, in some cases, victims of serious psychological trauma in childhood often do not remember it, since large segments of time can be forgotten or repressed. The brain literally deletes the connections that make the memories accessible because reliving them just introduces further trauma (Pincus 2001). This can have considerable impact on behaviour, although I am disinclined to believe that Brady was seriously abused in early childhood and has repressed this, because his memories of this period in his life are for the most part extremely detailed and vivid and benign. I asked him some questions about his early years. Children can sometimes be cruel, and cruelty to animals is often cited as an early symptom of murderous ambition for many serial killers, but this also can be something of a red herring. Richard Chase, the 'Vampire of Sacramento', when captured expressed remorse about some animals he had killed but none whatsoever for the six human victims he hunted during his short murder spree in January 1978.

Brady has been accused of animal cruelty more than once. I asked him about this and he explained:

> As a child in WW2 I explored a bombed-out church in the Gorbals and came across a small bird lying in the ruins. I quietly approached it to avoid alarming it, near enough to see it was apparently breathing and asleep. I reached out to hold it. Suddenly something subconscious froze my movement. As I stood and watched its breast rise and fall I identified the sweet smell of putrescence and gingerly touched the bird with my shoe. It was a vessel of seething maggots. My first lesson in the deception of nature and life. Disgust gave way to pity and I built a tomb around it with bricks. I assume that gave rise to the stereotypical fable that I once buried a cat alive [2005].

More recently, he told me that the only creatures he talked to at the hospital where he is currently incarcerated were the mallard ducks that occasionally pass by his window, 'the only intelligent creatures in this place'. He told me he used to flick them crumbs now and again through a gap in the window until the Ashworth authorities did one of their routine shakedowns and confiscated the piece of stale bread he had in his cell for this purpose.

So Brady was not an especially evil child, but something was waking up and began to take form. As a young teenager, he started to take crime a lot more seriously, and so did the authorities when he landed in the 'grown-up' court for a more serious burglary.

'*At age 15 I was put in a "remand home" in Glasgow. The inmates pointed out the perverts on the staff.*' Having been released, he was caught later for another minor offence and he was put on probation, which was conditional on his moving to Manchester to live with his mother and her new husband, Patrick Brady, whose name he now took. Now he was an outsider in a strange land with a strange name and a strange accent, to the locals anyway. Reflecting on another uprooted serial killer, Ted Bundy, Brady offers some insight into how those aggrieved by what they consider to be judicial injustice can end up '*coldly examining the alien city from the heights, viewing the despised inhabitants as antagonists to whom one owes no mercy*' (2001, paraphrasing Balzac).

Brady was not particularly impressed with Manchester and its denizens. He lashed out and more (minor) crimes were committed. The authorities had finally had enough. They raised the stakes out of all proportion to the severity of his offences.

'*I had my "short sharp shock" in 1955.*' It still resonates decades later. He was caught handling some stolen materials at the market where he was working. He was sent to Strangeways, a totally adult prison. '*Strangeways opened my eyes and I opened library books, recruiting and organising.*'

Three months there was followed by two years in borstals. First was Latchmore House, a POW camp that had been used to hold captured Germans in World War II.

'*Barbed-wire fences, marching at the double. Natural*

resentment at arrest for nothing was channelled into getting even profitably' (2009).

Next came Hatfield borstal in Yorkshire for a while. This was followed by time in a particularly harsh establishment based in Hull Prison. At this time, people were still being hanged there. Brady was shown the gallows, perhaps as an object lesson in negative reinforcement. If that was the case, whoever authorised this must have had a somewhat shaky understanding of behaviourist psychology. It totally and predictably backfired and achieved precisely the opposite effect to what they might have naively intended:

'*I examined the bricked-up execution cells – open trap, planks for wardens to stand on, clutch lever on a ratchet, beam above trap with ringbolt for rope, empty cell below for assistant to swing on the legs. Pragmatic counter-responsive, emulatory mental note: Get guns*' (2004).

I suppose the motive might have been to scare the teenage offenders out of the momentum of a criminal career. You cannot inflict much more of a brutal 'short sharp shock' than revealing to a convict the apparatus that could and would be used to kill him if he continued with his criminal career. But in Brady's case the stupidity of the authorities was mind-boggling. They had picked on the wrong person. Brady, having been shown the hanging room, understandably took this as a direct personal threat, which I am sure it was meant to be. But his reaction was not what they intended. Rather than developing a fear of authority, he responded with a clear desire to get *them* before they got *him*. So many mistakes.

After that he was sent to an army medical admissions officer for possible conscription. Brady found the concept laughable, ludicrous. He told them he had just spent two years in jails marching up and down the square. They were totally wasting their time, as he had no intention of spending another two as a bottom-rank squaddie doing pretty much exactly the same thing (punctuated no doubt with learning to polish boots, peel potatoes and whitewash coal).

'Had they persisted I would have spent just long enough to identify the armoury and saved time, energy and money travelling to Europe for supplies' (2004).

In prison he had convicted criminals for vocational guidance counsellors and many reasons to despise authority, so it is no great surprise that he wanted to arm himself.

> [M]y 'tutors' were adult professional criminals to whom I owe my eventual missions to Europe and America – as opposed to the dead-end labouring jobs shuffled to me by the Probation Service on release, posing a positive hindrance to two years of captive planning and organizing/recruiting. As I couldn't even leave the country without the permission of the state parrots, my false travel documents had to be supplied by a contact running a travel agency. The same scrutiny of finances prevented proper investment and other enterprises, except by proxy [2004].

Personally, I do not believe a word of this. I think it is nostalgic dreaming. Stock clerks from Manchester council estates did not make exciting international transatlantic journeys in the 1960s. But I did not want to derail his fantasies, so I just nodded politely whenever these kinds of grandiose embellishments came up in my interviews. Delusions of grandeur are not exactly rare with serial killers. Henry Lee Lucas, convicted of 11 murders, confessed that he was responsible for literally hundreds more. He also claimed that he had travelled to Spain and Japan on killing missions, although the truth was that he had never even left the United States. False confessions can be an effective defence strategy that can confuse law-enforcement agencies, and Lucas was an expert at this (Norris 1993).

One thing Brady *is* honest about, though, is the effects of incarceration on people. After all, he has more experience of this than almost anyone alive.

'Prison, an expensive way to make bad people worse ... a complete systematic failure to prevent people already in the system from re-offending' (Soering 2004).

'If you start with a man whose behaviour is already erratic and strip away all the elements of normalcy in his life, giving him more anger to motivate him and more time to fantasize, you are creating a recipe for disaster' (Douglas and Olshaker 1998).

Brady described prison life and the inevitable effects it has on long-term prisoners to me repeatedly:

'Having deprived prisoners of all that is worthwhile outside, they then next deprive them of all that makes life bearable inside' (2004).

'I met hundreds in prison straining at the leash with unfocused vengeance ... that is the price the public will pay for their indifference' (2007).

'In almost fifty years I have lost count of the disaffected seeking revenge against official ignorance and regression' (2009).

Anger and retaliatory responses do not usually take years to develop in a penal environment: they can occur in a matter of days, they can occur in a matter of hours, they can occur *instantaneously* and then slowly ferment and coalesce. In almost all cases, the convict leaves the prison ready and prepared to instigate further mayhem and with a dark vengeance in their heart.

Some incarcerated serial killers are on record as literally begging not to be released when/if they reach the end of their sentence. They know what is likely to happen and sometimes try to warn the authorities. Multiple murderer Henry Lee Lucas was released from Ionia Prison in 1970 (due to 'overcrowding') after serving a sentence for stabbing his mother to death. 'I told them that if I got out I would go back to killing if they let me out, and that is what I done.' He was true to his word. On release he immediately killed two women within sight of the prison gates (Lucas, cited in Norris 1993). Manson Family leader Charles Manson also begged not to be released from prison when one of his sentences for conspiracy to commit murder was completed. Aileen Wournos (see Chapter 7) made the same prediction, although in her case she was executed before this could happen.

It is amazing that the authorities often ignore the warnings from the actual criminals themselves regarding crimes that they predict they would commit if released. Instead, they prefer to rely on the advice of so-called professionals, although sometimes professional psychologists and criminologists are ignored as well. Lucas was arrested at one point and given a psychiatric evaluation, after which psychologist Newton Johnson predicted, 'It is very likely that further difficulties with the law will be encountered by him in the foreseeable future.' He was right. When Lucas was released, he moved from state to state murdering people at random for over a decade.

ZIMBARDO PRISON EXPERIMENTS

Volunteer Stanford University psychology students participating in an experimental programme in 1971 were randomly selected to be either a 'guard' or a 'prisoner' in a prison environment, and then had to live the role full time. The prisoner volunteers were 'arrested' at their homes by (real) police and then taken to a realistic simulated prison and locked up in cells. This was meant to be a series of controlled experiments, but they did not remain controlled for very long. The trials had to be stopped within a few days after they got extremely ugly in ways that even the most cynical psychologists conducting the mechanics of the experiments had not anticipated. The 'guards' started inventing and inflicting sadistic punishments, and the 'prisoners' quickly fought back in every way they could think of. It would not be long before almost everyone would lose control and someone would end up either seriously injured or even dead. The research was halted, much to the relief of everyone concerned. Once everything was over bar the shouting, it is interesting to note that it was the 'guards' who ended up with the serious psychological issues. The 'prisoners', on the whole, were just glad to get out of there, but the 'guards' had behaved in ways they had never expected to be capable of, and many were left with some serious psychological conflicts concerning their behaviour.

Brady comments on the research, '*As the (Zimbardo) experiments demonstrate, the creation of criminal behaviour applies both to staff and inmates equally. Not to mention the effect even on visitors, as you yourself experienced*' (2008).

He was certainly right in my case: my visits to Ashworth were always disturbing and occasionally outright frightening. I do not know why they even bother calling these places hospitals any more. Everyone involved with Ashworth, Broadmoor and Rampton knows that the 'special hospitals' are really prisons, in every sense of the word.

Prisons offer a calcification of human emotion, an emotional wasteland. When something dies – and hopes die very quickly in prison, with a life sentence and no conceivable possibility of parole – something comes to replace the vacuum that has been created and that something is unlikely to be anything positive for the prisoners or those who may come into contact with them. Brady accepted this with a certain resolve: *'Better to have no hope than false hope.'* Very few people who have experienced prison survive psychologically unscathed, whether they work there or are confined there.

THE PSYCHOLOGY OF
A SOCIOPATH

After the penal overkill of Strangeways, Hull and the POW camp, the authorities probably naively thought they had broken Brady and, if anything, he would just continue with a meandering catalogue of minor crimes and probation violations. If so, they had miscalculated, and had seriously underestimated the level of resentment he had learned to conceal as well as the length of time it had been crystallising.

'Why stick to rules made by others? Especially religious precepts, which branded you an outcast from the day of conception' (2001).

This seems to be fairly logical but take a different perspective and some doubts starts to emerge. Author John Douglas has little time for explanatory theories. After all, even those who come from broken homes or abusive childhoods or who have had head injuries or a dominant mother or who have been to jail (or maybe even all of these put together, all the clichés) may eventually emerge as law-abiding adult citizens rather than homicidal, antisocial, reactive individuals who break any restrictions on their behaviour that they encounter. It is true that most (but not all) serial killers have had to endure horrendous childhoods, but lots of people have terrible childhoods. Serial killers *choose* to attempt to pass that pain on to someone else (Davis 2005).

The psychopathology of a sociopath cannot usually or easily be put down to one conveniently blameworthy event, or even a series of events.

'Despite bad background or any other mitigating circumstances or explanatory factors, they [serial killers] choose to commit violent predatory crime ... Once they aggress against others they instantly forfeit whatever claims they had to victim status' (Douglas and Olshaker 1998). Perhaps. Brady shrugged off victim status every time it came up in our conversations. Although he has continually pointed out that he had been subjected to inhuman treatment in the penal system and repeatedly reminded me of the regime he has to contend with at the hospital, he stubbornly insists he was always in control and made his own decisions, control perhaps being one of the most important psychological foundations he uses to keep his mind from crumbling.

If Brady had pleaded guilty while on trial for multiple murders, it is possible that explanatory factors might have been presented as mitigating circumstances during the sentencing part of the trial, but it almost certainly would not have made any difference to the end result. As it was, both Brady and Hindley lied all the way through their trial, stubbornly insisting they were both not guilty in the face of a massive amount of incriminating evidence against both of them. Now he takes full responsibility for the crimes he was convicted of and does not even try to offer any explanation other than his conscious decision to kill people because he wanted to kill people at the time:

It's a fashionable excuse to blame ones [sic] *crimes on tales of abuse by others. I thought I had heard the last of that pathetic piffle straight from a tupenny* [sic] *dreadful but it is a fashionable deus ex machina for ones* [sic] *crimes nowadays to blame it all on tales of abuse by others. Prior generations had more spine and dignity but they are catching the whining syndrome from the present. God used to be the popular coat hanger for personal responsibility but he is totally discredited now and of not even any use as a scapegoat anymore in intelligent circles. In fact I tried to portray myself as svengali at the trial, to sway the jury in favour of Myra, but evidence by both defence and prosecution witnesses and that of Myra herself revealed the emotional relationship and ruined the effect* [2001].

In the trial transcription, Hindley is questioned and undermines the portrayal of her involvement in the murders as that of an innocent dupe under Brady's hypnotic control:

Mr Heilpern (examining): 'Could you tell us, Miss Hindley, what were your feelings for Ian Brady?'

Hindley: 'I became very fond of him. I loved him. I still ... I love him.'

Brady claims to see imprisonment as both an occupational hazard and a self-fulfilling prophecy, but neither of these offers a full explanation. Yes, he ran into some very bad people at a very bad time, and I don't just mean the criminals he was incarcerated with but also the people who were doing the incarcerating. But, even if circumstances dictated that he had to reinvent himself, it was his choice as to how he might do this.

'*Revenge ferments revenge*' (2004). '*After borstal, I resolved never again to be involved in anything trivial*' (2008).

Mad as hell? Yes. So mad you could even *kill someone*? Brady comments on Ted Bundy's being perceived as a problem to be managed: '*A problem? Managed? I'll show you what a problem is, I'll show you managed!*' (2001).

Brady's anger had finally boiled over and he responded laterally and murderously, and as with nearly all cases of serial killing it did not take long before the murders got out of control. He admits that he may have overestimated his own callousness. Believing that he possessed enough intellectual and emotional strength to deal with the ramifications and unfolding events, he became inexorably drawn into a killing momentum that almost immediately ran at a velocity that would have been hard to predict and equally hard to contain.

But why did Myra Hindley actively participate with Brady's crimes? There have been a number of experiments in social psychology that show how powerful, manipulative individuals or circumstances can influence and overwhelm the behaviour of others, whether the targets are meek and gentle or powerful and self-confident. The mechanics of manipulation might be different, but the result is often the same.

Perhaps the most famous illustrations of these effects come from the Milgram conformity/obedience experiments conducted in the 1960s and 1970s in America. The psychologist Stanley Milgram was interested in exploring the question of what might be the most direct technique one person can use to change the behaviour of another. He wished to explore the factors that could cause individuals to obey commands that would normally go against a basically nonaggressive nature (by all accounts, Hindley, although rather feisty as a teenager, was not especially aggressive before she met Brady but, then again, neither was he).

In a number of experimental scenarios, Milgram recruited volunteers who thought they were participating in a learning experiment (which in fact, they were, but they did not realise *they* were the subjects – psychological experimentation was rather more radical and unethical in those days than it is now, and many experiments involved deception). In the standard experimental scenario, the volunteer would arrive at the university and be taken into a formal laboratory situation. They would be introduced to a person who they believed was also a volunteer. They drew straws to see who would be the 'teacher' and who would be the 'learner'; of course, this was rigged, and they always ended up being the 'teacher'. Then they would witness the 'learner' being taken into another room and wired up to an electric-shock generator. Then the volunteer would be asked to read lists of words over a microphone to the 'learner', who had to remember which words were paired together to form a correct answer.

At this stage, the volunteer could hear the responses but could no longer see the man delivering them. Each time a mistake was made, the volunteer was instructed to administer an electric shock as a 'punishment' using the electrical generator, each jolt getting higher in voltage up to and beyond levels that could cause death (this possibility was clearly labelled on the generator). The man who was apparently being shocked was not actually receiving any shocks at all, he was an actor, an accomplice of Milgram, but the volunteer administering them did not know this. An

frequently someone who lives very close to the address of the killer or killers. This is why it is essential for investigators to move very quickly, because, if it is a serial cycle, the range will spread out further with each murder and linkages will become stale. One rule of thumb in forensic investigation is that, if an abduction/murder is not conclusively solved within the first 48 hours after a person is noticed missing, the probability of this happening drops radically. After decades, no matter what clues have been gathered, the trail has gone beyond frozen. Pauline Reade was taken a few miles away to Saddleworth Moor on a pretext. There, Brady cut her throat and buried her. Neither Brady nor Hindley have ever been charged with her murder, although both of them have admitted accountability.

23/11/1963: Twelve-year-old John Kilbride was abducted from Ashton market, which was a few miles away from Brady's and Hindley's homes. He was taken to the moor, strangled by Brady after he had discovered his knife was too blunt to cut the child's throat, and then buried.

16/6/1964: Twelve-year-old Keith Bennett was abducted from a street in the general area and taken to the moor. He was killed and buried and his body has not yet been found.

26/12/1964: Ten-year-old Lesley Ann Downey was abducted from a Christmas fair, taken to Brady and Hindley's house, stripped, gagged, photographed and then strangled by Hindley. Her body was then driven to Saddleworth Moor and buried.

At that point Brady was almost beyond caring about the consequences. He had completed his '*existential exercise*'.

'Contrary to popular belief, the "Moors murders" lasted less than two years.'

So there was a gap in the murder cycle, this is not unusual with serial killers, but in most cases the gaps between murders get shorter, not longer. The so-called 'cooling-off' periods diminish on a timeline. In Brady's case, this did not happen: it went the other way.

So their next killing was out of sequence and it went badly wrong for pretty much everyone concerned, not least their victim.

6/10/1965: Nearly a year after the Downey killing, 17-year-old Edward Evans was invited back to Brady and Hindley's house in a badly planned robbery involving Hindley's brother-in-law, David Smith. It was a half-baked plan to rob Evans, who had nothing worth taking, anyway. The murder was sloppy and left a ton of clues. Brady had changed his MO and killed Evans with 14 axe blows in their living room. When questioned at the trial, Brady said, 'The first two blows were not hard ... after that they were hard ... if he died from axe blows, then ... yes ... I killed him. There was blood all over the place at that time – on the walls and there were pools of it on the floor, he was gurgling, blood I suppose. Then later I suggested getting the place cleaned up, the blood was being walked in all over the floor.'

When Evans finally died, his body was hidden in Hindley's bedroom wrapped in polythene. Evans's burial was planned for the next day but by then David Smith had informed the police who arrived the next morning and arrested Brady before this could be accomplished.

There had been one murder approximately every six months, then a gap of nearly a year, and then it stopped.

Brady had finished, and it seems highly likely that if no further murders had been committed they might never have been caught. It is conceivable that their victims might never have been found and would have remained missing persons to this day. Brady could have gone on to different pursuits. I asked him what he would have done if none of this had ever happened, if he had not been caught and convicted for the murders, what career might he have developed. He replied, *'Journalism or politics.'* I would imagine he could have been quite successful in either of these, but it was not to be: serial killers very rarely stop killing until they are either captured or die.

By strangling Downey, Hindley had equalled Brady in terms of homicidal freedom of expression, maybe even surpassed him. As I have stated, it seems possible that they were both trying to get the upper hand, to outdo each other with their capacity to kill in cold blood. Brady's *'existential exercise'* had been concluded as far as he was concerned, although, like most serial killers who have been permanently incarcerated, Brady occasionally drops hints that there may be other murders that have not been discovered. As far as Hindley was concerned, with the Downey killing, she had proved she could be just as deadly as Brady and the stakes were raised again. Everything was running out of control and the killing had to stop one way or another. By this time, it was almost inevitable that they would finally be caught.

But why commit a murder in the first place? A murder of a stranger? Why this rather than a robbery, a fraud, a kidnapping, or some other kind of criminal act of revenge? Occasionally, when I start a forensics lecture course, as an icebreaker I ask the students some questions. 'Who in this room has ever considered killing someone?' Most people have thought about it at some point in their lives and usually about half the people in the lecture theatre put up their hands. They make jokes: husband/wife/mother-in-law/Jehovah's Witnesses, etc. Some people actually get upset if you suggest they are not capable of killing.

So then I say, 'How many of you have considered *how* you might do it?' Some hands go down, but not all.

Next, I say, 'Might you use poison?' Most of the men's hands go down, but interestingly none of the women's does. It seems this may have crossed their minds before.

Then I say, 'How many of you have considered how you might get away with it?' Usually that finishes it. They have not thought it through that far. But one time there was a student whose hand stayed up right until the end of my questions. After the lecture, I questioned her about it. She had it all planned. She was going to disable the CCTV camera where she worked, kill her boss by flinging her down a flight of concrete stairs and then escape via a back door to complete an already established alibi. I asked her why she wanted to kill her boss and she replied, 'Because it is necessary.'

Of course, this was all hypothetical. If she was really going to do it, she certainly would not be telling me and a room full of police, prison officers, social workers and lawyers, but the idea for her was a little more than just an intellectual exercise. I did not take this too seriously. This was just a fantasy conception of a single murder with a specific target with whom the student presumably had some major personal grievance. The systematic murder of *strangers* is much more difficult to rationalise, but some patterns emerge when you compare various case scenarios.

THE DYNAMICS OF SERIAL MURDER
STAGE 1: Recreational

We all have multiple personae that we shift among, sometimes consciously sometimes unconsciously, depending on where we are and whom we are with and what we are trying to achieve. These are as diverse and unpredictable as our personalities. We also all have our breaking points, and for certain people this breaking point can be the start of not just one but a whole cycle of murders. This might be a complex plan rehearsed and refined over months or years, or a snap decision made in a second. With crimes of passion, there is usually very little premeditation. Something devastating occurs. People kill without planning or calculated precision and almost invariably get caught.

The first murder in a serial cycle, whatever the motive, is analogous to stepping on to an exceptionally scary rollercoaster. The perpetrator may have been thinking about it for some time, perhaps toying with the idea, developing a plan, but they are scared to step on the ride because they know that, once they do, there is no way they can get off until the ride is finished. The consequences are uncertain but they are aware that, if they get caught, they are more than likely to wind up in jail, or worse.

For some, however, pressure builds up until one day, when they might be feeling especially nervy, angry and reckless, they finally decide to try the ride. They somehow get through it and then get off at the end frightened and breathless. Whether they are caught or not or whatever the motive or justification, there is no going back. With the first murder, the killer is likely to be sick with terror at having done something irrevocable, almost certainly amazed that it has happened and most likely wishing it had not. Most perpetrators do not perceive the gravity of their actions at

45

first, but after a little while it starts to sink in. The course of many lives has been changed forever, the killer is in effect suffering from a form of post traumatic stress disorder (PTSD) and will usually experience many of the symptoms associated with the psychological/emotional rebound that is generated by extremely stressful situations.

Henry Lee Lucas comments on his first recreational murder, that of a hitchhiker he picked up in east Texas: 'That killing was my first, my worst, and the hardest to get over ... every time I turned around I would see police behind me. I would always be watching for police and be afraid they were going to stop and pick me up (Lucas, cited in Norris 1993).

If they are not immediately apprehended (and, as stated, most murders are solved within 48 hours, after which the case becomes more difficult to solve), and if the police do not immediately turn up and arrest the person or persons responsible, then it appears that the killer entertains the possibility that they might indeed have got away with it. Then they will try to forget the experience, seal it off in their mind. This of course is impossible. Take, for instance, my student who said she wanted to kill her employer. Suppose she achieved this and managed to escape undetected. What then? A number of things would happen. First, there might be something on the television news, and then in the newspapers the following day. Next, she would have to keep up appearances by going to work as if she knew nothing. Everyone would be talking about it. The police would interview everyone who worked at her place of employment, including her. She would have to account for her movements on the day of the murder, probably more than once while attempting to keep her story straight. Every instance of action, inaction or reaction would be fraught with the danger of possible apprehension. Life would become an intolerable game of cat and mouse. Combine all this pressure with memories of unsettling images and sounds from the murder itself, and – for most people anyway – life would become unbearable.

But serial killers are different for two important reasons. First, they usually kill strangers and, if there are no witnesses and no link between them and the person they have killed, then far from being the work of the criminal mastermind they might like to think they are, their killing of a stranger has been as easy as falling off a log. Second, they are usually sociopaths. So, for the most part, they have no compassion for their victim or their victim's relatives. They simply could not care less about what anyone thinks other than the authorities who might be trying to capture them.

Even the most cold-hearted sociopath must feel a little apprehension at first, but very slowly and cautiously they may start to feel a little more confident. At this point, the details of the murder begin to blur or are reconstructed in memory. However, the potential consequences remain an irritating threat, persistently emotionally disturbing. What if the body is discovered? What if there was a vital clue missed that could link them to the killing? Something they missed?

Conscious reality breaks through and the individual now has limited choices: deal with it; call a lawyer; turn themselves in and accept the horrible consequences of their actions, the condemnation from society and the victim's relatives, probably the loss of their home, friends, family, employment, freedom and future all in one go. Their life is ruined if they are caught, when they would almost certainly be facing a prison sentence or incarceration in a mental hospital for an undefined term. In most states in America or in China or the Middle East, the perpetrator could also easily lose their own life. If *you* had the option of going to prison for years and maybe being executed, or *not* going to prison, which would you choose? Maybe there would be a distant possibility of redemption or at the very least attrition of some kind depending on the nature of the crime, some murders being more forgivable than others (although this varies from place to place and time to time) but, whatever the potential outcome, all of these inevitabilities seem pretty miserable or even impossible to contemplate. Certainly, nothing positive seems likely; it is not going to go away; the culprit has crossed a line and can never retrace their steps.

This momentum makes it possible for some killers to believe whatever lies are necessary for them to pursue and indulge their fantasies further, even to the point of believing they have not been mentally imprisoned by their actions, but that they have actually become more 'free'. Cognitive dissonance again. Some gradually develop confidence in their expertise and invulnerability. So, for these individuals, what now? Do another one? But this time better? Once they make *that* decision, there seems to be no going back until their luck runs out. This is how serial murder begins and progresses, and once the cycle is started it is almost immediately out of control.

Recreational murder is now commonplace, a practical solution for boredom and frustration.

For example, South Carolina serial killer Donald 'Pee Wee' Gaskins described his first killing in his autobiography *Final Truth* (1993). He had been snubbed rather rudely by a hitchhiker after he had picked her up on the highway. He had suggested to her that he could give her a lift to her destination and on the way he would buy her dinner and they might spend the night together. He was anticipating consensual sex with this girl, a one-night stand perhaps, but that was *his* fantasy, not hers. She laughed in his face and asked to get out of his car. She could not have picked a worse person to humiliate or a worse time to do it. He was seething with anger, resentment and lust at the time although, of course, she was unaware of this.

For Gaskins, who perhaps had not had a good look in the mirror for a while, this rejection was a brutal psychological slap in the face. When reality for the killer does not live up to the fantasy, this is when the victim faces the greatest danger. If his victim had managed to read the situation she would have played along, waited until they were in a public place and then easily escaped. But she did not. You cannot really blame her for falling into his trap. We all like to think we can pick dangerous people out in a crowd and then steer clear of them, but many serial killers look and behave just as we do, in fact more so. By laughing at his clumsy attempt to seduce her, she unwittingly crafted her own death sentence. Gaskins had something of a revelation. He explained what happened:

> The answer was simple, what I had to do was kill her. I remember smiling and wondering to myself why I had not ever thought of that before. If she was dead, she couldn't never tell nobody nothing. I could do anything I wanted with her. Anything.

So he did, he punched her senseless and drove her deep into a forest where he tied her up, brutally raped her and stabbed her, and then he killed her and disposed of her body at the same time by weighing her down with a heavy logging chain and pushing it into a swamp. 'I watched until she had sunk so deep there weren't no trace of her. She didn't make bubbles for very long' (Gaskins 1993).

When he had disposed of all the evidence to the best of his ability, he drove away extremely pleased with himself. He went into a truck-stop café and bought a meal with her money. 'Afterwards I was so damn hungry I ate the biggest steak on the menu. All my bothersomeness had sank into the marsh with that girl.'

But this euphoria did not last. The calm that Gaskins and other serial killers experience when they have killed for the first time does not last for very long, and in almost all cases they are quickly beset with fear and anxiety. The next day, Gaskins was terrified and panic-stricken. He had horrible nightmares about mistakes he might have made or clues he might have left. The night after the murder he was terrified, but, gradually, over the next few days, he cautiously began to accept that he was not going to get caught. Why would he? There were no witnesses and nothing to connect him with the disappearance of this woman. So what happened next? He wanted to try it again. So he did, haunting the South Carolina coastal highways for a number of years, a rolling death trap for naive hitchhikers, killing approximately one every six weeks. His final 'score', according to Gaskins, was 31 people he knew (confirmed) and between 80 and 90 strangers (unconfirmed).

People, including the killers themselves, hunt for explanations. Gerard J. Schaefer, the convicted Florida serial killer we met earlier, came up with the following when trying to explain his psychology to baffled journalist Sondra London:

> You don't understand ... because ... you are not a
> serial killer. What I tell you is inconsistent because

the experience itself [killing] is inconsistent. It's like
... I am throwing rocks at your window ... and
you're trying to figure out where they are coming
from ... and you can't ... because they are all
different colors. But you see ... they're different
colors ... because they are coming ... from different
places [Schaefer 1989].

No wonder London was confused: he was projecting
multiple personae and manipulating her for his own
amusement.

Gaskins is not quite so eloquent but perhaps more honest
about his dishonesty: 'I talk to everyone differently
depending on who they are and what I want from them'
(Gaskins 1993).

Joel Norris and Nan Cuba conducted an intensive
investigation into the life and crimes of Henry Lee Lucas,
who was eventually convicted of a total of 11 murders in a
labyrinth of legal permutations that lasted for decades.
Lucas would change his story almost every time he was
interviewed, at one point saying he had never killed
anyone, then later announcing he had killed more than 600
people. They likened Lucas's eternally shifting persona to a
kaleidoscope, where 'chips of glass shift and settle, and then
resettle according to the current viewer's whim'. They
concluded that Lucas, like the others, had learned the skill
of transformation and adaptation at an early age in order to
survive (Norris 1993).

So, basically, what all these people are saying, albeit in
different ways, is that you should not believe anything they
say. The information they are prepared to release is
carefully crafted and modified depending on whom they
are speaking to and what they want to achieve. Having

interacted with Ian Brady for more than six years, I am inclined to view his shifting personae from a similar perspective. This is not mental illness. We all do this in our day-to-day interactions with others, and it is usually subconscious. However, with serial killers, it seems to be a *lot* more pronounced, a *lot* more calculated. It is under conscious control, and control is one of the major factors to consider when trying to understand these people. A number of researchers in this field seem to have missed this essential aspect and blame these crimes on uncontrollable libido. This is a mistake. With serial sex crimes the sex act itself can be almost incidental, peripheral; it is the *control* over another human being that is the major motivating force.

So it can be argued that the only thing that remains consistent within the psychology of serial killers is *inconsistency*. This is not multiple-personality disorder (MPD) or dissociative identity disorder (DID). These are neurological conditions that can cause people to lose all control and are extremely rare and stand out a mile. Brain damage can sometimes be identified by CAT (computerised axial tomography) scans, which can identify neurological brain damage, or MRI (magnetic resonance imaging). The computer builds three-dimensional images of a person's brain from a series of calibrated X-rays. Any damage revealed may be the result of a number of different factors: high-impact head injuries, tumours, aneurysms, strokes etc.; but these are extremely expensive procedures that have little use in serial-killer detection except perhaps in retrospectively trying to isolate possible cause after the killer has been captured.

You cannot run CAT or MRI scans on hundreds of suspects: they take hours and cost a fortune. Even if you could find evidence of brain abnormalities, the data produced cannot be used with any predictive certainty of homicidal intent. Plenty of people have brain abnormalities and do not turn into serial killers, so even if you could run sophisticated scans on all your suspects, in most cases it would be unlikely to prove anything useful.

Lots of people with brain damage do not go around strangling people and chopping them into pieces with axes; and the results from those who *are* tested show that most serial killers do not have brain damage, anyway. They know exactly what they are doing. Even the umbrella term 'schizophrenia' is not terribly useful. Schizophrenia literally translates as 'split mind', the stereotypical Jekyll-and-Hyde scenario. This is far too simplistic. People who have MPD or DID do not have one mind that is split into two or more pieces: they have many minds that are contained in one cortex, which is not the same thing. Fairly recently, psychologists have started using the term 'antisocial personality disorder' (ASPD). This is a catch-all term for all kinds of unusual mind functioning that professionals cannot understand, and therefore is just another essentially useless category. It is certainly nothing new; Carl Jung summed it up nearly a century ago:

> The persona is a complicated system of relations
> between individual consciousness and society,
> fittingly enough a kind of mask, designed on the
> one hand to make definite impressions on others,
> and, on the other hand, to conceal the true nature
> of the individual [Jung 1928].

Schaefer's 'rocks' were different colours because he chose to throw them from different places. He projected the appropriate persona for the particular situation. Masks were worn when they were required and discarded or exchanged according to circumstance. So even experienced investigators who have the most promising clues find that they rarely lead to an understanding. They usually lead only to more clues which are even more perplexing. The personae that the killer expresses are driven by an undercurrent of shifting motivations that even the killers themselves have difficulty explaining, comprehending or understanding, even if they want to. They are just playing another game and thinking three moves ahead.

Danny Rolling, the 'Gainesville Ripper' (now executed for killing five people, although suspected of more) described pretty much the same psychological pattern – conscious decisions to project personae in specific ways for his own advantage: 'You see, I had multiple personalities at a very young age. I would go off to myself and then change over. It was a defense, the only way I could deal with the pain and confusion in my life' (Rolling and London 1996).

Rolling called himself 'the man of many faces' and actually had a name and description for each of his personae: Danny: 'Good-natured, friendly, loving, intelligent, troubled, tormented'; Ennad: 'Strong, self-willed, daring, Ennad might rape you, but he does not want your blood'; Gemini: 'Darkest night, evil, destructive. Gemini came from all the hatred, all the pain, everything sick and insane that happened.'

Rolling describes a typical experience of Gemini emerging: 'Danny's out, I'm in, Danny's out, I'm in. Let's go hunting … my hopeless friend' (Rolling and London 1996).

Rolling was diagnosed by a psychiatrist, Dr Elizabeth McMahon, as having a 'dissociative disorder known as possession disorder or possession syndrome'. This can occur with people who are intensely involved with Christian fundamentalism, as Danny Rolling was. For some individuals, try as they might, they discover that their blind faith in an interventional God is not supported or confirmed by any evidence whatsoever. Blind faith is a rare commodity, understandably. Brady lost all faith in God at a very early age when his prayers went unanswered, so he is not really comparable to Danny Rolling. Brady figured out the shortcomings of organised religion very early and developed his own philosophy which made him ultimately a lot more dangerous.

People like Rolling reach a crisis point where sexual impulses and violent tendencies breach the crumbling ramparts of their faith and everything falls apart. Despite clear evidence to the contrary, they are unable to accept that they could possibly be the instigator of rape or murder so they blame it on external dark forces: 'The devil made me do it. I was possessed.' Rolling was at least honest enough to not try to use an insanity defence in court. He knew that he consciously gave his killing nature free rein when it suited him and no jury would be likely to believe otherwise. He admitted (most of) his crimes in court. He was just trying to make sense of it all for himself.

It is interesting that he talks about himself using the third person. This is quite common with convicted killers. It is a way of talking about their crimes without either confirming or denying personal responsibility: 'Back at the hotel the man changed his clothes, and with them, his personality' (Rolling and London 1996). So it is a *conscious* decision, the core human identity almost stands back and lets its alter ego take centre stage. When describing his murders, Danny, the unifying component, sits back and watches. It is a psychological distancing mechanism: 'I did not do it, that was Gemini', etc. Many serial killers feel the need to give names to their murderous alter egos. Rolling had 'Gemini'; Ted Bundy had 'the Hunchback'; William Heirens – who admitted three murders in Illinois in the 1940s – had 'George Murman'; David Berkowitz had 'Son of Sam'; John Wayne Gacy – the 1970s serial killer – had 'Jack' or 'Pogo'; Yorkshire Ripper Peter Sutcliffe had, absurdly, a 'talking Polish gravestone'; and Zodiac – active in California in the 1960s – had, well, 'Zodiac' (he was never caught as far as we know and his real identity has never been confirmed). These were not nicknames or concepts given by the press while they tried to build up a mythology in order to sell newspapers: these were ephemeral entities invented by the killers themselves and summoned up in their trial presentations as part of insanity defences. But, as stated, this is not evidence of multiple personalities: it is more likely a kind of coping mechanism that might help them dodge the most serious consequences of their crimes. Also, they can be seen as an attempt at subtly shifting the blame and possibly stabilising their fragmented psychological equilibrium while simultaneously staying off death row (in the case of the US killers) and winding up in the relatively better conditions of a mental hospital. However, winning an insanity plea and ending up in a mental hospital rather than prison may well be something of the proverbial frying pan/fire analogy. Brady fell into that one in a big way.

Brady tried to blame his murders on external, supernatural forces, but with his tongue firmly in his cheek. He told both Fred Harrison and Colin Wilson (cited in Brady 1990) a story in which he described cycling to a job interview and, while pausing in a shop doorway, seeing a mysterious green 'face of death':

I have seen death, a green face, warm, not unattractive – attractive in fact. I'll do it a favour, and it will do me favours. Like it will do [for me], in the end. Green, not black – people always associate death with black. The face is not really formed, it's a radiation, a warmth. Warm green ... I had conversations with it. Everybody has something in them that they converse with, at the purely personal level. Everybody needs something that they are committed to, inside them [Brady, cited in Harrison 1987].

I asked Brady about this mysterious face of death in 2009 and he came back laconically, '*SPIN!*'

I burst out laughing. He had been just playing games with both of them, as I am sure most of the other killers I have mentioned above have also done with researchers trying to understand them. There was nothing occult involved as a direct motivating factor in Brady's crimes, at least nothing that he or anyone else can identify, explain or quantify. Rolling, Berkowitz and Sutcliffe all had supernatural stories to explain their crimes: a 'possessed dog', a 'ghostly voice from a Polish gravestone'. Serial killers are forever changing their stories – it goes with the territory.

Weapons Fixation

This concept can be seen from more than one perspective. In addition to naming their various personalities, some killers even go so far as to christen their favourite weapons. American Marines are encouraged to give their rifles names; some serial killers do it without being ordered to do so. Edmund Kemper, the California 'Co-ed Killer' who was convicted and imprisoned in 1963 for shooting both of his grandparents dead for 'fun', called his favourite knife 'the General'. Donald Gaskins called his 'the Toothpick'. Rolling, while not choosing a name for the KA-BAR Marine fighting knife he used to kill his victims, certainly imbued it with some aspect of personality: 'I will say this much. Once a knife's blade has tasted human flesh, it becomes transformed from mere metal and leather to an entity which thirsts for more … and more … blood' (Rolling 1996). The enormity of responsibility is diverted to alternate personae and in some cases additionally to weapons that might be used. Rolling even went so far as to describe how his different personality projections had different preferences for the type of weapon they would use for various occasions ('Ennad liked guns for robberies, Gemini preferred knives for killing').

Brady likes guns. He constantly referred to them in his letters, although he also carried a knife. Referring to a scene in a bar in Manchester when, out with Hindley, he had encountered some aggressive males, Brady describes his response:

> …. the 'black light' began to operate. Casually, I slipped my hand into my overcoat pocket and with thumb and forefinger, opened the lock-back knife I always carried, made entirely of stainless steel, devoid of ornament and with the functional purity of scalpel. I felt marvellous, delighted, and ready to hack the half-wits [2001].

Luckily for everyone concerned, nothing more apparently happened in this encounter. What is interesting here, though, is that, although his knife had no ornamental appeal and he had not given it a name, it certainly had an aesthetic/fetishistic appeal. Otherwise why use phrases such as 'functional purity of scalpel'?

Discussing the date of Brady and Hindley's apprehension by police, he said,

> *One came politely to our door, dressed as a bread man to gain entrance for the other twenty five dressed only in civilian uniform. I, and others, respected police back then. No wonder and no surprise that guns are regularly being carried by criminals today. Our rule was never to even show [our guns] unless absolutely necessary – axes, shotguns, iron bars were more psychologically effective back then, people just did not take revolvers seriously in those days, thinking them fake by their rarity, or just not used in Britain, only in America. Now, they think and act otherwise. The silver .38 snub-nosed revolver looked like a toy; the .45 and others were more convincing visually. But for convenience the .38 fitted nicely under my waistcoat, in easy reach when straightening my tie.*

Weapons fixation, again. Wilson, cited in Brady (2001), claims Brady told him that in 1999 a sharpened bucket handle was found taped under a sink in his ward and that he was blamed for this and subsequently moved to a psychotic ward where he went on hunger strike as a protest. Brady told me that the bucket handle had nothing to do with him. Who can be sure? Although I am inclined to believe him. Why lie about something like that when you freely admit to being a serial killer?

I mentioned I had tracked down some photos of him posing with a rifle.

> *Those few photos of the rifle (the licensed one) were an exception to the rule never to photograph, but I*

developed them personally and kept the only copies, which Myra's mother was supposed to destroy as instructed. What a family! A police informer sister, a spineless brother-in-law, a mother who deceived her own daughter. We, the two 'criminals', were the only ones who believed in family loyalty. And even Myra turned eventually. I had a weakness – I always gave first move before acting.

Gaskins carried a gun to gain the psychological upper hand over his victims: 'Nobody argues with a gun,' he stated. 'I drew out my Beretta and pointed it at her ... that always scares them into being real quiet, like their first look at the "Toothpick" always makes them piss' (Gaskins 1993).

This is known in routine forensic psychology as 'weapons fixation'. It is akin to a deer being immobilised by oncoming headlights on a road. The victim freezes. If someone is pointing a gun or an especially evil-looking knife at someone who manages to survive the encounter without getting shot or stabbed, the chances are that they will usually be able to recall the exact details concerning the appearance of the weapon, yet they will probably have a highly unreliable memory for details about the person who was holding it. The perception of the person being threatened is immediately fixated on the object of the fear.

Some serial killers even adapt their vehicles as weapons. Ted Bundy drove a number of (stolen) Volkswagen Beetle cars. It was a model he had discovered by trial and error was the best to trap his victims in when they accepted a lift and had climbed into the front seat. He had removed the door handle on the passenger side so the door could not be opened from the inside, and the small size of the car made it easy for him to jam the person up against the dashboard so that he could easily jump into the back seat and then strangle them from behind. Lawrence 'Pliers' Bittaker and Roy Norris – operating in California in 1979 – used a van, their portable murder 'comfort zone', which Bittaker christened 'the Murder Mack'. The van had no side windows in the back, so that once a victim was captured it would be virtually impossible for them to draw attention to their plight as they were driven to a deserted location to be raped and murdered (Davis 2005).

Although Brady has an aesthetic fascination with guns, as far as I am aware he has never admitted shooting anyone. Why? He could easily have shot many of his victims. It is highly unlikely that anyone would have heard gunshots at the location of the murders up on the moors. There are a number of reasons. He was, for instance, forensically aware of the problems associated with using a firearm to kill someone. No two guns are exactly the same. Even two seemingly identical guns made by the same manufacturing equipment on the same day will have unique forensic characteristics. Brady knew this. Bullets are easily linked to the weapon that fired them and ballistics evidence stands up as solid forensic evidence in court. If he shot someone and the gun was later found in his possession, this would be very hard to explain. So he would have to dispose of a weapon that he may have been particularly fond of at the time and/or he would have to retrieve the bullet embedded in the victim's body, which may not be a terribly easy thing to do.

Obtaining the handguns they wanted was no easy task. Myra Hindley had to join a gun club in Cheadle in order to buy revolvers, passing herself off as an innocent and somewhat unlikely amateur target-shooting enthusiast and befriending other club members before being in a position to buy revolvers covertly (Brady may not have been able to join because of his criminal record). Brady also mentions travelling abroad to buy firearms equipment. I have not discussed this in depth with him but his appreciation and knowledge of weapons came up on a number of occasions. For example:

> Shot guns were more persuasive and ballistic safe (only the firing pin marks on the empties to worry about). We also had adapters for the revolvers, enabling smaller calibres to be used in larger calibre guns (.22 from a .45); adapters being cheaper to replace than used guns [2004].

Weapons fixation works both ways. This is not unprecedented. Gaskins, in full knowledge that the police were breathing down his neck, could not bear to part with his favourite weapon, 'the Toothpick'. He actually packaged it up when he thought he was about to be arrested and then went to the post office and posted it to himself.

Brady chose ligature strangulation for most of his murders. For the last one, he used an axe. There could be other reasons for not shooting his victims, which are less palatable than simply not wanting to dispose permanently of his beloved guns. Death by strangulation is much more up close and personal for the killer. The majority of serial killers choose to strangle or suffocate their victims, almost as if the death is somehow more satisfying if they use their hands. With the murders being very much a power/control experience, strangulation allows the killer to take as long as they want to complete/appreciate the murder. Some serial killers, e.g. John Wayne Gacy, Ted Bundy and the policeman Gerard Schaefer, all enjoyed taking their victims to the point of death through strangulation, then loosening the ligature and letting the victim revive to consciousness before proceeding. This way the murder could be prolonged for as long as they wanted. Dennis Nilsen describes enjoying 'the extremity of the death act itself. If I did it to myself I could only experience it once, if I did it to others I could experience the death act over and over again' (Masters 1985).

But this is all detail, murder aesthetics. As far as the killings are concerned, regardless of what weapon they use and no matter how much they try to avoid responsibility and blame, serial killers *decide* to kill, they make rational decisions, rational to them at least, and the realisation that they are actually capable of killing and getting away with it is something of a surprise, even to them. It really is that simple; it is a matter of *choice*. The answer was staring me right in the face all along. They do it because they *want to* and because they *can*.

Can serial killers control themselves? Yes, they can, but they choose not to. Do they have difficulty controlling themselves? Obviously yes, they do.

Other patterns started to come into focus.

STAGE 2: Murder Becomes Routine
'Soon, everything seemed dull ... There was not a clear identifiable emotion within me ... my depersonalization was so intense, had gone so deep, that the normal ability to feel compassion had been eradicated' (Ellis 1991).

Behaviour based on fantasy has an overwhelming tendency to escalate. Once the first murder has been achieved without capture and the shock starts to subside, the balance between fear and desire tilts. The first murder can be very frightening, while at the same time being

63

something of a disappointment for the killer. It may not have been quite what they expected or fantasised about. Afterwards, if a body has not been found, there will be no splash headlines in the press, nothing more than a missing-person report in a police file, so the aftermath can be something of a letdown and the murder itself something of an anticlimax, especially if it was based on fantasy.

'It is invariably the case that actions bright and exciting in the imagination are unfortunately, often disappointing or farcical in practice ... real adventure – of the neck-on-the-line variety – is unsettling ...Riding the whirlwind is an acquired taste' (Brady 2001).

Some individuals acquire the taste. Somehow, everything happening becomes progressively easier to ignore. Usually the killer becomes psychologically derailed by the first murder. Then the level of violence escalates and a new set of dynamics comes into play. This next stage seems (at first) almost too callous to comprehend. This is a slide into indifference as the body count rises. The novelty of getting away with a murder has quickly grown stale, especially if hardly anyone has even noticed. This is where many killers elaborate their crimes in order to try to accentuate the intensity. As with an addiction to a drug, the serial killer needs to increase the dose in order to replicate and enhance the effect. Once a serial pattern has been established, the so-called 'cooling-off' period between murders gradually becomes shortened and the level of violence escalates. Schaefer (1989) describes this escalation:

> By the time I nabbed Jessup and Place [two of his victims] I had been in the ghoul game for almost 10 years . . . By then I was into doing double murders and an occasional triple when the opportunity

arose. Doing doubles is far more difficult than doing singles, but on the other hand it also puts one in a position to have twice as much fun. Neither wants to be the one to go first and they don't mind telling you quickly why their best friend should be the one to die.

This escalation got Schaefer caught. This is where some serial killers start becoming careless and making mistakes.

In the 1960s, around the time Brady was emerging from his chrysalis in prison and developing his game plan, an American rapist and serial killer, Ted Bundy, was also developing a kaleidoscope of projected personalities and fantasies. He was a student, lawyer, psychologist and, rather alarmingly, a worker on a rape-crisis and suicide helpline, which apparently he was rather good at (Rule 2000).

Bundy was initially exhilarated by his crude sexual attacks and murders. He was careful for a while, shifting kill sites to different states, switching identities. He covered his tracks leaving very little for the police to work with. Once he got the hang of recreational murders and the emotional shocks of the early murders had become routine, it turned into a game. He started killing two female victims at a time and on one occasion attacked five women in one night, three of them ending up dead. Planning and precision became irrelevant and he became bored, disorganised and lazy, taking risks, driving the same type of (stolen) car and leaving behind clues and witnesses.

At this point, he could not really care less if he got caught. He was indifferent, perhaps even looking forward to it. This is not rare. This pattern repeats itself within the history of very many serial killers. Gary Ridgway, the 'Green River Killer', basically threw in the towel when he finally got arrested in 2001 for four murders in Washington state, and confessed to an additional forty-four others. This was no miracle of police forensic endeavour. It seems everyone involved, killer and detectives alike, had just got fed up with the whole thing and decided to bring it to a close. Brady has a chapter on the 'Green River Killer' in his book, where, interestingly, he suggests more than one person was involved. He may well be right, although I suspect that Ridgway may have been doing different styles of murders in different ways, depending on the mood he was in when it was time for him to kill.

After conviction in Florida, Schaefer and Bundy were briefly on death row together in Starke prison. They recognised comparable psychology and, while not exactly becoming friends, each could see aspects of his personality reflected. They exchanged routine serial-killer shop talk: moaning about the chore of digging graves, cleaning up after a killing, getting the urine smell out of the car. Police thought Bundy's regular removal of the death seat from his car was part of his 'trap'. Not so: he was just trying to get rid of the smell and attempting to wash the visible bloodstains away (this was before luminol was used by forensic investigators to detect the presence of bloodstains that cannot be seen with the naked eye).

Schaefer said, '[Bundy] knew for sure that I knew there was a really boring side to death work. That it wasn't all raging sexual release as the media likes to portray it.' (Schaefer and London 1989).

Schaefer and Bundy are both dead now – Bundy electrocuted, Schaefer stabbed to death by another convict – so we have only scraps to work with. However, the growing feeling of indifference towards the fate of their victims or even their own fate can be seen in the case histories of other killers. Edmund Kemper was only 14 years old when he decided, on a whim, to shoot both of his grandparents. 'I just wondered what it would be like to shoot Grandma.' Released in 1969, he soon continued killing, now with randomly selected victims initially kidnapped in university campuses and later hitchhikers picked up on the freeways. His killing skills were initially refined to avoid capture: he selected strangers for victims, avoiding leaving links or clues that might tie him to the disappearances. But this controlled phase did not last very long. In the 1970s, he attended his psychiatric appointments with the decapitated head of one of his new victims in the boot of his car. 'At that diagnostic interview, two psychiatrists agreed that Kemper was now "safe" and recommended that his juvenile records be sealed to permit him to live a normal adult life' (Leyton 2001).

In 1973, he murdered his mother, who was probably the person he wanted to kill all along. He cut her head off, raped the body, cut her larynx out and ground it up in the kitchen waste-disposal machine, and then stood the head up on top of a bookcase and used it for a dartboard. Even *that* got boring after a while, so he phoned one of his mother's friends, Sally Hallett, and invited her to the house for a 'surprise party' for (the already dead) Mrs Kemper, and it certainly was a surprise for Mrs Hallett. When she arrived, Kemper bludgeoned her, strangled her and cut her head off. Having finally run out of ideas, Kemper then burned out in a psychological meltdown and turned himself in. Again, no high-profile exercise in forensic investigation here. He had had enough and wanted to turn himself in. He phoned the police and asked them to come and arrest him. They put the phone down, assuming he was yet another crank caller. It took more than one call, but finally they turned up and took him into custody, where he remains to this day.

you. I think serial killers have these tremendously exciting experiences, but no one to share them with. So they spend a lot of time cultivating people they hope they will be able to talk to. They start out small, and they build up, hoping to get to the point where they can tell you what they have been doing, and you will accept it (Kelly, quoted in Schaefer and London 1989).

By an unforeseeable turn of events, Ian Brady met Myra Hindley. Despite all the danger signs from his criminal history, I do not think anyone could have predicted that the lethal factor that started Brady's infamous murder cycle might have been this woman. Hindley was a young secretary employed by Millwards, a chemical supplier in Manchester where Brady worked. She was assigned to assist him. Without Hindley, the Moors Murders probably would not have happened. Although Brady was initially indifferent, eventually they fell in love – at least as far as 'love' is possible for sociopaths – and they became inseparable, 'almost telepathic'.

To help Brady get the equipment he wanted for robberies (conceived conceptually, but never fully realised), Hindley obtained the weapons they needed. Once they had these, they needed reliable transport. Brady had motorcycles, but those are not much use for the types of crimes that were being considered. Hindley learned to drive a car, passed her test, and they began hiring vehicles occasionally. This is when their murders commenced. Eventually they bought their own car.

Neither of them has ever been able to offer a comprehensive explanation as to why they started killing. While I have tried to identify causal factors (with Brady at least), there is no magic solution. It was a unique combination of factors. Perhaps at this point they were both showing off, each trying to outdo the other. Hindley was infatuated with Brady's gangster façade and tried to flatter him by demonstrating that she could be just as ruthless as he could, and Brady may well have been trying to impress her by demonstrating that he was actually far more ruthless than she could possibly have imagined.

I recently asked him why he had not included any case studies of female serial killers in his analysis of serial killing in his book, *The Gates of Janus*, and he said that he had not done so because he did not want the reader to think he might really be talking about Hindley. So maybe it is not the case that Brady is unable to explain why their murders occurred. Perhaps he had never really been given an opportunity to explain. Brady conceived and conducted most of the murders on his own, but not all of them. He formed a partnership with someone he could trust to explore possibilities and who in some ways was even more murderously adventurous than he was.

After Brady had been arrested, police searching the house found a left-luggage ticket for two suitcases that had been stored at Manchester's central railway station. In them were photographs of ten-year-old Lesley Ann Downey taken in Hindley's bedroom and three copies of an audiotape recording of the minutes immediately before her murder. The original tape had been made on the night of her abduction, but Brady had copied it at least twice. Her mother later identified one of the recordings as being that of her daughter's voice screaming for help after she had been kidnapped and taken to their house. While sound engineers claimed they could identify the voices of only Brady, Hindley and Downey, there has always been a suspicion that there was another person there, but this has never been proved and almost certainly never will be. Both Brady and Hindley claimed at their trial that the child had left their house unharmed, but more recently Brady stated that Hindley had *'insisted on strangling her'*. At the trial, when Brady was asked why he had kept the recording and duplicated it, he replied, *'because it was unusual ... that is the best adjective I can find at the moment'*.

Also in one of the suitcases was a brunette wig, simple but effective misdirection. If anyone had remembered seeing a child getting into a car, they may not have been able to recall the exact make of the car or the registration number but they would almost certainly remember that the woman inviting the child into the car had dark hair. Myra Hindley, a platinum blonde, would have been swiftly eliminated from any police inquiry. As it was, no witnesses to any of their abductions came forward and the wig in the suitcase was, at best, circumstantial evidence. However, Hindley's fingerprints on the photographs of the child were certainly not circumstantial: this was solid evidence of her involvement, which was ultimately used to convict her.

Hindley could have easily testified against Brady as a prosecution witness and he might well, at that time, have corroborated her story. If she had done so, she would almost certainly have received a much lighter sentence and would probably have been released at some point. But she did not. Like Brady, she pleaded not guilty to all charges, but with the amount of evidence piled up against them it was pretty much inevitable that any jury would convict both of them and they would both receive the maximum penalty available under the law at that point in time, which they did.

Modi operandi

Brady and/or Hindley would lure a young person into their car on some innocent pretext. Friendly couple in a nice car offer a lift home (with a small detour)? Why not? Nobody knew much about serial killing or abductions in those days, bar really exceptional cases. It was a time when you could leave your front door open and let your children play in the streets unsupervised. Sometimes Hindley would drive the victim up on to the moors, with Brady following behind on his motorcycle; other times they would both be in the car.

Once all these pieces were in place and they arrived at the moors, it was all over for the victims. They were led out away from the road to admire a view or help look for something. Isolation was used for several reasons. First was the element of control – 'Control by environment rather than by weapon' (2001). Even if the victim became aware of the danger they were in and tried to run, where were they going to run to? There was nowhere to run. One police officer who was involved with the search for bodies on the moors remarked that the place was 'like the surface of the moon' (Williams 1968). Second, it was highly unlikely that there would be any witnesses passing through such a desolate area. The victims were killed and buried at designated spots and the couple drove home, before returning at a later date to photograph the grave sites and ensure the bodies had not been dug up by animals.

More murders came to light after both Brady and Hindley had been convicted, and another body was found in 1987, but neither of them was ever charged with any of these. At the time of their capture, Brady had absolute faith in Hindley. He had witnessed her killing and knew she would follow him down any road of criminal activity he chose and could also be trusted to keep her mouth shut. During the murder period, though, boredom started to set in and, a couple of murders later, it was time for some aggressive expansion.

At this point, there was nothing much to anticipate other than more murders, which by then had become routine. '*I felt old at twenty-six. Everything was ashes. I felt there was nothing of interest – nothing to hook myself into. I had experienced everything.*' Expansion was considered by including David Smith, Hindley's brother-in-law, who had a (relatively minor) criminal history. It was a way to progress, but it was a massive error of judgement that got them both jailed. Operating as a pair, they were quite literally getting away with murder; but expanding their enterprise by including Smith was a serious tactical mistake.

STAGE 3: Post-capture

In November 1985, after 19 years in prison, Brady was declared criminally insane and transferred to Park Lake Hospital in Liverpool, which is now Ashworth Hospital, where he remains to this day and is likely to remain until his death. When I initially wrote to Brady, I knew enough about his history to know that he could not be quantified using standard psychometric testing tools (if indeed anyone can with any degree of certainty), and it would have been pointless and unprofessional for me even to try. Anyway, I was not planning to do a psychiatric diagnosis and held no lofty medical pretensions along those lines because I am not a psychiatrist: I am a psychologist. I was interested in his views on serial killing because I thought that, as a convicted serial killer, he might have some insight into the field I was researching, the psychology of serial murder. So, I just tried to relate to him as a human being and see what I might be able to learn. At the same time, I was also intrigued by the possibilities of experiencing first hand what is actually going on in the 'special hospitals'.

I wrote to him for the first time in 2002 after reading his book on the analysis of serial killing. My letter was just an enquiry to see if he was going to continue research and write anything else. I had no idea whether he would reply. He wrote back to me. After we had established a modicum of mutual trust over the next two years, I asked him again if he might be considering writing further material and he elaborated on my initial question:

> Creativity in adversity? Discussed this concept with [Lord] Longford when he was writing a book on the possible merits of suffering. I argued that comfortable academic contemplation of such was quite different from the direct unrelenting, hopeless experience that nullified possible objectivity and distorted sensibility and personality. Therefore suffering, on the whole, was primarily negative and held little merit other than self-indulgent or aesthetic rationalisation of the unavoidable. Other people's suffering is always so much more philosophically acceptable [2004].

We started exchanging letters frequently. Once we had established a framework, our conversations went in lots of different directions. This type of research cannot be done effectively in a short space of time. It took me years to gain any credible trust, but eventually he wanted to talk about crime and murder; he wanted to talk about institutional corruption; and he wanted to talk to *me*.

Brady called himself *'The resident folk devil of Ashworth'* in his first letter to me, and the focus of hostility towards him has increased since the death of Myra Hindley, aged 60, in

2002. With Hindley gone, he is the only one left with any answers, and the only one left to blame. At this point, I had to consider how this research could affect my own life. From reading forensics texts, it became apparent that some of the people who work with killers and look into the abyss, regardless of their experience, find the abyss is looking back into them in alarming and unexpected ways. This can be disconcerting and potentially dangerous. Let us look at two examples.

Final Truth (1992), the autobiography of Donald Gaskins

Author Wilton Earle edited and published Donald 'Pee Wee' Gaskins's autobiography, which is possibly the most intensely graphical depiction of the life and crimes of a serial killer I have ever come across. Gaskins had an incredibly vicious introduction to the American penal system. He was gang-raped and brutalised to the point where he would either have to kill or endure further rapes and beatings and accept a subservient role as a prison 'punk' – basically, a meat puppet to be used, raped, bought and sold among the prison wolves.

When he was finally released, he had discovered that pain endured could be cancelled out (temporarily) by pain inflicted with what he called his 'recreational murders' or 'coastal kills' in South Carolina. The fact that most of his victims were perfectly innocent strangers did not seem to matter, and later made it easier for him to commit his 'serious murders' (people he knew). Gaskins gloated about his 'special mind' to Wilton Earle in a series of recorded interviews which were published after Gaskins died in the electric chair. Gaskins's confessions are terribly brutal and do not contain one shred of compassion for the men, women and children he raped and slaughtered (including members of his own family). Wilton Earle, while forcing his composure to remain professionally neutral as he patiently listened to Gaskins giggling and bragging about torturing people to death, found the whole experience shattering. It half killed him; he had a serious breakdown and was very ill indeed.

The Last Victim (1992)

Then I came across another case which had similar elements, *The Last Victim* (Moss with Kottler 1999). Their work details Moss's relationship with 'Pogo the Killer Clown' John Wayne Gacy, which progressed through letters, phone calls and eventually visits while Gacy was pitching his last-ditch appeals against execution. Jason Moss (1975–2006) most certainly *was* Gacy's last victim and some have argued that he set himself up. Moss was only 18 at the time and was corresponding with a number of high-profile killers, Wisconsin serial killer Jeffrey Dahmer, Los Angeles 'Night Stalker' Richard Ramirez and Charles Manson among them. He finally selected Gacy as his central research theme. What he rather naively failed to notice was that Pogo had his own agenda and selection process, as 33 young men, very much like Moss, had already found out. Twenty-eight of them were discovered buried in Gacy's cellar. When Gacy ran out of room, he started simply throwing the bodies in the local river. Unbelievably, Gacy claimed at his trial that all 33 deaths were 'accidental'. The jury was understandably unconvinced. Twenty-eight bodies buried in his cellar and five floating down the river were somewhat difficult to explain as 'accidents'. He was sent to death row but he wasn't quite finished killing yet. Gacy continued to kill even after he was caught, reaching out from his death-row cell and crafting someone else's doom, which would occur *after he himself was dead*.

After a number of years, Moss noticed the trap he was in: 'I began to realise [the danger] and knew if I didn't bring things to a close soon, there would not be much of my mind left' (Moss with Kottler 1999). Sadly, he was too young and too late. It seems incredible that he was admitted to death row to spend time alone with Gacy in the first place, but he was and he could not cope with it psychologically. It finally tipped him over the edge.

I trawl through files, minimising and maximising and sliding images around the screen until I come up with three pictures:

1. Moss stands on a sunny American suburban sidewalk, smiling, being handed a letter from one of his killer pen pals by a mail lady. He looks fit and happy, as if he is about to go and play baseball or something.

2. Moss is now pictured looking rather uneasy standing on death row next to a handcuffed Gacy. Moss's discomfort is understandable: Gacy had just threatened to rape and kill him and there had been no guards in sight to intervene. Gacy does not look nervous. He looks smug.

3. Slide cursor across the screen to the next image: a couple of years had passed and for Jason Moss things didn't look so good any more.

Click and enlarge.

You can tell it is Moss only by the eyes. Everything else has changed: in this picture he is now bald (totally), ashen, haunted; his posture is crooked; he looks about 50. Shortly after this photo was taken, he shot himself in the head. There was no note, but the date of his suicide (6/6/2006) has not gone unnoticed by Internet conspiracy theorists. Riding the whirlwind can be a one-way experience and you are unlikely to get home safe at the end.

Then I got an invitation from Brady asking me to visit him at Ashworth. He had said, *'Never doubt your experience in favour of other people's opinions.'*

So I went.

CHAPTER THREE

ASHWORTH HOSPITAL

I had read that Brady would communicate only selectively. His early letters focused on conditions, a common gripe with those caged. Brady cannot even bitch about the weather, having not been outside since 1975, so it is understandable for him to focus his contempt on the suffocating environment where he is incarcerated. Ashworth Hospital has fluorescent lighting and incessant noise 24 hours a day. He wanted me to come and experience it for myself.

In an early letter written to me on Christmas Day 2003, he had given some rather ominous warnings concerning the hospital:

> Take care not to become sick or sectioned if ever on safari through darkest Liverpool and the pygmy auspices of the Merseyside Care Trust. Carry a first aid kit and elephant gun. They'd sell your organs for a percentage bonus. One advantage, being on hunger strike avoids the badly cooked swill which would cause riots in a maximum security prison.

During my twenty years in prison, I saw six riots, food trays flying freely, governors and screws skating and falling flat back on chunks of gravy and custard – I had more freedom, trust and intelligent company in prison back in the 1960/70s than exists in this self-dramatising limbo of the walking dead, a penal anachronism.

Inmates are complaining about their miserable, badly cooked Christmas day fare! Before this parasitic regime stopped food parcels, I used to live almost entirely on outside provisions, so I'm missing nothing now. I hang Christmas cards out of respect for the senders, as against the contamination of surroundings. The word 'patient' is only retained: a) to infer mental incapacity and discredit all valid complaints and charges against staff, b) to maintain the prestige of calling this a 'hospital' and warders 'nurses'.

Travelling to the hospital was a five-hour crawl up the motorway into the dark. I pulled off the motorway junction and into the Ashworth complex: massive electrified fences with razor wire. Puzzle your way to the visitor centre. Lots of loosely connected single-storey buildings with bars, gates, CCTV cameras. Later, I concluded that it would be harder to break *into* Ashworth undetected than to break *out*.

Visitors' entry, bulletproof glass. Put your possessions in a sliding tray, which slams through to their side. I am wondering if I have to talk to Ian Brady through a glass shield. Am I allowed to smile at anyone? Visitors' lounge is ugly hospice yellow. I got some water in a strange pointed cup. You cannot stand it on a table (they do not want you to stay).

Security checks: I anticipated a standard airport check-in.

80

Not quite. I have to remove my jacket, my watch, empty my pockets, walk through a metal detector, walk back through and remove a ring, finally get through that successfully. All my things are taken from me and put in a plastic box. They go through an X-ray machine and disappear into the abyss for the duration of my visit. They take a mugshot of me.

Next is the body search. Arms cruciform up against a wall and I am frisked from head to toe. A huge sign orders 'DO NOT PET THE SNIFFER DOGS', and in they come – not the huge snarling Alsatians I was imagining but rather two diminutive mongrels.

What now? Retina/iris scan? DNA test? I have been here only about an hour as a visitor and am already feeling processed and nervous.

Finally, they decide I am not a risk to their security and move me to the next bit. Here, I have to enter a series of what can only be described as air-locks. I move into a chamber, the door seals and locks behind me, and then, after a while, the door in front of me opens, air hisses in and I can proceed (and breathe again). I walk down a little barbed-wire corridor and then into another enclosed air-lock. I glance through the wire: there are a couple of tennis courts. Four-foot-high weeds have burst through the playing surface and the nets appear to have long since rotted away. This is not exactly what I expected from looking at the Ashworth website, which shows a lot of smiling people enjoying a nice sunny afternoon.

I get to Ian Brady's ward. Single-storey building heavily barred, more locks to be opened before me and then locked behind me. The guards lead me along a corridor into an office. Inside is – guess what. Another guard, who takes more details (the same as I had already given two 'airlocks' ago). No handshake, no smile. I am then taken into a room, which is apparently where Ian Brady is force-fed every day (a procedure that takes a number of hours). It is small, about 12 foot by 10 foot. Dirty table with a constellation of cigarette burns. Small barred window. A couple of old chairs, nothing else.

A guard yells, 'Get Brady!', slams the door and I am alone. Not much to look at. No pictures, no anything. I feel as if I am in a cell. Which in fact I am.

Where should I sit? One chair looks rather gross. Caked in crusts of yellow stains, which frame a shadow-like silhouette of a human torso and arms. It looks as if it belongs to someone, so I take the other. I hear shuffling footsteps. Doors being slammed and locked, jangling keys.

The door flies open.

Ian Brady.

What is he like? Well, tall. I would guess about 6 feet tall. Black suit, scarecrow frame, but not emaciated, not yet. He shakes my hand, introducing himself. He is the first person since my arrival to acknowledge my presence as anything other than a nuisance, disturbing the routine. Brady sits down into the outline on the force-feeding chair. He has tinted glasses and a tube hanging out of his nose.

At the time, smoking is still allowed in Ashworth. Brady chain-smokes through the whole interview, flicking ash on the floor or simply letting it fall into his lap. He stubs his cigarettes out on the table with undisguised contempt for his surroundings. With no other option, I do the same. He mentioned smoking in his first letter, which was mainly concerned with the misery of spending Christmas at the hospital when he would rather be dead: ' ... *smoking will hopefully accelerate the so far laggard* deus ex machina *of cancer – the "smoking kills" tobacco logo, in my case, contravenes the trades description act*'.

That hope has now been extinguished, along with his cigarettes, when smoking was banned at Ashworth in 2008. I later asked him about this.

'*Stopping smoking was not the problem. However being stopped by the admin here is another more emetic matter*' (2009).

Back to our meeting. I shift to neutral researcher mode. He is going to give me a mental tour of his situation. He takes the interview in any direction he wants and, under the circumstances, I am not going to argue.

He asks if I have an agenda for the meeting. I say no, I just want to talk to him. At this time, I make a point of not asking idiot questions such as, 'Tell me about the murders.' It would be intrusive and rude. At later interviews, he *did* talk about his murders, his '*existential exercise*' or '*that Moors business*' – the terms he uses for the crimes he was convicted of, but at this early stage I had to concentrate fully on using an extremely objective and non-judgemental approach.

He describes his capture and conviction for killing as almost an inconvenient glitch in his criminal career rather than the life-terminating event it was for him and Myra Hindley and a lot of other people as well. At this meeting, as far as his crimes are concerned, he speaks only of the day of his capture. I make it clear that I am there simply to talk to him. I see no symptoms of any instability; in fact, these are rather conspicuous by their absence when you consider that I am talking with someone who has been locked in a concrete box for nearly half a century and is now incarcerated in the psychotic ward (as Brady calls it) of the most notorious mental hospital in the United Kingdom.

We talk for over three hours. Occasionally, a face appears at the window in the door, patients shuffle up and down the corridors, but we are left alone and uninterrupted. During the interview, he remains calm. Only once do I see him express deep emotion. We are discussing the day of his capture (7 October 1965).

His house had been surrounded after a tip-off to the police from Myra Hindley's brother-in-law David Smith (who would become the chief prosecution witness, and who had been present when Brady killed Edward Evans with an axe the previous night in the living room in the little house at 16 Wardle Brook Avenue in Manchester). Smith had phoned the police the next morning. There had been a mysterious gap between Smith's leaving the house the previous night after witnessing the murder and making the call to the police the following morning (Brady has never understood *'what happened in those missing hours'*).

Brady demonstrated to me what happened when police officers from three forces had arrived (one officer disguised as a bread-delivery man). They had pushed past Hindley and entered the living room, where he was in bed writing a letter in green ink to his employer explaining that he could not go to work due to a damaged ankle (injured during the Evans murder, although obviously he did not mention this in the letter). Brady leaned forward and showed me how, after calmly finishing the letter and with the house swarming with police, he had leaned down while sitting on the bed to put his shoes on with one hand while simultaneously reaching underneath with his other hand for his revolver. Fortunately for the police, Brady had left it upstairs in the bedroom, where Evans's body had been carried by him and David Smith the previous night. Brady had discarded his gun in Hindley's bedroom with the body because the heavy revolver had been getting in the way in its shoulder holster when they were struggling to carry the corpse upstairs and hide it while trying not to involve the grandmother, who had been woken by the noise of the murder.

Hindley kept guard at her door while the men stumbled past with the body. If you can overlook the gravity of the situation, it sounded almost farcical, almost as if a closer look might have revealed a glimpse of Alfred Hitchcock on a ladder cleaning the window behind them as the body was concealed in Hindley's bedroom.

But there was nothing funny about the situation as far as Brady and Hindley were concerned. The police were there, the evidence was there, they were pretty much busted for this particular murder. However, if the gun had been there, he and Hindley just might have been able to evade capture. When this realisation sank in, and certainly not for the first time, Brady's expression changed. I have never seen a human expression quite like that and I do not think I will ever forget it: utter desolation and regret. If they *had* shot their way out, their plan was to escape by, ironically, the one route the police had not covered, a small path between the houses across the street. This Brady and Hindley had christened 'Rain Lane' after an experience when they got drenched walking along it and getting caught in a downpour when they had been so free.

Brady quickly regained his composure. Later, he dismissed this observation in a letter (2004):

> *I only recall the interrogating teams of three forces. At the trial the police testified Smith warned we were armed – hence the 25 police and six cars that surrounded the house. Unlike today's posing exhibitionists with German machine guns, in my day the police were more discreet, merely supplying a*

couple of selected detectives with revolvers kept out of sight. We had the same insurance policy of concealment unless forced to use. Back then the public didn't take firearms seriously.

During the interview, I had asked him why they did not take evasive action earlier when the police were trying to enter the house. Hindley could have slammed the door on the police; they could have got to their weapons. Maybe.

'*Why I didn't shout and block, when she opened the back door to the police unwittingly, is an imponderable still. Even with the sprained ankle I might have reached upstairs in time.*'

'If you had managed to get to your guns, what would you have done?'

Brady looked over his glasses at me. '*What do you think?*'

They would have shot as many police as they could and then sprinted down 'Rain Lane'.

Later, in a letter, I asked him: 'If you both had made it through "Rain Lane" without being shot or captured?'

'Rain Lane' was one route north by car once you hit Ashton. The second route was a quarter of a mile distant for emergency by foot, a railway track, we'd checked it prior. Having used tracks for jobs, I had a map of the whole Manchester network installations for use in disappearing acts to suit all occasions [2004].

More recently I asked him again about this: 'What if you had managed to escape?'

'*Difficult to know how the future would have evolved if we had not been interrupted. We certainly intended to retire young or die in the attempt*' (2008).

But all this is hypothetical. Despite all these plans, their luck had finally run out. They had been caught red-handed with a dead body in the house and a witness who saw the murder – not the easiest thing to talk your way out of in court. There were some possible escape opportunities. Hindley was not even arrested for five days after the murder investigation started. She had plenty of time to run, but she did not want to leave Brady to face the consequences of their crimes alone. Myra Hindley, much later after conviction, would try to orchestrate an escape from jail. For Brady, though, the opportunity for escape came much earlier while he was being held at Hyde police station shortly after his arrest. He was left alone in a canteen with an unbarred window while an officer took a telephone call. Brady did not move. '*I could have stepped into the parking lot and got away.*' His second chance came after Hindley had been arrested and they were both being held at what was then Risley remand centre. Brady was escorted to the women's section for an interview with his solicitor.

> *They came to take me over, and there were no handcuffs, no walkie-talkies, no police dogs or television cameras ... there was a pea soup fog which was so bad we were bumping into cars ... you could not even see the beams from the searchlights. All I had to do was one step forward, one step sideways, and that was that. It was a cinch* [June 2008].

Again, he did not try it, although at that point he had not been convicted and the police were still trying to figure out the basic details. Perhaps there was still some hope that a legal manoeuvre might cause the case to collapse, or, if not, then perhaps they would be convicted of manslaughter, which typically results in a sentence of about four or five years. Or, if successfully convicted, then perhaps even a 'normal' life sentence (for a single murder, in the United Kingdom, this is typically about 13–14 years, depending on premeditation and mitigating circumstances).

It seems likely at that point that Brady did not fully realise the shattering repercussions of his crimes and that both he and Hindley would be spending their entire lives in prison without any possibility of parole or release – ever. If he had, I guess he would have at least attempted to disappear into the fog. At that time, however, his loyalty to Hindley was still paramount, as hers was to him, and neither of them wanted to leave the other to face the music alone.

The third possibility of Brady's escaping happened many years later at Ashworth when someone apparently, and unbelievably, forgot to lock the doors and some of the inmates stumbled outside into the grounds. I cannot vouch for the truth of this, it may well just be wishful thinking, but this is what Brady told me:

A slight breeze wafted my 70 year old frame towards the wall. But a passing doctor in pajamas, suffering from Münchausen-by-proxy syndrome and using stilts to increase his stature, managed to grab my feed-tube and anchor me to a couple of beach ball patients training to be garden gnomes in the grounds. But seriously if all the doors to wards were left open at night, no captives would escape, and even if ropes were left dangling over the walls to boot, most of the Michelin zombies wouldn't get six-feet off the ground without a trampoline. That's the truth being concealed by this pathetic security charade; no one escaped even when there was maximum freedom inside under a decent regime and inmates were being released weekly direct into the community [June 2008].

Shortly after receiving this letter from Brady, I received another one, this time very angry and bitter. I had suggested he might embark on some more writing. He dismissed my suggestion. *'Every attempt at escape, even in writing, is at present impossible'* (July 2008).

In my initial meeting with him, I asked him directly about his sanity. This is rather a dangerous question but at this point I had reason to believe that it could well be my one and only chance to talk face to face with him. He is not the easiest person to get to see, as I am sure you can imagine, and anything could have happened. The Ashworth authorities might not let me in to see him again. Brady might not *want* to see me again. I was not going to waste what could be my only opportunity to ask questions, so I gambled, took a deep breath and then asked directly, 'Do *you* consider yourself to be insane?'

He replied, *'Perhaps the absence of any obvious symptoms of insanity after being locked up for life could indicate that I might very well be insane.'*

A circular argument, as in the scrupulous covering up of any signs of insanity might well be proof that he actually *is* insane. Catch-22.

It is now evening and the guards have finally got fed up with my being there and terminated my interview. Brady is searched and marched back to his cell, and I have to get out of the complex, which I soon discover is not an easy task to achieve. Leaving Ashworth is in some ways more difficult than arriving, which I suppose makes a certain amount of sense from a security perspective. I am escorted back across the deserted compound and then left at one of the airlocks. I can make out a few shadowy figures. Who are they? Escaped patients? Guards? Too dark to see. Through the airlocks to the visitors' exit point. Property is returned and I walk out of the door into a hailstorm. I head in the direction I can half remember from arriving, while trying to use my mobile phone to get picked up.

I get to the gates, razor wire, no mobile-phone signal, locked in. I cannot see very much. So, back to the visitor centre, which is now closed, all the lights are out. I ring the bell. No, the place is closed and they 'do not have a telephone for public use, goodbye'. Click! What on earth do I do now?

I wander around the complex. Finally, I find 'staff entrance'. Inside are four men sitting around in security outfits watching football.

'I need to make a call, how do I get out?'

'We don't have a telephone.'

Maximum-security asylum for the criminally insane and they *don't have a telephone*? I don't think so, but they will not budge. I finally get a mobile signal and make a call to organise my evacuation. I am told to walk around all of the buildings to finally escape the complex and thank heaven I find the exit gate. The car turns up to rescue me and we drive south. I get home and collapse into bed, although I do not get to sleep until dawn.

This was just the beginning. Brady wanted to see me again.

PART II

SHATTERED LIVES, HOMICIDAL INFECTION

CHAPTER FOUR

PROFILING AND VICTIMOLOGY: SWIMMING WITH SHARKS

Within the confines of a maximum-security hospital or prison, meeting someone like Brady can be dangerous for a number of different reasons. Interacting with people who have been diagnosed as being insane beyond hope of redemption is a psychological minefield. In any novel social encounter when you breathe a mental sigh of relief in discovering that the person you have just met seems quite normal and certainly easy to communicate with, you can easily let your guard down and can become vulnerable to manipulation that you might not even be aware of. This awareness is especially important when conducting interviews with individuals who almost certainly have their own agenda and motivation for portraying themselves in a certain way. Brady just seemed so *normal* that now and again I had to remind myself why he was there. I did this by looking at his hands.

In mental hospitals for the criminally insane, you are relatively safe as far as your physical welfare is concerned (if you keep your wits about you). There are guards everywhere, many more guards than patients as far as I could see (this was later confirmed by Brady). On a superficial level, the guards at the hospital seem more threatening than the people they are supposed to be guarding, but you still have to be careful. In my next visit, I was left alone in a room with about eight Category A patients for at least ten minutes in a maximum-security ward while the guards went off to escort Brady to a visiting room. Category A prisoners in a mental hospital are those diagnosed as being the most dangerous criminally insane patients in the country, labelled as unredeemable violent people who might murder pretty much anyone who walks across their line of vision without a second thought. I just smiled politely at them and they smiled back. I waved a 'Hi, nice to meet you'; they smiled and waved back. I did not feel threatened by any of the patients, and I am sure that, if anyone had threatened me and I had yelled, the guards would have eventually turned up in force with straitjackets.

STOCKHOLM SYNDROME

Meeting the patients in the hospital, I felt as if I were talking to people who had been kidnapped and seemed to have resigned themselves to the fact that their lives had been more or less written off and who had accepted that they were stuck there pretty much for good. In order to survive and achieve a bearable lifestyle within the hospital, the patients tend to cooperate in order to complete the picture that validates the existence of the hospital and their presence there as legitimate members of a therapeutic environment. They do not really have much choice other than to play along. But there are cracks in the façade if you know where to look. For example, the patients' artwork in the visitor centre looked forced. It was certainly ugly to the extent that I was amazed that the hospital staff would present it as evidence of warm and positive rehabilitation. To me it looked very angry or at the very least negatively inspired. I mentioned this to Brady, who responded, '*Any creative activity in this place is regarded as subversive*' (2005). Brady told me he had given up painting, and this is unsurprising under the circumstances.

In the hospital, where there could be danger of physical threat, anybody who might seem to be running to your aid might not be coming to overpower your assailant: they could possibly be coming to support the assailant and help them to overpower *you*. So the patients learn to submit quickly to the regime. Psychologists call this mechanism of self-protection 'learned helplessness'. The person quickly learns not to draw any attention to themselves and to roll over and expose their soft underbellies in order to defuse potential danger, a behavioural characteristic that can be observed in most mammals when they are threatened by a more physically powerful adversary. Point a weapon at someone and they will usually immediately put their hands up; and, if the weapon is suitably threatening, they will obey pretty much any order they are given in order to avoid getting hurt. Of course, serial killers are aware of this and select any weapons they use accordingly, to gain maximum threat.

A number of dynamics can be present in various situations when psychological and physical power-and-control games come into play. One of these is known as 'Stockholm syndrome'. This was named after a famous case in which the people who were working in a bank that was being robbed, rather than acting as victims, decided to side with the robbers in order to save themselves and also to join in for a share of the proceeds. This effect was termed to describe a paradoxical psychological phenomenon wherein hostages express adulation and have positive feelings towards their captors, emotions that might appear irrational to those watching from the outside.

So, what we have is basically a psychological response to the perception of potential threat, especially the unexpected threat of suddenly being confined and being unable to do what you want to because someone is pointing a weapon at you, an armed robber, a potential rapist/murderer or a 'nurse' with a club and a syringe and the power to lock you in a cell and dictate the terms and conditions of your confinement. The syndrome can operate on a number of different levels. When confronted with life-threatening situations with people who appear to be potentially dangerous, the inevitable (and sensible) response is to try to assimilate the point of view of those threatening you. This is initially a self-preservation mechanism but can quickly develop into a psychopathic neurosis (Fuselier 1999). In extreme cases, some kidnap victims go beyond empathising with their abductors to the point where they might possibly even fall in love with them. Is this what happened with Myra Hindley?

The Patti Hearst case is possibly the most high-profile example of Stockholm syndrome. Having been kidnapped in California in 1974 by the Symbionese Liberation Army (SLA), Hearst – granddaughter of William Randolph Hearst, the American publishing magnate – ended up siding with her captors and eventually helped them to rob a bank. Her cooperation was initially an act of self-preservation, but this soon developed into a neurotic empathy with her kidnappers and their cause. When caught, she attempted to use 'brainwashing' as a defence, but it did not work. The SLA are not serial killers; they are political activists. But some of the same psychological principles can apply in serial-murder cases. The fact that serial killers can appear non-frightening, non-threatening, even attractive, is a clear illustration of the duplicity that enables them to get away with not just one murder, but a whole string of them without anyone noticing anything much out of the ordinary, other than perhaps the fact that people were mysteriously disappearing, which could be the result of a number of different and non-criminal reasons.

Most serial killers are not stupid. They are highly manipulative chameleons; they blend in with the herd either as lone predators or operating in tandem with accomplices. Like any natural predator, they do not want a fight. They want to bring the victim down quickly, quietly and privately, with no clues or obvious connections that might bring them under suspicion. If the victim cooperates, that makes it much easier. When bodies *are* found, the common reaction from people who know the suspect/accused is disbelief. There must be a mistake! Finding out that the nice next-door neighbours have been systematically murdering people for fun on the other side of your living-room wall is initially unbelievable. But it happens.

Harold Shipman, the British general practitioner who was convicted in 2000 of having systematically murdered patients, was well liked, a pillar of the community. His living patients (the small handful who were left when he was finally caught) were amazed when the truth about his murders emerged. One, incredibly, even went so far as to state that he would be happy to still have Shipman as his doctor, and this was *after* Shipman had been convicted of the murder of 15 of his patients – although suspected of a considerable number more (Whittle and Ritchie 2000).

MISSING PERSONS

Harold Shipman was something of a unique case. With most serial killers, people just vanish and there is no homicidal doctor like Shipman signing their death certificates. When someone goes missing and there are no clues, no body found and no credible witnesses, there is very little to work with. Disappearances are filed away as missing-person reports, and even that tiny step does not always happen. If there is an inquiry, the police will interview friends, relations and colleagues, but, if no one is actually reported missing, then even this is obviously not going to happen.

Dennis Nilsen (see Chapter 2) was convicted in 1982 of killing 15 people in London and nearly all of them disappeared without anyone ever reporting to the authorities that they were missing; and, anyway, even when victims *are* reported to the police as missing, there is no standard procedure for an investigation and there will probably not even *be* an investigation if the missing person is an adult and there is no obvious suspicion or evidence of foul play. So, for an investigator, there is often virtually nothing to work with. No person reported missing, no suspect, no crime scene. Well? Where do you go from there?

If someone *does* notice that a person has disappeared, this is where profiling might be useful, and the first thing to do is to try to whittle down the list of possible suspects. By necessity, criminal investigators often use the fourteenth-century tenet of Occam's razor. This involves the use of a heuristic (a rule of thumb) that is applied to reduce the number of possible suspects and explanations to a level that can be effectively and practically investigated. You eliminate assumptions to a set of conjectures that are practically possible to investigate. When a murder or kidnapping is suspected, the ideal procedure would be to interview every single person in the area at the time within a 100-mile radius, including all those who had entered or left that area at the time of the murder. Of course, this is impossible, so untestable assumptions are removed as quickly and logically as possible. The trick is to find one item, one detail, and then focus on it until it is an exhausted possibility, then eliminate it and move on to the next anomaly, another detail that seems slightly out of place. But Occam's razor as an investigative procedure has a double-edged blade. The razor is not much use if it cuts out the target from the investigation, and this is a huge danger in the process of criminal profiling.

CRIMINAL PROFILING

'Criminal profiling' is a term used for the process of investigating criminal factors and analysing physical and behavioural evidence in order to attempt to identify the person or persons who might be responsible for a crime. It is a multidisciplinary approach (or should be) that has generated a lot of controversy and misconceptions. Even professional practitioners have stated that the process is fraught with danger and the possibility of disastrous mistakes being made. A bad profile can be worse than no profile.

'Profilers tend not to agree on anything ... they tend to keep their cases to themselves and do not publish them due to information sensitivity and confidentiality issues ... and there are no professional profiling organisations working on the development of uniform ethics, standards, and practices' (Turvey 2002).

I can certainly vouch for the authenticity of this statement from my own research.

Turvey then goes on to state that, as profilers have limited mechanisms for professional discourse and the sharing of information, it is no surprise that many working in the field conclude that profiling should remain more of an art than a science. At the time of writing, the profiling of serial killers is something of a hit-or-miss enterprise that is potentially dangerous for everyone involved. While psychology may help us to explain and understand certain types of crimes retrospectively, after they have happened and the person or persons responsible have been apprehended, it is not so useful or reliable when employed in an attempt to predict what crimes might occur in the future and who might be likely to commit them. 'Solving' a crime before it has actually been committed remains in the realms of science fiction for the time being, and this is probably a very good thing too. It is bad enough convicting innocent people of crimes that have occurred, but if you include crimes that have not even happened yet a million mistakes could be made.

A psychological profiler trying to develop an efficient plan of action in order to identify a realistic assessment of the likely perpetrator of a violent crime will run into any number of frustrating limitations and restrictions. What tends to happen, at least at the time of writing, is that the profiler will be begrudgingly brought in almost as a last resort when all other lines of criminological inquiry have been exhausted.

For example, an apparently 'motiveless' murder has occurred. Regular law-enforcement methods have failed to identify a suspect and the police have basically given up on the investigation. Then more murders are discovered and the authorities finally have to admit defeat and bring in a psychologist. This is certainly not going to look very good for the police investigators, who have to admit they have hit repeated dead ends, have got nowhere and have essentially failed to do the job they are paid to do. This is also not very fair on the psychologists, either, who are brought into a very hostile and frustrated investigation as a last resort. Nobody likes the idea of an 'expert' being brought in to tell them how to do their jobs. It is tantamount to an admission of failure. Typically, the psychologist is given a dustbin bag or a cardboard box containing the stale, incomplete and poorly labelled dregs of the evidence, evidence that has been mauled by half of the police in the jurisdiction.

The following two real examples from forensic research highlight how easily incompetence can completely derail an effective investigation before it has even started. These show how easily a crime scene can be contaminated by alarming levels of human error.

In the first, police were called when a shooting had occurred. A man was found shot dead at one end of a room. The gun that had been used in the killing was found on a mantelpiece at the other end of the room. This was immediately treated as a murder investigation rather than a suicide until a police officer casually mentioned that he had moved the weapon from beside the body and put it on the mantelpiece 'in case it got in anyone's way'.

The other is even more bizarre. A man was transported to a mortuary, having been found, presumed murdered. A forensic scientist visiting at the time noticed that the man was still breathing and was in fact still alive, so he notified the mortuary assistant. The next day the assistant telephoned him and informed him that he had dealt with the matter and put the body in a freezer overnight – that the man was now most definitely dead and they could come and collect the body in order to conduct the autopsy (Erzinclioglu 2000).

Cases show the fragility of effective forensic investigation and the massive pitfalls of underestimating the propensity for human error in crime investigation. The forensic investigator has to attempt to identify not only any errors the perpetrator might have made, but also those the police might have made that might have derailed the inquiry before it has even started.

Cases such as these are not uncommon. In an ideal scenario, the criminal profiler is brought in right at the beginning, when the crime scene is untouched, the body has not been hauled off to the mortuary and the blood is not yet dry. A profiling endeavour is much more likely to yield useful results if the investigator can see the murder scene *exactly as the murderer has seen it*. Unfortunately, this very rarely happens, almost never in fact, especially if any serious (and obvious) errors in an investigation come to light that are then swiftly concealed by those in charge. Nobody likes to have to admit they have made stupid mistakes and basically failed at the job they have been trained to do, and the police, like anybody else and any other profession, can get very defensive. Additionally, in a serial cycle, with each murder, the sense of urgency and pressure constantly escalates for everyone involved in the investigation, and you can end up with a group of individuals working from different perspectives, all using different approaches, and bickering that someone else is to blame for the lack of progress and resolution. This, of course, is great news for killers who can carry on murdering while everyone involved in the investigation is busy arresting and interrogating innocent people, blaming each other, denying that their particular strategy might have been responsible for wasting everyone's time, missing vital clues and basically getting nowhere.

As far as psychologists are concerned, and to compound problems even more, there are a number of different approaches to profiling.

First, there is *profiling by hypothesis*, a top-down approach based on distinct psychological 'types' or categories. Profiling by hypothesis is probably the most common method, the one that most people are familiar with. The question this method poses is: What sort of person might have done this?

Second, there is *profiling from forensic evidence*, a bottom-up approach utilising the hard forensic facts from crime scenes as the main pieces needed to build a legally watertight case against the individual you are hunting and have caught (assuming you have actually apprehended the right person). The question here is: What clues has the person left behind that will stand up in court to positively identify and convict them or at least prove beyond reasonable doubt that they were there?

Then we get *profiling by behavioural analysis*. Here the focus is on the behavioural dynamics that may be considered from analysis of the crime scene. Here, the profiler attempts to surmise the point of view of the killer. The question here is not so much what type of person might have done this. It is more akin to speculation as to what might have happened at the crime scene and why. Then you work backwards to the second approach. A million misconceptions can occur. This is not terribly scientific.

Finally, there is *profiling by synthesis*, which combines all three of the above (multidisciplinary). This seems to me to be the most potentially creative way forward, integrated converging operations.

No particular method is infallible on an individual basis. DNA, fingerprinting, eyewitness testimony, even an outright confession cannot be relied upon. So use all of them. You have to be receptive to all of the evidence coming in from lots of different angles, even if some of it appears to be extremely unlikely. As far as psychology is concerned, certain factors can be quantified, but it is essential to avoid limiting the parameters of a profile unless you absolutely have to. Everybody is different, and everybody behaves differently at different times in different places and for different reasons. While some factors can be indicative of behavioural predispositions, cause-and-effect models have limited hypothetical probability or validity. Life events that might inspire one person to kill might have completely the opposite effect on another person. Just because *you* might behave in a certain way when confronted with a particular set of circumstances, it does not mean that anyone else will behave in the same way.

Here are some outlines and some of the potential problems of profiling by synthesis as it is commonly used at present if a serial killer is suspected to be actively operating.

A person is found dead in suspicious circumstances. First, who might have committed the crime? Psychologists usually use three categories.

1. ORGANISED OFFENDER

This offender is usually male, 18–35 years old. Same race as victim. Normal to above-average intelligence (which is sometimes used as a convenient retrospective explanation for why the profile being used turned out to be completely wrong ('he/she was too clever and calculating'). The person is probably employed and used their own vehicle. (Before you read on, ask yourself how many people *you* know who could fit this basic profile.)

So then you introduce forensic evidence and psychological motivational factors that might be surmised from the crime scene. With the organised offender, the murder is usually planned, rehearsed, sometimes for many months or even years. The perpetrator brings and takes away their own murder weapons and/or rape kit (handcuffs, duct tape, mask, gloves, knife, gun, rope, etc.). Donald Gaskins (see Chapter 2) after his first abduction had his victim, still alive, in the boot of his car. He stopped at a hardware store to buy some essential tools for the murder, such as clothes line to tie up the victim. He realised later how idiotic it had been to park outside a store with a live victim in the boot, and decided that from then on he had to be sure that whatever he needed for his killings he should have readily available in advance.

'I started buying stuff to put in a duffel bag I could carry in whatever car I drove ... I never bought much in one place ... It got to be kind of a hobby, looking around whenever I was in a hardware store, figuring out how I might use tools and other stuff in ways different from what they was made for' (Gaskins 1993).

He was becoming *organised* and bought items such as hoses, a hand pump, a blow torch, acids, lighters, hammers and hatchets so that he could have all these things ready for when he wanted them.

If the victim is not buried or sunk at the place where they are killed, the organised offender will usually transport the body and bury or conceal it somewhere else, or else the victim is lured, alive, to a preplanned location to be murdered. This was Brady's usual MO (method of operation) and is a lot more convenient for the killer. It is not so easy to transport a dead body, far easier to get them to walk to the place where they are going to die, although, of course, it is much more risky in that the victim will have more opportunities to escape, more clues may be left behind and more witnesses may notice something.

Some enterprising killers may even have dug a grave in advance (Gerard Schaefer did this often; see Chapter 2). The killer makes an effort to establish alibis and eliminate clues that might lead to their being connected to the crime or that might link two separate crime scenes. Any similarities that link two separate murders would be likely to attract a lot more police attention than a single missing-person report would, but not always. So are we looking for an 'organised' serial killer? In criminological investigation, the term 'serial killer' does not become an operational concept until three or four bodies are found with crime-scene characteristics that very clearly imply that they might have been killed by the same individual or individuals. The evidential links have to be very clear in such cases and police have a terrible reputation for failing to link identical crimes that happen at different locations.

Next you might want to consider potential suspects, interview them and check alibis; this can be a further filtering tool. Police are immediately suspicious if someone comes up with a detailed and precise alibi for a day when a murder was committed. If someone has killed, especially if it was for the first time, the events of that day are likely to be ingrained in their memory with unusual clarity. With a murder, as with most life-shattering events, a reinforcing effect on memory occurs. Unless something unusual or exceptional has happened on a particular day, people are usually very vague if questioned about where exactly they were and what they were doing on a specific day. Can *you* remember exactly what precise events in your life occurred three Thursdays back? Probably little more than vague assumptions: 'went to work, watched TV in the evening' and suchlike. But, if you can remember the events and times precisely on that day, this could well be a clear indicator to a shrewd investigator that *something* dramatic happened on that day, and murdering someone is certainly a dramatic event for all concerned. An innocent suspect is likely to make mistakes or be unsure and contradict themselves if asked the same question more than once. But the person with a fixed alibi sticks suspiciously to their story. Memory is fluid, so a precise and unchanging recollection of detailed events suggests careful rehearsal.

The more detailed the recollection of events described, therefore, the easier it is to find flaws in the account given (if an investigator is suspicious about the precision of memory for a day when a murder happened, a useful strategy can be to ask the suspect what they did on the previous or following day and compare the level of precision recall). Brady, who had considerable forensic awareness back in the 1960s, even jotted a note to remind himself that, two weeks after he had killed, and, if questioned about that day, he should state his memory for that day was vague. A sensible course of action as long as he could remember to throw the note away! The police found it in Hindley's car and when it was read out in court, it was irrefutable damning evidence for the prosecution to use, but I shall get to that later.

To an investigator, using an 'organised' profile is of little help if you have no idea who might be a likely suspect. You cannot interview everybody so when more evidence comes up, you need to go back and refine the profile, and this takes a lot of time.

The organised category of offenders – once over the initial emotional shock of their first murder – usually manage to keep up appearances and keep control of their lives for a considerable amount of time. In many cases, a number of years might go by with relatively low-risk murders happening on a regular basis and with no obvious indicators to people around them, but this cannot last. Despite getting better at killing, with each murder, serial killers are developing a pattern that law-enforcement agencies will eventually pick up on (not always, but usually). The paranoia and anxiety of the killer often increase, along with their compulsion to continue killing, while at the same time their attention to detail and their forensic awareness start to erode. They become overconfident, they start making mistakes, leaving clues, acting bizarrely, and once this happens it is usually only a matter of time before they miss something critical, as Brady did, and they usually get caught as a result of routine police work, luck or a tip-off.

2. DISORGANISED OFFENDER

This is the second category for profiling, usually male again. They have a history of psychiatric illnesses. They might possess a rundown vehicle, if they own one at all, or use a stolen car or public transport. Most murders committed by disorganised offenders happen in the daytime, which may suggest that the perpetrator is either unemployed or works at night. These murders are not usually planned or rehearsed. The perpetrator is unlikely to have prepared an alibi. The killings explode out of a flash of rage, an impulsive overreaction to stress, frustration, lust or impotence (these last two usually being closely related).

The disorganised offender uses whatever weapon is available at the time and drops it at the crime scene, usually a blunt instrument of some kind rather than a weapon brought along specifically for the purpose of a premeditated killing. The 'Green River Killer', Gary Ridgway, having not brought along a murder weapon, improvised by strangling at least two of his early victims with their own jeans. Ted Bundy, at least initially, would bludgeon his victims with any blunt instrument he had to hand; it was only later that he, like Gaskins, started collecting tools specifically obtained for the purpose of murder. There may be evidence of overkill with the disorganised offender (many more blows, stab wounds or shots fired than are necessary to kill the victim). The body lies where it falls and there is usually little effort to conceal it.

This catagory of killer is most likely simply to run or drive away as fast as possible and may leave behind witnesses and clues. They are not interested in souvenirs but might take any cash the victim has on them, although this is not usually the primary motive for the crime.

Bundy and Gaskins did not stay in the disorganised category for long, though. Once they had figured out they were capable of killing and getting away with it, they quickly became a lot more cunning. Both of these killers switched categories very quickly. However, with most disorganised offenders – people like Henry Lee Lucas and Arthur Shawcross for example – the murders are not often planned with any care or attention to detail. They do not fantasise about them and rarely tell anyone about them in advance. They just kick off and do them. Rape, if it happens, is almost an afterthought. Such people may rack up a few deaths in a furious momentum and as a result they usually get caught fairly quickly, unless they quickly develop cunning, as Bundy and Gaskins did.

These first two categories, then, seem logical, maybe even useful, up to a point, which is when you get to the third category.

3. MIXED OFFENDER

This one has characteristics of both types.

'It should be emphasized that the crime scene will rarely be completely organized or disorganized. It is more likely to be somewhere on a continuum between the two extremes of the orderly, neat crime scene and the disarrayed, sloppy one' (Burgess 1997, cited in Turvey 2002).

Great! A terrific amount of help, then – or not. The 'mixed-offender' category makes a nonsense of the other two. Turvey (2002) calls the first two categories a 'false dichotomy'. Follow such rigid analytical distinctions and all you have is a bunch of assumptions. You cannot quantify or measure these people with such precision because motivation and pathology are fluid, yet psychologists continue to try. The patterns are not that obvious or consistent and often even the killers themselves cannot explain them. The organised offender can become disorganised as the murders continue. The disorganised offenders can become more organised as they learn by their mistakes and become better at avoiding apprehension. If the profiler is working with categories such as these, it can do more harm than good. It is not like painting by numbers, because there *are* no numbers, motivations are carefully hidden and a bad profile is worse than no profile at all. You could be eliminating the person you are hunting from the inquiry.

Myra Hindley, for example, would have been eliminated as a suspect in the Moors Murders case (being female), and in fact she was initially eliminated from the inquiry and was not even taken into custody for a number of days after Brady had been arrested. Jeffrey Dahmer, the Wisconsin serial killer, would have been eliminated as a suspect for his murders of 15 people because nearly all of his victims were African-American, Hispanic or Asian, and Dahmer was a white Caucasian. Dahmer was so convincingly normal that, even when one of his victims managed to escape and ran down the street naked and bleeding and the police were called to the scene, he managed to convince the police that it was a lovers' drunken argument, and the police promptly escorted the victim back to Dahmer's apartment and left him there. Dahmer thanked them and said good night, then he locked the door and quickly drilled a hole in the victim's head and injected acid, finishing the murder.

Peter Sutcliffe *was* eliminated from the Yorkshire Ripper investigation even after being interviewed on more than one occasion because a dangerous and interfering person had been tracking the murders in the media and decided to send a hoax tape to the police – a 'joke' that horribly backfired. When the police received this and believed it was from the actual killer, they broadcast the recording on television and radio and revised their profile. As it was not Sutcliffe's voice, he was no longer considered to be a suspect and remained free to continue killing.

The categorisation of profiles using the rigid methodologies I have described is very much hit or miss. I suppose a working knowledge of these types of patterns might be used to streamline an investigation where there are far too many suspects to interview, but it is very dangerous to rely on such simplistic forensic templates.

Most honest psychologists will agree that, apart from there being a couple of incredibly lucky guesses in criminological history, there has not been a single major case solved using a psychological profile of the killer (Newton 2000). As stated earlier, the only thing that is consistent with serial killers is inconsistency. That is possibly the only thing you can *definitely* be sure of.

Another common mistake that some profilers seem to make is assuming that all murderers do is think about murder. Most serial killers go to work, watch TV, have relationships. They weigh up their actions and the risks they are taking. Having killed for the first time and got away with it, they refine their plan for their next murder and eliminate the mistakes that may have nearly got them caught at the start. Many get better at it, at least for a while. They do not want to get caught before the game has really started. Why would they? Even the emotional ricochets of the murders are effectively disguised to people who might even be sharing their beds. If your wife or husband does not notice you are murdering people, then what chance have the police got? With Peter Sutcliffe, for example, Sonia Sutcliffe, his wife, had no idea her husband was the Yorkshire Ripper even though he fitted the initial photofit picture and had been repeatedly questioned (although incompetently) by the police. That is what she claimed at the time, anyway, although maybe she just did not want to believe it.

In another case, Fayina Chikatilo, the wife of 'Rostov Ripper' Andrei Chikatilo (convicted in 1992 of 52 murders in Soviet territory), described him as 'a perfect husband'. She claimed that she had no idea what he was doing. People will reject any possibility that their partner might be the person the police are searching for, and in some cases even when they have accepted the truth they might try to hide them or give them alibis rather than face the consequences that they will have to deal with and that will undoubtedly turn their world upside down. The family, friends, colleagues and neighbours of Brady and Hindley were all completely amazed when the case broke. None of them had the slightest idea. They would almost certainly have seen the newspaper bulletins and posters about the missing children, but none of them connected these reports to the nice young couple they thought they knew. 'Beyond belief!' was the typical reaction when the story was finally revealed.

Modern serial killers build intricate webs of duplicity. The shocking discrepancy between the person you think you know and what they have done disturbs people greatly to the point of either outright denial or, at the very least, disorientation. Killers are very rarely foaming-at-the-mouth knife-wielding crazies who randomly stab anyone within reach in a blind frenzy. If this were always the case, they would not remain undetected for long. Profiling would be laughable: 'In my professional opinion, the screaming bloodstained man running down the street stabbing people with a carving knife might fit the profile of a possible suspect.'

It is nonsense, it does not work like that, and this is what makes sociopathic killers – people who have no conscience – so very dangerous. Most of the fear and surprise evoked in both the victims and people who know the killer is a consequence of there being very little about them that might warn anyone of what they are capable of until of course it is too late.

The writer Brian Masters, best known for his biographies of serial killers, comments on Dennis Nilsen's 15 murders:

One of the most astonishing things about the case is Nilsen's ability to go about his daily work with energy and enthusiasm, to go out for drinks, walk the dog, and even entertain people peaceably at his flat, while all the time there was a collection of bodies under his floor or in the cupboard [Masters 1985].

Ian Brady and Myra Hindley managed to keep up appearances too. Going to work every day, walking the dogs, decorating their house, just the nice young couple next door, a bit reserved perhaps, but nobody suspected anything out of the ordinary.

This façade of normalcy extends the active kill cycle of sociopaths beyond even their own expectations, and makes it that much easier for them to continue killing, sometimes even beyond their apprehension and imprisonment. The murders can sometimes go on after they have been captured, but now on a much more sophisticated level. The concept of serial killers continuing to murder people after they have been caught has been used in crime fiction on more than one occasion. In Thomas Harris's book *The Silence of the Lambs* (1988), the antihero Hannibal Lecter kills a man in an adjacent cell by persuading him to swallow his tongue. In an earlier Harris novel, *Red Dragon* (1981), the same character, Lecter, while incarcerated, nearly gets the family of an FBI agent killed by revealing details of their location in a coded newspaper contact advertisement intended for another killer who is still free and actively killing. In the David Fincher film *Se7en* (1995), the serial killer literally walks into the police station and turns himself in, but that is not the end of the killing. This is just fictional, isn't it? No, it happens in real life.

Here are some examples.

After receiving a number of life sentences for multiple murders, Gaskins (the South Carolina killer mentioned in Chapter 2) continued to murder after he was imprisoned. In 1982, he handled the contract killing of a man, Rudolf Tyner, who was being held in solitary confinement on death row. Gaskins managed to kill this man without even being at the crime scene. At the time of the murder, Gaskins had a perfect alibi: he was locked in a different cell in another part of the prison. People thought that the murder of a man in solitary confinement was simply impossible.

How did Gaskins do it?

It was done, after a number of failed poisoning attempts, with explosives that had 'walked' into the prison hidden in the heels of a pair of boots after various prison officials had been bribed. The explosives were concealed in a plastic cup that Gaskins managed to have smuggled into his victim's cell along with instructions. Incredibly, Tyner followed the instructions and held the cup to his ear at a precise time thinking it was some kind of homemade jailhouse radio. Gaskins checked the time carefully and then detonated the explosive remotely from his own cell and blew the man's head off.

These people can be incredibly ingenious in their dark designs. Gaskins died in the electric chair in 1991 for this crime after the truth finally came to light.

Of course, people get killed on death row all the time. That is the whole purpose of the place. But the killings are not usually committed by another prisoner. It seems reasonable to conclude that Tyner was a gullible moron who did not even realise he had been targeted. However, in some cases, there are other factors to consider: murders and other serious crimes can be committed with the active collaboration of the victim. This is not as outrageous as it may at first appear.

HYBRISTOPHILIA

Hybristophilia is a recently documented paraphilia, or psychosexual disorder with affective/emotional elements. 'Hybris' means a condition of hysterical psychological blindness that may be partial or complete; 'philia' means an intense or unusual attraction. It is similar to Stockholm syndrome but there is one major difference: the hybristophiliac seeks out their psychosis, whereas the person with Stockholm syndrome has it thrust upon them. So, it is a matter of choice, but the symptoms are more or less identical.

In the most pronounced form, the illness has an attention-seeking pathology a little like Munchausen's syndrome, which is a term used for factitious psychiatric disorders where people pretend to be either physically or mentally ill in order to draw attention or sympathy to themselves. Their strategies of deception can become incredibly elaborate and can involve painstaking research in order to make their fake illnesses as realistic as possible. With psychiatric variants of Munchausen's, the sufferer spends so much time and effort mimicking the symptoms that they eventually develop the disorder for real and present symptoms realistic enough to fool specialists.

Hybristophilia is perhaps more closely related to Munchausen's syndrome by proxy (MSBP). This is a rather strange disorder to comprehend or diagnose. It refers to the abuse of another human being, usually a child but it can also be an adult invalid or a very old person. The sufferer of MSBP enjoys all kinds of special attention, even adulation, as the people around them praise their ceaseless efforts to care for the person who appears to be afflicted with a terrible illness that cannot be conclusively diagnosed. For people who have MSBP, the frequent visits to hospitals and specialists are seen as exciting developments in their life, and all the attention and empathy they receive as a result of being perceived as a dedicated carer reinforces their desire to keep the poor victim as ill as they can for as long as possible.

In severe cases, the actual symptoms of the psychiatric disorder that is being projected will start to appear in the child/relative, who is now in a psychological trap. More than 1,200 cases are reported yearly in America with comparable numbers reported in other countries depending on their population (J. Gregory 2003). Not everyone succumbs to Stockholm syndrome and not everyone develops hybristophilia, but those who do are juggling with some very similar behavioural dynamics.

Hybristophilia is unique in that it is the attention that association with a murderer brings that is the primary driving force. The hybristophiliac gets plenty of attention from the killer they have fixated on. Bored people on death row or locked up for life know how to recognise the propensity for these obsessions in other individuals and expertly exploit them, just as they managed to recognise and manipulate their victims while they were still actively killing.

Why do certain people develop romantic feelings for infamous murderers? It usually starts out as curiosity about someone who has committed exceptionally outrageous crimes, but once contact is made it can turn into something much more sinister and can develop into a malignant obsession. Issues of safety can become cosmetic and may be dangerously overlooked. The hybristophiliac craves attention, and they get it by proxy, not just from the killer they have befriended but also from people around them who are fascinated by the dynamics of the situation. They become semi-famous by association. The true hybristophiliac can then become psychologically infected with the drama of murder and this can introduce factors that can complicate and confuse an investigation. In an even more bizarre manifestation of the illness, murders can occur with the active collaboration of the victims. In some cases, it is not only serial killers who are searching for victims, but also victims who are seeking out their killer.

Here are two examples of how hybristophilia can evolve.

In 2001, Armin Meiwes – the German 'Rotenburg Cannibal' or 'der Metzgermeister' (which translates as 'the Master Butcher', and this was his Internet pseudonym) – posted contact advertisements on websites asking, quite openly, for people who wanted to be killed and eaten, or killed by being eaten. He got more than 200 replies. After interviewing and turning down a number of applicants for various reasons, he killed and ate Bernd Jüergen Brandes, a Siemens computer technician from Berlin, with complete consent on both sides. Brandes had taken steps to orchestrate and then cover up his *own* murder in advance. He had actually advertised himself as a victim and even ate his own penis, which Meiwes had cooked before Brandes finally bled to death. At the trial, the judicial officials could not clearly decide what crime had been committed and what precisely Meiwes was actually guilty of. When both killer and victim had consented and carefully planned the murder, it was only a matter of arrangements. The jury sent Meiwes to jail, though, to be on the safe side.

Most hybristophiliacs do not actually get murdered, although they certainly become victims in many other senses of the word. A typical case is that of Richard Ramirez, the Los Angeles 'Night Stalker'. Profiling did not work in his case, as he had killed randomly with no preference for age, race or gender. After conviction on 13 counts of murder in 1985 he attracted a huge fan club of hybristophiliacs. His dark magnetism held a special fascination for a number of women. His trial had to be relocated from Los Angeles because his fans were having catfights outside the court and flinging naked photographs of themselves to him during the trial sessions. Even one of the jury members who sentenced him to death fell under his spell and started to visit him in jail. After voting on the jury for his execution, she now claims he did not get a fair trial (typically). Another woman, Doreen Lioy (not a jury member), married Ramirez after a postal romance with him while he was held at San Quentin prison in 1989. She has stated she will commit suicide when Ramirez is executed, although I would hope that her fantasy might be shattered when he is dead if it has not been already.

The hybristophiliac wants to be close to the action, pathologically focused on someone who is completely unobtainable. Truth becomes irrelevant; it spoils the fantasy that the hybristophiliac is carefully and obsessively constructing. The individuals who develop this focus on an unobtainable, and therefore safe, 'love' object (who ironically would probably never interest them in a more routine situation). This becomes the driving force behind the disorder. That is the key. So you have to be extremely careful when working with serial killers and people who might be under their influence. No matter how well prepared and experienced you are, you have to remain emotionally neutral or at least try to be.

This is not as easy as it might seem at first, but it is

critical. Look what happened to Jason Moss (see Chapter 2). Serial killers are expert at setting elaborate psychological traps, they have no qualms about lying through their teeth or crashing and burning with passengers on board, it just makes the whole thing more fun. Once captured for good, what is there to lose? Emotional vulnerability is quickly identified by serial killers and they play games with their hybristophiliac groupies just as they have with their murder victims. Why not? Prison is boring and prisoners will do anything to alleviate the numbing stasis of their circumstances. Another serial killer, Lawrence 'Pliers' Bittaker, sells his toenail clippings to obsessed fans and probably laughs all the way to the prison canteen.

There are further complications with chronic cases of hybristophilia. Sometimes these people are quite willing to commit their own crimes in order to get more involved and cement their relationship with the killer they have fixated on. Possibly the most famous case is that of Veronica Compton. She fell for Kenneth Bianchi, the LA 'Hillside Strangler' who was convicted of ten murders in 1983. Compton was never convicted of any murders as far as I am aware: she just fell in love with Bianchi, tried to orchestrate a scam to get him released from prison and ended up on an attempted murder charge herself.

Emotionally shallow like most serial killers, Bianchi wanted to be in love only when it suited him. Most serial killers dump their lovers as casually as the bodies of their victims. This emotional void is known as ahedonia, as defined in the fourth revision of the *Diagnostic and Statistical Manual of Mental Disorders* (*DSM-IV*), published by the American Psychiatric Association, and used to quantify mental illness. The killers take care not to personalise their victims, or their lovers: it complicates things if they perceive either category as human beings. They can flatline emotionally when it suits them, as can the hybristophiliac. Compton moved on as well when Bianchi dropped her, switching her attention to another doomed fantasy relationship with Douglas Clark, known, among other things, as the 'Sunset Slayer'.

So was Myra Hindley a hybristophiliac? Although we cannot be sure, it certainly looks like it. She showed many of the typical symptoms. She was infatuated with Brady and fell madly in love with him very quickly. His shady criminal background may have held some fascination and it certainly made him a lot more interesting than the local Manchester lads she was bored with dating at the time, but I do not think she was fascinated with murder, at least not at first. Linking up with him romantically, though, was a critical event for both of them. I doubt either of them had any idea about what they would end up doing together or could have predicted the shattering consequences of their relationship.

Brady comments, '*I have never experienced the need to corrupt anyone. I simply offered the opportunity to indulge extant natural urges*' (2001).

Brady has more than his share of hybristophiliac groupies. He receives 'fan' letters from all over the world, as does Peter Sutcliffe and pretty much all high-profile serial killers who have been incarcerated. You only have to search on the Internet and it becomes apparent how strongly the public fascination concerning crimes of serial killers remains in the collective consciousness. There are literally thousands of entries that relate to Brady's murders, many of which are almost tributes, thinly disguised as condemnation. However, there are many cases of multiple murder in criminal history, often with a higher body count, which the average person on the street would not recall or even recognise. Why does the Brady–Hindley case remain so firmly in the public consciousness? Brady himself explains it:

Atmosphere ... The mention of Jack the Ripper immediately conjures up streets congested with horse-drawn carriages ... Whitechapel, the sordid slum district in London frequented by prostitutes, where all the Ripper's murders were committed, its cobbled narrow alleys swirling with fog and lit only by bleary gas lamps, offered a perfect dramatic setting for the horrendous savage murders. The public love being 'horrified' ... The Moors Murders ... took the brooding, desolate, Yorkshire moors, treacherous with bogs and shrouded in deathly mist ... to penetrate the public psyche ... [Brady 2001].

On my next visit to see Brady at Ashworth, the grounds of which are certainly brooding and desolate after dark, I was escorted to a new location. After the metal detectors, body searches and routine interrogation, they decided that a different room would be allocated. I was escorted across the compound to what is termed the 'family room'. This was not his force-feeding room where I had talked to Brady previously. It seemed unlikely that the 'family room' had ever been host to a familial visit and I doubt it could have been a very happy one if ever it had. Visitors are conspicuous by their absence at Ashworth. The room has a cheap nylon sofa and a couple of ugly chairs which both Brady and I realised had been nailed to the floor when we tried to move them into a more comfortable position. I guess the pseudo-normality of the room is meant to make the patient and visitors feel more comfortable and avoid the atmosphere of incarceration. In fact, the reverse occurs. The room is stuffy, ugly and fake, and it smells bad. '*Humid in this bunker. They keep the air conditioner turned off so that the patients can enjoy the full therapeutic stink*' (2004). I could not have put it better myself. You leave the hospital with a horrible taste in your nose and mouth, which takes a considerable amount of time to eliminate.

It is almost impossible to relax in such a setting. While you are sitting there on the nylon sofa, all you have to do is glance up at the tiny barred window with the guards peering through the Perspex slot and any illusion of normality, comfort or privacy is shattered. I suppose this can be justified for security purposes, but it is very unnerving, making it impossible to relax. The 'family room' was like sitting in a cheap film set. If you are entering a prison, the fences and bars and guards and jangling keys are part of the entire scenario. They are not unexpected and therefore easier to accept as part of the situation. The force-feeding cell from the last visit, although certainly gruesome, at least felt honest on a rudimentary level and ultimately more comfortable.

Brady was released from his cell and let into the room.

As my cigarettes had been confiscated for the duration of my visit (along with everything else I had on me), Brady offered me one of his unfiltered roll-ups, explaining that they were made of pipe tobacco that he would leave to dry out on the radiator in his cell overnight to make them as strong as possible. He was not kidding. After I stopped coughing, we laughed, and a guard, who was lurking outside, peered through the plastic window with a puzzled expression. Normal behaviour in the mental hospital is not expected.

The interview went in lots of different directions. Brady can talk about pretty much anything with a certain amount of authority. We discussed gambling, horse racing, politics, media, censorship, law, crime, prisons, sanity, history, music, regrets. Nostalgia came up a lot in his letters, which is completely understandable given the circumstances: he certainly has no fond memories about his time at the hospital, and has hated pretty much every single minute of it: *'Ashworth, the Millennium Dome of Liverpool, without the entertainment'*. He hates all the staff as well: *'I wouldn't spit on a member of this administration even if they were on fire. I'd look for petrol!'*

Brady made it crystal clear how much he hates the hospital and everyone in it, without exception, but I knew that already from his letters, and, anyway, what on earth could I do about it other than acknowledge that it was indeed a seriously unpleasant place to reside? I was relieved when it was time to leave. I said goodbye and then started following him off down the wrong corridor thinking he was directing me to the way out of the labyrinth. Brady noticed, spun around, smiled and said, *'You're going the wrong way.'* We both laughed.

Brady told me in his next letter that the guards hanging about did not like this at all. He said that they did not like the fact that we seemed to be at ease talking, even though a relaxed conversation is always far more productive in such circumstances than a formal question-and-answer session. Brady does not *have* to talk to me (or anyone else for that matter) and it seemed essential to keep things on a friendly basis rather than fire questions at him. I certainly learned a lot more than I would have done if I had given him a pile of questionnaires to complete.

When the guards terminated my visit and put me into the

airlock, Brady was searched and marched back to the '*Planet of the Apes*', as he calls it, and I was shown the door. Before they would let me leave, they insisted on taking another photograph of me and photocopying my passport and driving licence. There was no reason at all why they should do that, but I let them get on with it as it seemed to keep them happy and I wanted to get out of there as quickly as possible. It was something of a relief to depressurise and resurface outside after the interview and get away.

A week or so later, Brady wrote to me:

> *Re-entering planet of the apes* [after I had visited], *mutterings of staff resentment were distinct. Resentment that the continuity of my isolation had been punctuated by intelligent life. Any outside 'intrusion' that disrupts the gestalt created by the collective pathological delusions of staff disturbs the administration. The next day over twenty security prison warders raided this cellblock and searched cells and inmates all day* [2005].

A couple of days after this, Brady wrote to me again. I felt rather guilty, as apparently my visit seemed to have resulted in *all* the patients' cells being shaken down. I had no idea that something like that might happen. I was searched so carefully on the way into the ward that there is no way that I could have smuggled anything in – or out for that matter. I had been sniffed and prodded and scanned and photographed and was not even allowed to take a paperclip or a pen in there. I imagine the guards got their bonuses for donning their 'control-and-restraint' gear the following day even if they never managed to find so much as a contraband plastic spoon.

VICTIMOLOGY PROFILING

Victimology certainly has many of the dangers that can undermine the profiling of a killer, but the advantage of focusing on the victim is that the profile can sometimes be directly confirmed with hard forensic facts, not assumptions. If a person goes missing, the questions to ask would be: Who were they with when they vanished? Where were they going? What was their state of mind? etc. – information that can be quickly and accurately gathered and confirmed. Such information can only be guessed at if you are attempting to compile a profile of a murderer. You can ride with the FBI Violent Criminal Apprehension Profiling system (VICAP) or the similar British Home Office Large Major Enquiry System (HOLMES) until the wheels fall off without getting anywhere close to the killer you are hunting. Do a scientific profile of the victim, however, and you are likely to solve a case much faster. Angling to identify some shadowy UNSUB (unknown subject/suspect) from crime-scene evidence – which, for all you know, might be inaccurate, poorly recorded by police or even staged deliberately to mislead an investigation – can waste thousands of hours of investigative time and might even get an innocent person convicted while the perpetrator carries on killing. This has happened very many times in criminal history.

Perhaps forensic profiling of a killer is a useful starting point, often the only method of investigation possible, but it by no means offers a guaranteed solution. Analysis of physical forensic data can help to solve some of the mechanics of a murder investigation and help build an analysis of what may have happened, but for me as a psychologist the question of *how* it happened is much less interesting than *why* it happened, and that question may well be effectively addressed using a victim profile as a key aspect of a criminal investigation.

Bringing in a profiler as a last resort when all other lines of enquiry have been exhausted is fair on neither law-enforcement officers, who have to admit they have reached a dead end in their enquiries, nor the profilers, who get thrown into the mix without the data necessary to complete a comprehensive analysis effectively.

'The operative goal of a [profiling] unit is to solve a murder within forty-eight hours after it has been reported. Statistically, if a murder investigation goes on for a longer time, the chance of its being solved drops significantly' (Du Clos 1993). Can you give a psychological profiler a plastic bag of bones and a pile of fuzzy photographs of the trampled scenes of crimes that occurred months ago and expect them to come up with an accurate composite of the perpetrator? Well, how much can they expect? Unless the profiler notices some critical clue that has been missed by the frontline investigative team, or can come up with inspirational guesses, it is hardly surprising that sometimes the best they can come up with is a fractured, vague and speculative analysis of the dynamics of a murder. This is not likely to be very scientific or to lead law-enforcement officers to the perpetrator. Given scenarios like this, is it any wonder that psychological profilers are tentative about revealing their ideas or conclusions?

But, before we all despair and throw in the towel for good, there are still some things that can inspire. Profiling is a relatively young science and I was not going to waste any opportunities, even if the Ashworth visits were horrendous. I realised I had to go back to the hospital, and this time I knew they would be ready and waiting for me.

PROFILING CONCLUSIONS

Profiling by synthesis – despite the flaws I have identified – is perhaps the most potentially creative way forward, converging operations. While trying to profile a shadowy figure from fractured puzzle parts of crime-scene forensic material or from half-glimpsed unreliable accounts reconstructed in memory from eyewitnesses, the profiler can do more harm than good. You cannot rely on flashes of preternatural inspiration. As we have seen, a bad profile can be worse than no profile at all. A bad profile can get people killed. If one wanted to attempt to conduct an effective profiling investigation then the following, I believe, should be the most critical areas of interest.

First, victimology. Profile the victim. You are going to get a lot further a lot faster with detailed evidence about the victim, which can be confirmed forensically, not guessed at. This stage might also include an analysis of potential hybristophiliac influences.

Next, comfort zones. I think a lot can be learned from the crime *scene*, not just victim positioning/posing, bloodstains and DNA body secretions. An analysis of those is important and might reveal useful evidence, but the investigator needs to take a step back and consider the entire crime environment and context. Holistic approaches seem to work better (comfort zones are explored in more detail in the next chapter).

Third, signature. What is it about a string of murders that links them all together? Or, more subtly, what is *missing* from a string of murders that provides a link? If you notice *that* then you might be on the right track. With most serial killers, the signature is nearly always there. With the marginally more clever ones, the absence of a signature *is* the signature, just as the absence of fingerprints suggests that fingerprints have been deliberately wiped clean or the perpetrator was wearing gloves (which is obviously suspicious if the weather is not cold). Neither of these signature patterns is easy to spot. You could be looking for something as innocuous as a tiny repeated detail or lack of one; but, if you can recognise this, it might save a lot of time and possibly some lives. It is often the case that there might be some apparently irrelevant aspects of evidence that when identified can link a series of case profiles or at least help investigators in tracking an elusive UNSUB. The perpetrator is creating a picture. They may well have a particular style of brushstroke or preference for a particular colour or a preference for a particular type of victim. All of these, when combined, might give you a reasonable profile to work with.

So victimology plus comfort zones plus signature might give aspiring criminal profilers a head start, but it is early days yet. Some criminal profilers will (almost certainly) disagree with these conclusions. However, one thing most researchers seem to be pretty much in agreement on is that we do not know all the solutions yet and there is a lot more to learn: 'We need to keep studying them and looking for answers ... because we *know* we have got to be able to stop them quicker and more effectively' (Douglas and Olshaker 1998).

Of course, Brady and Hindley's crimes would have been unlikely to have been effectively solved using victimology profiling. Out of the five murders, it was only the last, Edward Evans, who might have put himself at risk as a victim by visiting a gay bar and allowing himself to be picked up by a male stranger (Brady). All the other victims in the Moors Murders case were perfectly innocent children who had been quietly abducted off the streets. As we saw earlier, in 1960s Britain the serial killing of strangers was neither recognised nor understood. Perhaps the only indication of a growing phenomenon might have been reflected by a handful of films that were becoming popular and had started to utilise the murder of strangers as a viable plot device. Films by directors such as Alfred Hitchcock (*Psycho*, 1960) and Michael Powell (*Peeping Tom*, 1960) were being screened in British cinemas. For the first time, audiences were seeing the random murders of strangers in modern settings outside of traditional war and western contexts. However, not for one second would I support Emlyn Williams's laboured implication in his book about the Moors Murders, *Beyond Belief*, where he suggests that films may well have had a causal influence on Brady and Hindley during the time of their killings (Williams 1968). Brady did not need to watch violent films for inspiration. He probably just enjoyed them in reflection, and, since thousands of other people were frequently watching films such as these and not turning into serial killers, implying causation is ludicrous. Serial killers like watching films, just as anyone else does. Brady's current favourites include *The Shawshank Redemption* (apparently very popular among long-term prisoners, perhaps due to the portrayal of the lead character who manages to outwit a horribly corrupt prison system and finally escape). Brady also likes Oliver Stone's *Natural Born Killers* and has mentioned this film to me on more than one occasion. He also sent me some of the songs from the soundtrack on a cassette.

Despite what some forensic profilers might believe, we cannot use a simple blueprint or template and simply tick boxes in order to narrow down the probability that a person hunting or being hunted is the perpetrator or a victim of a series of murders. However, it is possible to ascertain some general trends that go beyond analysis of victims, comfort zones and signatures (yes, there may be more than one signature to complicate an analysis further). Here are some of the more popular ones.

UNSTABLE FAMILY BACKGROUNDS

This comes up a lot in many serial-killer histories. Jeffrey Dahmer was more or less abandoned by both of his parents, who divorced and went their separate ways, leaving him on his own in a lonely house in Milwaukee to brood and obsess and then finally kill.

Dennis Nilsen's father left when he was very young and Nilsen has no memory of him. His grandfather, of whom he was particularly fond, died a few years later while Nilsen was still a child: 'I was sickened by the past, the present and a doubtful future' (Nilsen, quoted in Masters 1985). Charles Manson never knew his father and was passed from place to place as an unwanted child. Ted Bundy never knew his father, either.

Ed Kemper, again with no father figure as a significant presence in his life, was rejected by his mother when he grew to 6 feet 9 inches tall, weighed over 20 stone and had taken to dismembering his sister's dolls. He was banished to the cellar of their house because of fears that he might attack family members, who were getting increasingly disturbed by this huge hulk lurking in the cellar and what he might do. These fears were confirmed when Kemper strangled his grandparents and later strangled his mother. There are lots of others. Nowadays, coming from a single-parent family is no big deal really; in fact, it is becoming almost the normal course of events. But decades ago it was considered a terrible stigma to be born a 'bastard' and for certain individuals it was perhaps a highly significant factor in the development of uncontrollable levels of resentment.

Brady, having never had any kind of relationship with his father, whom he had never actually met, almost certainly had to undergo all kinds of persecution from his peers and had little choice but to accept the role of outcast in the pious and conservative Scotland of the 1940s. He refuses to talk about this, understandably. He may not remember many of the details of his childhood. Few of us can. We may perhaps recall a handful of meaningful or traumatic events if they happened, but often we cannot remember with any certainty or precision. Details are distorted and reinvented when they are recalled, and Brady's memories of his childhood are as typically vague as most people's are. However, the stigma of having no father seems to come through very clearly when he discusses Ted Bundy. When describing his views on Bundy's psychology using analysis by hypothesis, he may perhaps be talking about himself by analogy; but this is just speculation, and nothing he says can be verified with any degree of certainty.

FRUSTRATED AMBITION

Of course, lots of people are born into single-parent families and do not grow up to kill, which brings me to a second factor that, when combined with the first, can result in an amalgam or focus of resentment which in certain cases can result in a violent backlash against the world and humanity in general. This is the problem of frustrated ambition, where ambition exceeds capabilities. Here are some of the more obvious ones.

Ted Bundy was a terminal overachiever. But successfully completing college courses in law and psychology constantly elevated his ambition beyond his abilities. An engagement to a girl from the rich and socially upmarket group he aspired to join went disastrously wrong when she unceremoniously dumped him. He was furious and probably felt like killing her, but obviously could not because he would be the prime suspect. So he started killing women who *looked* like her.

Dennis Nilsen had a mediocre career in the army and then a year in the police force, which was terminated when he realised he was not really getting anywhere there either. Then he worked as union representative in a government employment commission where his colleagues were pretty much indifferent towards his efforts to help them with their disputes with management. A long-term relationship failed when his partner moved out. He was desperately lonely and, after a one-night stand with an anonymous stranger he had met in a bar, he lay awake next to this man knowing that when the morning came he would be left alone once again. Nilsen finally cracked: 'I was afraid to wake him in case he left me. Trembling with fear I strangled his struggling body and when he was dead I took his young body back to bed with me and it was the beginning of the end of my life as I had known it' (Nilsen, quoted in Masters 1985).

Then he started killing regularly using the same MO: get the victim drunk, strangle him and then put him in the cupboard or under the floorboards, take him out occasionally for company for a few months until the maggots or smell became unbearable and then burn him on the bonfire in the garden and hunt a new one. This went on for a number of years before he was finally caught.

Gerard Schaefer saw his police career in tatters, having lost his job and being arrested after an absurd kidnapping/pseudo-arrest of two young women. Luckily, this went wrong when both victims, who had seen his face and could identify him, escaped, and went to the authorities, ending his career in law enforcement. He cracked and started killing, making sure he did not make the same mistake again by executing his victims before they could get away.

Even Charles Manson, the failed musician who had been trying to assert his talents with indifferent members of the Beach Boys and the Hollywood film community, had overestimated his abilities. He finally realised what everyone knew anyway: that his music was, well, just garbage. Like the others, he started killing, or in his case got other people to kill *for* him (technically, Manson was not a serial killer according to the usual definition of the term, although he was certainly accountable for a number of deaths).

There are others, but what about Brady?

Being sent to prison at such a young age was certainly not the best start in life. He was mixing with hardened career criminals. These people he looked up to were not exactly going to accept a 17-year-old petty thief into the upper echelons of their dubious fraternity, but these were the only role models he had, and he aspired to be like them. On release from jail, he managed to find employment in a situation that for someone with Brady's unreachable aspirations must have seemed to be a very dull, restrictive and meaningless state of affairs.

'Outside, in my less prophitable [sic] *role, I singly controlled multiple stacks of industrial chemicals in six rail stations and three warehouses. Now I am being controlled by 2000 staff engaged in counting plastic spoons'* (2004).

This reference to his earlier role relates to his time employed at Millwards Merchandise, the tiny administration office where he worked as a stock clerk and met Myra Hindley. He was hardly the linchpin of an international industrial corporation, as he might want to believe in retrospect. In reality, it was a boring, poorly paid job in a dusty little office in Manchester with half a dozen staff. No one, apart from Myra Hindley, was going to notice him there. Even if he persevered for 40 years, the best he could expect would be retirement with a miserable state pension and a fake-gold watch. Frustrated ambition again. Brady wanted his 15 minutes of fame. Unfortunately, 15 minutes of fame/infamy has its price, and, due to the appalling nature of his crimes, it was inevitable that he would have to pay for it for the rest of his life. And that is exactly what happened. Brady got a lot more than he anticipated when he decided to abduct and murder children for recreation, although I doubt very much that at the time he seriously realised that his actions would shatter so many lives, including his own, and that there would be no going back, ever.

When he was finally captured and sent to jail for good, the criminal fraternity would have nothing to offer him other than hostility and violence. People convicted of crimes such as Brady's do not have an easy time in prison. It is quite the opposite: from the minute the iron doors slam behind them, they become a target for both inmates and guards. Child murderers and rapists are the lowest of the low in the criminal hierarchy. 'Beasts' used to be the commonly used term, and the hardcore bank robbers and suchlike will have nothing to do with them other than making and enacting plans to maim or kill them. Brady was shunned and/or physically attacked by the very people he had aspired to become one with. Criminals such as the Kray twins, John McVicar and Ronnie Biggs – those he so much wanted to emulate – would have treated him as the lowest of the low, not even worthy of taking a single step up the criminal ladder.

London serial killer Dennis Nilsen would occasionally open a cupboard door and an arm or a leg would fall out and remind him he had forgotten to dispose of a victim, or he might notice flies crawling out from under the floorboards where most of the bodies were hidden, not to mention the appalling stench that got worse and worse as the body count went up. His immediate neighbours living in the flats in the same house complained to him about the smell but with no real conviction, and accepted his explanation that there must be something wrong with the drains. There certainly was. They were blocked with rotting human flesh that Nilsen had attempted to flush down his lavatory.

It is incredible that Nilsen somehow managed to maintain a psychological equilibrium while all of this was going on. He had been living in a house full of corpses for a number of years, but finally this fragile balance began to slip: 'A fly buzzing around would sometimes remind me of another dimension under the floor' (Nilsen, cited in Masters 1985).

Interestingly, it was not the presence or the smell of the decaying bodies that upset him most; they were just objects to him once they had been killed and the disposal of the remains was to him simply a practical problem. It was the *personalities* of his victims he remembered from his time spent with them while they were still alive that finally began to fragment his emotional stability. Nilsen became frightened to go home to a house full of ghosts that he had created. At an office party one night, he was shocked to hear the same music he had been listening to during one of his murders. This particular victim was hidden under the kitchen floor at the time. Nilsen was terrified to go home: 'he was back there, waiting for me'. This victim was apparently listening on headphones to the London

Symphony Orchestra's recording of sound bites of popular classical music set to a disco beat: *Hooked on Classics*. Nilsen strangled him with the cable of the headphones while he was listening.

Nilsen killed 15 people in four years and hardly anyone suspected anything. Only one of these missing persons was the focus of a serious investigation (which did not achieve any useful results). This is not untypical: many serial killers and their crimes go unnoticed, even by people living in the house where the murders occur. Neighbours might notice uncharacteristic late-night digging in a garden or a patio being resurfaced (think of Fred and Rosemary West), or in Nilsen's case a midnight mission into the drain in the garden to try to unblock the sewage system before Dyno-Rod turned up. It is ironic that Nilsen's four-year murder spree was solved by a drain repairman from Dyno-Rod rather than as a result of any high-profile professor of forensic criminal investigation.

When murders occur, people might eventually start wondering about smells or strange noises they might have heard or unusual comings and goings they might have seen; but, even if such things are noticed, people are unlikely to pay much attention to them. Perhaps Brady and Hindley's neighbours wondered about the couple's late-night trips to desolate parts of Saddleworth Moor, but they would have been unlikely to comment or even think twice about them. People on the whole tend to mind their own business concerning other people's behaviour unless it adversely affects them. In most cases, people do not do anything even if they do notice something unusual. Would *you*, for example, contact the police if you saw someone arrive at your neighbour's house and you did not see them leave? Probably not for a very long time, if ever. The chances are there would be a simple explanation and you would end up looking stupid and possibly get involved in an argument. Nobody wants to get involved in other people's lives. It just causes trouble. So, unless you have especially nosy and forensic-aware neighbours, it might well be some time before anyone bothers to pick up the phone and report anything to authorities, no matter what they have seen, and no matter how bizarre it might appear.

This is exactly what happened with Brady and Hindley. What they were doing was out of the scope of most people's understanding, beyond the comprehension of the workaday neighbours who were more interested in how they were going to pay the gas bill or what might happen in the next episode of *Coronation Street* or *Doctor Who*. In 1960s Britain, people did not kidnap and murder children for fun. It was simply beyond the realms of most people's comprehension, and this is why they managed to get away with it for so long.

Psychologists call this indifference to the fate of strangers 'bystander apathy', and it seems to be a lot more prevalent now than ever before. These days, when the sun goes down and almost everyone is locked up safe in their houses, they are most likely to be too focused on their television programmes or Internet chat interactions even to notice the neighbours hauling a dead body past their living-room windows.

Most of Brady and Hindley's murders occurred in the dark on desolate ground on the moors. At such a location, there would almost certainly have been no one within earshot, so no matter how much noise occurred it was highly unlikely that anyone would have heard anything. With their last murder, when their victim was killed in the living room of their semidetached house, there was almost certainly a lot of noise made from the victim's screams. David Smith testified in court that the victim was screaming while he was being bludgeoned with an axe, and I tend to believe this was probably true. Anyone would scream when being hit with an axe, and it took 14 blows before Evans died – plenty of time for him to make a lot of noise. This racket was enough to wake Hindley's grandmother, who had been asleep upstairs, and who promptly went back to sleep after the murder without finding out what was responsible for the noise until the police arrived the following morning.

In 1973, Albert Brust, a Miami killer, having murdered some people, committed suicide with poison while sitting in a garden chair on his lawn. The neighbours repeatedly walked past his corpse but apparently just ignored it until much later the following day, when they finally had to acknowledge he was still sitting there (in the rain, in a cloud of flies). Finally, they reluctantly contacted the police, who turned up to search the premises. They found that Brust had been dead for some time. Investigating officers also discovered the body of a missing teenage boy cemented into his bathroom wall, and that Brust's garage seemed to have been turned into a soundproofed 'kidnap room', the comfort zone for his murders (Owen 2006).

As far as the neighbours were concerned, not reporting a motionless figure sitting outside in a lawn chair for over a day seems horribly callous, but it is not unusual. Indifference to the fate of others is becoming endemic. Approximately 25,000 people go missing annually in the United Kingdom alone (Erzinclioglu 2000). They disappear without anyone ever reporting anything. Most of these people are never found.

Even the murderers themselves can be indifferent. Nilsen was not even sure of the exact number of people he had killed. He had to count the number of ties he had left in his wardrobe to work it out, one tie being used for each strangling and then discarded.

Another alarming example of total indifference to murder occurred in New York in 1996. Michael Alig and an accomplice, Robert Riggs, committed a totally idiotic murder in the infamous 'party monster' case (St James 1999). Together they murdered a Hispanic drug dealer, 'Angel' Mendeles, in their New York apartment with a hammer in a stupid argument over rent money and drug debts. The body was dumped in their bath, cut in half and then stored in a cardboard box in their living room while Alig and his friends continued partying with their friends. The box (with the dismembered body in it) was apparently used as a coffee table. People would ask, 'Where's Angel?' and Alig would say, 'I killed him, his body's in that box.' And everyone would laugh, assuming this was a joke or a publicity stunt.

This went on for about a week until the box started to smell. Alig and Riggs then carried it out to a taxi. The driver helped them lift it into the boot and then drove them to a bridge over the Hudson River, where they threw it in. The legs had been tied up into dustbin liners; these sank and were never found. But the box with the torso, head and arms in it happened to be lined with cork (the killers did not realise this), so it floated off down the river and was washed up a couple of days later on a Staten Island beach. Although the police now had the top half of the body, the arms and the head, these remained in the morgue for nearly eight months before being identified.

Alig and Riggs were indifferent to the gravity of the situation and the potential consequences. Alig had announced to friends in advance that he was going to do the killing and afterwards cheerily confessed to anyone who would listen, and even went as far as to attend a New York club party with 'guilty' written all over his face with a magic marker pen while the investigation was in progress. He then went on a binge with his victim's drugs and money for a number of months until the police finally identified the body and arrested Riggs, who immediately confessed without even being interrogated. Reality finally sank in for Alig, who made a last-minute cross-country run for it, but was soon caught because he had held a 'party press conference' about the murder, where he had told everyone what he had done, where his hideout was and which route he was taking to get there.

Alig and Riggs are now both locked up in jail and are likely to be there for some considerable time. Most 'ordinary' non-serial murders are so stupid and the perpetrators so foolish that identification of those responsible should be fairly easy, but it is not if nobody really cares. There is no need for sophisticated profiling in cases like this, just routine police investigation and basic forensic awareness.

When the perpetrators openly admit their guilt, or, as in Alig's case, boast about it, it is hardly surprising that nobody believes them. Ed Kemper had to call the police a number of times before they took his claims of multiple murder seriously. Colin Ireland did the same, calling the police and newspapers about his multiple murders and getting increasingly exasperated that nobody seemed to be in the least bit interested (Gekoski 1998). Donald Gaskins (see Chapter 2) at one point transported his dead victims around in a hearse he had bought and in which he had placed a sign in the back window that read, 'WE HAUL ANYTHING, LIVING OR DEAD'. The police thought this was hilarious, at least until their missing-persons files started piling up. Additionally, as we have already seen, the presence of death can act almost as an aphrodisiac for certain individuals. It definitely did for Brady and Hindley.

Gaskins explained his own perspective: 'I have to say that I got more ass in the back of that hearse than in any vehicle I ever owned. Fucking a killer in the back of a hearse truly turned-on them women who liked the smells of violence and death' (Gaskins 1993).

Of course this is Gaskins's own account of the situation, his fantasy. It seems much more likely that most of the women he abducted would probably have been almost comatose with fear and would be willing to behave in any way imaginable in order to try to save their own lives.

Such blatant indifference to the enormity of serious crimes can act as a camouflage or misdirection. I mean, nobody could be *that* stupid. And if the killers themselves become indifferent to their murders and the potential consequences of their acts, then you can hardly expect other people to believe their improbable claims or show any more concern. In another more recent case, residents in a block of flats in Southern California had ignored a dead body propped up on a neighbour's patio for a number of days. When it was finally identified as a dead human being, they came up with the lame excuse that they 'thought it was a Halloween display' (*Los Angeles Times*, October 2009).

People just do not want to get involved if they can possibly help it. Probably the most famous case of bystander apathy that is documented in the psychological literature was that of Kitty Genovese. This 28-year-old woman was stabbed to death in 1964 on a busy New York street. Thirty-eight people reported later that they had heard her screaming for help as she was being murdered. Not one of them intervened or offered assistance or even made a call to the police. In fact, one witness was reported as saying that he had turned up his radio to 'drown out the screaming' because it was getting on his nerves.

It may well have been the sheer number of people who had heard her murder that had led to a diffusion of responsibility. The more people who witness a situation that might require intervention, the less likely anyone is to do anything about it. This has been tested rigorously in controlled experiments (Darley 1991).

With the Moors Murders case it is almost certain that at least one, if not more, of Brady and Hindley's five known victims may well have been seen being invited into Hindley's car. However, anyone who saw this would have no reason to think anything was out of the ordinary and by the time the story broke the chances are that witnesses would probably not remember anything more than a vague impression. If there was no obvious argument or physical coercion, any witnesses would be highly unlikely to remember specific details, and even if somebody did notice something, eyewitness testimony, as we have seen, has been shown to be extremely unreliable. This has been demonstrated many times. Perceptual limitations combined with the reconstructive nature of memory makes reliance on the recollections of witnesses today very weak evidence in a court of law which can be easily undermined by an astute defence lawyer within the dynamics of the courtroom. However, in the 1960s, the reliance on witness statements was paramount in the course of a criminal trial. In those times, if a *credible* witness was to point at the accused and say confidently, 'It was him/her', then the jury would almost always believe them. Which is exactly what happened with the Moors Murders case, despite consistent attempts from Brady's and Hindley's defence lawyers to undermine the reputation of David Smith, the chief prosecution witness who had watched Brady kill. Not that it would have made any difference anyway, even if the jury had not believed Smith. There was just too much evidence stacked against Brady and Hindley, much of which Brady had deliberately preserved. Most serial killers do like to hang on to their souvenirs.

To recap, even if you might have neighbours who would not notice if your house was burning down or bother to intervene if they did, killing people in your own home is a forensic minefield. It is pretty much impossible for all the evidence generated in almost any kind of murder to be concealed. If the location comes under suspicion as a potential crime scene, modern investigative tools are likely to find trace evidence generated before, during and after the murder, even if no body is found and the murder site has been scrubbed with bleach, which in itself would be suspicious, especially if the rest of the house has not been so carefully cleaned.

LOCARD'S PRINCIPLE OF TRANSFERENCE

There is an important theory called Locard's principle of transference (1920), which relies on one of the most fundamental principles of forensic science, which is that every physical event in a murder scenario, any contact between the killer, the victim or the location of the crime, no matter how fleeting or unnoticed, leaves some kind of a trace.

Dr Edmond Locard was a twentieth-century forensic scientist who built the first forensic crime laboratory in Lyon, France. He came up with a basic premise: even if the perpetrator is incredibly thorough when attempting to eliminate all the trace evidence from a murder or other serious-crime scene, they will almost certainly leave something behind that will link them to the event. At the same time, the chances are they will almost certainly have taken some forensic evidence away with them.

> Wherever he steps, whatever he touches, whatever he leaves, even unconsciously, will serve as a silent witness against him. Not only his fingerprints or his footprints, but his hair, the fibres from his clothes, the glass he breaks, the tool mark he leaves, the paint he scratches, the blood or semen he deposits or collects. All of these and more bear mute witness against him. This is evidence that does not forget. It is not confused by the excitement of the moment. It is not absent because human witnesses are. It is factual evidence. Physical evidence cannot be wrong, it cannot perjure itself, it cannot be wholly absent. Only human failure to find it, study and understand it can diminish its value [Kirk 1953].

Locard's principle of transference holds up today in almost all cases.

Brady was forensically aware; he knew most of these pitfalls and even went so far as to compile meticulous lists of instructions, to himself, to try to make sure he was eliminating any forensic evidence he might have left behind after his murders. He carefully tried to cover his tracks before, during and after the murders. The lists Brady had written reminded him to check all the details and make sure nothing had been missed and anything incriminating had been destroyed. However, carelessly, he forgot to destroy what was probably the most important evidence that was used to successfully prosecute him: the lists themselves! By making these lists (which the police quickly found), and by trying to conceal other evidence in suitcases left at the railway station left-luggage storage (which the police also quickly found), he might as well have called the prison and made a reservation. The lists were found in Hindley's car by the police after Brady had been arrested, and these were especially damning when read out in court by the prosecution, who referred to them as 'body-disposal plans', which they were. One list even had 'destroy all lists' as an item, a reminder to himself that it should be destroyed, which he had forgotten to do. This was impossible to explain away in court and Brady did not even bother to try. Instead, he tried to cast doubt as to when they had been written in order to undermine their existence as evidence of premeditation. He said that they were written *after* the last murder. The jury were not convinced; they did not believe a word of this explanation.

Having attempted to clean up the crime scene after an indoor murder, the killer then of course has to try to conceal the body or somehow get it out of the house, as well as perhaps trying to establish a credible alibi if they have not done so already. Each of these activities just adds to the clues that might be found, the number of possible witnesses who might see something out of the ordinary, and, consequently, the intensity of any investigation that might be instigated. After the last Brady and Hindley murder – the Evans axe murder in the living room of their house – David Smith, who had been there at the time and witnessed it, apparently suggested stealing a wheelbarrow to get rid of the body. Brady stated in court that he had dismissed this as 'ludicrous', which of course it was. Perpetrators of serious crimes are often caught by additionally committing a relatively minor crime in the process of trying to conceal evidence relating to the first. The process of attempting to eliminate clues ironically and invariably multiplies their number and variety and so decreases the odds that the perpetrator will escape undetected.

Today, buried bodies are easily discovered with a methane probe, provided the search area is not huge and the body is not buried too deep or has not been buried for too long. Recent grave sites can even be identified from a helicopter if it has modern thermal-imaging technology. None of this technology was generally available in the 1960s, when Brady was killing. In those days, once a body was buried, it was almost impossible to locate unless there were obvious signs that could be seen with the naked eye. In Brady's case, delaying removing his last victim from the house and burying the body was his downfall. If he had successfully managed to transport it to Saddleworth Moor and bury it with his other victims there is a very real possibility that the Moors Murders would never have come to light at all and his victims would still be listed as missing persons to this day.

Forensics was relatively primitive in the 1960s when Brady and Hindley were killing, at least compared with today. Forensic evidence in murder cases at that time was limited mainly to fingerprints, the discovery and identification of the murder weapon, footprints, visible bloodstains and witness statements. Forensics is much more advanced now to the point that anyone with modern forensic-detection awareness would know it was madness to use their house as a murder location. There are just too many details that can be overlooked and microscopic evidence left behind that is invisible to the naked eye is admissible in court. Well-organised serial killers with forensic awareness are likely to choose multiple-murder and body-disposal sites that cannot easily be related to their routine movements. Ted Bundy stated: 'To the [nomadic] serial killer, mobility is very important' (Du Clos 1993). The more thinly the evidence is dispersed, the more useless it is likely to be in a murder investigation. Of course, Bundy ignored his own advice and insisted on driving the same model of stolen car and carrying his murder tools in the boot, just waiting to be pulled over by the police, which is exactly what happened. Maybe he *wanted* to get caught.

NOMADIC KILLERS AND COMFORT ZONES

Multiple murders in a single location do still happen occasionally (Nilsen, Gacy, Dahmer, the Wests, etc.), but these are rather rare because modern serial killers often travel a lot between different cities, states or even countries. These nomadic killers still operate territorially, but their use of a number of different territories makes them much more difficult to catch. These people have comfort zones in multiple locations, environments where they feel safe to kill and abduct, and where they know or have a good idea about the potential layout of the environment. Many like places of transit such as railway stations, shopping malls, public areas where lots of people are coming and going and nobody is likely to notice a quiet abduction taking place, or, even if they do see something strange, they might not realise they are witnessing an abduction. I doubt very much if Brady ever committed any crimes while he was abroad, if indeed he ever went.

I recall the impact of freedom and relaxation when I first visited the continent. The pavement cafés were bustling, contrasting with the pasty-faced drudges and robots of England, sitting in dim, funereal pubs sipping their half-pints of warm mild sludge. America was even better, finally space to breathe and borders to cross [2004].

This seems highly unlikely. As I mentioned in Chapter 2, I am disinclined to believe Brady made any adventurous journeys other than railway trips between various Northern towns in England and in Scotland – Manchester and Glasgow, obviously – and there is one confirmed trip to the Lake District. However, there is no evidence that he ever went abroad other than to Parkhurst Prison on the Isle of Wight where he apparently played chess with the convicted poisoner Graham Young.

He never mentioned many details of these exciting transatlantic adventures to me, anyway, and if it was a nostalgic dream I was certainly not going to deprive him of this by asking him to qualify the truth. Nostalgic dreams of freedom must be a fragile experience after the suffocating atmosphere of life in a grim Manchester overspill estate in the 1960s followed by nearly half a century of being shuffled about among various Northern English prison cells.

Serial killers recognise the absence of social patterns and easily blend into anonymity while moving through certain locations. If, for example, a witness was to see two people behaving strangely on a busy street or a railway-station platform, they would probably be unlikely to alert authorities, even if they thought they were witnessing an argument – in fact, *especially* if they thought they were witnessing an argument. Railway stations are perfect hunting grounds for serial killers.

Andrei Chikatilo, the Ukrainian Rostov Ripper (whom we briefly met in Chapter 4), found most of his victims at various railway stations. The Chikatilo case was horrendous for all kinds of reasons, not least the terrible mistakes made in the investigation where the Soviet authorities insisted that serial killing just did not happen on Soviet territory – it was a product of 'Western decadence' – and so they did not alert the citizens, even when mangled and chewed-up bodies were being found all over the countryside. A great opportunity for a serial killer. The authorities made other fatal errors. With Chikatilo's first murder, that of a nine-year-old girl, Lena Zakcotnov, in 1978, the authorities arrested, convicted and then executed Alexander Kravchenko for the crime. Kravchenko was innocent. He just happened to have a criminal record for a similar offence, was in the neighbourhood at the time and fitted the profile. After the police had beaten a false confession out of him he was convicted and promptly shot. When Chikatilo was finally convicted and executed, Kravchenko was awarded a posthumous pardon, which is not much compensation for him after being shot in the head for a crime he did not commit.

With modern transportation, serial killers can literally drive around taking their comfort zones with them. Gerald and Charlene Gallego, the 'sex slave' serial killers who operated in Sacramento between 1978 and 1980, and James Daveggio and Michelle Michaud used Transit vans. In both cases, it was the female partner who would lure people, usually teenage girls, into their van by offering them street drugs or to take them to a party. Once the victim had taken the bait and accepted a lift, it was usually too late. These vans had been modified so that they were not easy to escape from. They could be driven anywhere until the killers got bored of attacking/raping the person they had abducted and finally decided to transport them to a remote site for killing and body disposal and then drive away to hunt the next one (Davis 2005). So hitchhikers beware if a van pulls up to offer you a ride, at least take a glance into the back to see who or what might be there or who or what might *not* be there, unless you want to be taken somewhere which is not your original destination and where you most certainly will not want to go.

LINKAGE BLINDNESS

'Linkage blindness' is a term originally coined by Stephen Egger. It usually refers to the reluctance of law-enforcement teams to interact during investigations. It can also be applied to a failure to adopt a multidisciplinary approach. If tackled from a wide range of perspectives, this can potentially take investigations far beyond the tunnel vision of many homicide inquiries.

Nomadic killers usually take a long time to apprehend, often a number of years. It is very hard to compile information and come up with a decent profile if the perpetrators are operating in different jurisdictions, although linkage blindness is becoming rather less of a problem now that the Internet allows easy comparison of crimes in different states and countries. Internet links between law-enforcement agencies are becoming increasingly effective in tracking down nomadic killers and refining profiles of killers who may be operating internationally. (VICAP, HOLMES, etc. do have their place in criminological investigation, although there are a lot of teething problems that need to be resolved before these systems can be utilised with a high degree of certainty.) Of course, the flip side is that it may not be just law-enforcement professionals who have noticed the potential of the Internet. Like any technological development, the Internet has been immediately seized upon as a new and highly effective tool for serial killers to expand their comfort zones and extend their hunting grounds internationally, so it is a double-edged sword.

VIRTUAL HUNTING GROUNDS

Internet messaging, email, live-chat sites, dating software, social-networking sites, Yahoo!, MySpace, Facebook, Twitter – all of these have been involved in cases of stalking, rape and murder. Google Earth, a simple program to download, will give any user with Internet access a detailed satellite picture of possible kill locations. All they need is a postal code or rough description of an area and they can locate their victim's house, workplace (maybe even where and when they park their car) and the surrounding land and access roads to and from all of these locations. Those with more sophisticated computer skills and access authority can link into CC (closed-circuit) TV cameras and watch potential victims enter and leave their homes and workplaces. Serial killers have not been slow to realise this potential. The killer can sit in the comfort of their own home or in their car monitoring their victim's movements, their communications activities and daily schedules on their laptops and mobile phones. They can groom and select victims at their own pace with minimal risk.

Move up another notch and they can simply wait for potential victims to advertise their status as victims on the Internet (as we saw in Chapter 4). This *does* happen, the ultimate Internet dating experience! Log on to the cannibal websites and find the killer or victim who is 'just right for you! (enter profile)'. Only on the Internet! No wonder the Ashworth authorities withhold anything to do with communications technology from the patients there. They would not even let Brady have a copy of a music recording I sent him because it was on a rewritable CD.

The seductive anonymity of modern computer networking systems gives potential killers a sense of security, a whole series of masks they can hide behind while stalking. We see techniques such as 'hacking' (breaking into people's private accounts to gather sensitive information), 'identity theft' (assuming the identity of someone else for the purpose of financial fraud or misdirection when trolling for victims) and abuse of administration access to networking sites. There are plenty of other methods to locate victims precisely, contact them, manipulate them and plan attacks. You do not need a degree in computer science. All of these techniques and tools are freely available to anyone with Internet access and a rudimentary knowledge of computing skills. Nip down to your local computer store and you can buy a computerised stalking platform and set it up in 30 minutes. Now you can access international hardcore pornography and hundreds of thousands of people to hunt (or locate people who might want to hunt you, if you were so inclined).

One case worth mentioning reveals some of the many ways that a serial killer can use the Internet to their advantage during their murder cycle. John E. Robinson gained the dubious distinction of being the man responsible for the world's first well-documented case of 'Internet murder' (although there were other lower-profile cases before him). Originally based in Chicago, Robinson, who was convicted in 2003, started trawling for victims using newspaper dating advertisements but soon realised how much more efficient the Internet could be for the same purpose. He started visiting BDSM (bondage/domination/

sadomasochism) Internet chat sites, adopting the role of a 'slave master' hunting for vulnerable submissive females. It did not take him much time to find and then isolate them. 'Control by isolation' is one technique Brady and other serial killers used. Isolate the victim in a location with which they are unfamiliar and from which there is nowhere to run, and this is almost as effective as pointing a gun at them.

The predator removes the victim from their familiar comfort zone (victims have comfort zones too, as we all have) and then transports them to a place where there are no obvious or familiar exits, quite literally to somewhere there is nowhere to run. Brady used the desolate Yorkshire Moors in England. Ted Bundy used Taylor Mountain, a remote woodland in Washington. Robinson used an isolated ranch in Kansas.

However, possibly the undisputed 'expert' in control by isolation was Robert Hansen. Hansen owned a light aircraft and, after soliciting erotic dancers and sex workers in bars in Anchorage, Alaska, between 1980 and 1983, he would fly them out to a remote cabin in the frozen wilderness. After raping them, he would set them free to run away, but there was nowhere for them to run to. He would give them a head start and then hunt and shoot them. This went on for over ten years until one of his victims incredibly managed to escape and find help, and Hansen was finally arrested (Du Clos 1993).

Robinson's victims would travel to Kansas to meet him to play out the shared fantasies they had orchestrated together on the Internet. Of course, the victims had not realised the true nature of his fantasies. When they arrived to meet him in America they were quickly killed and robbed and their bodies were stored in barrels. Robinson would then adopt their identities and send email back to their families and friends at home pretending to be the victims and describing what a great life they were enjoying. However, pretending to be so many different people and having an extensive criminal record meant his entire house of cards finally and predictably collapsed and he was caught, tried and convicted. Sentenced to death in 2002 and pending further charges concerning three other bodies found on his premises, he currently awaits lethal injection in Kansas. Two books cover the case: Berry-Dee and Morris (2008) have a chapter on the case, and in much greater depth FBI agent John Douglas (2003) tells the entire sordid saga.

So, while the Internet might initially provide a comforting level of anonymity and safety for interacting with strangers, it is important to remember that it also provides a comfortable level of anonymity and safety for other people who might have a more sinister agenda. The Internet has one fateful flaw for potential victims of such predators, which is that nobody can ever really be 100 per cent sure that the person they are talking to and exchanging emails and photographs with is actually the person they claim to be. Most of the time these cases do not present any serious threat to the people concerned other than the embarrassment of being conned. There have been incidents where people have divorced their wives/husbands, resigned from their employment and then boarded an aeroplane to meet their Internet lover, only to find out that the person of their dreams turns out to be a different age, race or gender from that which they had been led to believe. The Brad Pitt lookalike who claims to be a film producer who owns hotels and yachts turns out to be a pimply 17-year-old geek who delivers pizza. Or the Angelina Jolie lookalike who claims to be a vivacious different places where murders have happened? Canter's work proposes a variety of different analytic models that could be useful in certain cases but the one thing he cannot explain is inconsistency. Once again, you cannot quantify these people with a painting-by-numbers approach. They kill whoever they want to, wherever they want to and whenever they want to. Usually the only pattern is the absence of a pattern.

I mentioned geographical profiling to Brady; he was familiar with the work and had seen Canter interviewed on television. He thought Canter's research was risible:

> It amused me to see Canter practically claiming patent for geographical profiling, ponderously proffering blinding banalities as original insight. Doesn't take too much to profile profilers. This particular one's 'reputation' rested upon deducing that a series of crimes all performed on or near railways probably were committed by 'someone connected with railways!' [2007].

So another unpromising theory. What else do investigators have to work with?

DNA

DNA was, and still is to a certain extent, considered to be the ultimate forensic evidence. However, a blind acceptance of the infallibility of DNA matching in forensics has got a lot of people killed. It has turned out not to be as foolproof in criminal investigations as people initially thought. It is no more foolproof than fingerprinting (easily fudged: wear gloves or take along someone else's fingerprints to leave at the crime scene and put them squarely in the frame). Similarly, blind adherence to DNA as *a priori* proof that a particular individual was at a crime scene does not stand up and can extend a killer's murder cycle. Chikatilo, who was suspected of being the Rostov Ripper, was eliminated from the investigation because his blood DNA did not match the sperm DNA found in and on the victims. Chikatilo was cleared and released to carry on an active and escalating kill cycle for 14 more years. Finally, he was caught, literally red-handed, washing blood from his hands and shoes at a railway station. At his trial, he had to be placed in a steel cage, not to stop him escaping but to stop him being torn apart by the furious crowd. He was convicted of 52 murders when he was finally caught and was condemned and executed in 1992.

As far as forensics is concerned, even if blood and sperm DNA *do* match with a person who has been apprehended, it is *still* not a foolproof evidential certainty that the right person has been identified. You need a considerable amount of trace material, and, anyway, DNA found might well belong to somebody else who was not even there (*New York Times*, 26 July 1994). DNA as an infallible test of judgement in murder cases has long been discredited, despite what people might think from watching *CSI* or similar fictional representations of criminal investigations that remain ever popular in the media. Furthermore, criminals with 'forensic awareness' have been known to contaminate a crime scene with DNA that they brought along specifically to derail an investigation before it has even got started.

To conclude, DNA evidence has acquired almost a magical confirmation of proof that a certain person was at a certain crime scene and therefore they are definitely the perpetrator, so much so that 'DNA evidence often appears to make some people, including scientists, override logic' (Erzinclioglu 2000).

Back to the drawing board.

SIGNATURE

Once a likely suspect has been caught, forensic evidence is usually necessary for a conviction; but, during an investigation of unsolved murders and looking for an UNSUB, an analysis of signature can be a lot more productive.

'The common threads that extend from crime to crime have come to be known as the killer's 'signature' and, more specifically, 'The killer's signature is his psychological calling card that he leaves at the scene of each crime across a spectrum of several murders' (Keppel 1997).

For example, Ted Bundy enjoyed killing women in America in the 1970s. He was convicted of 30 murders, although the actual number remains unknown; between 29 and 100 has been estimated. He was executed in the electric chair in 1989 so we can never be sure. Bundy repeatedly changed his MO. Did the suspect kill the victims in their own homes? Did he kidnap them using a vehicle? Did he use a particular weapon? Did he kill in a particular way? And so on. Bundy confused investigators for a number of years by alternating kill sites and methods of murder. Changing his MO made it extremely hard for investigators to link crimes but, if you look very carefully, you will see that there are some aspects that did remain consistent.

Bundy, like Kemper, hunted university campuses (their comfort zones), where, in Bundy's case at least, academic expertise enabled him easily to get enrolled on various courses and pass anonymously within campus society in a number of different American states. Bundy changed the courses he enrolled on more than once and changed his MO and appearance; but one thing he did not change was his signature. A killer's signature is not always easy to identify, and killers themselves might not even be aware of it. It could arise from some tiny psychological detail that investigators either miss or dismiss as trivial. But, if it can be identified, it might give an investigation something much more tangible than unsupported assumptions based on flimsy evidence from crime scenes that might have been trampled over and contaminated by police who have no idea what they are doing.

The signature then is a subtle psychological imprint that can help identify whether a single individual might be responsible for different crimes in different places, even if superficially there is little to link evidence and circumstances. Bundy was captured twice, and then escaped both times (once by leaping out of the court library window in a trial recess and running away down the street). Investigators had no luck tracking him down as he moved from state to state until they finally put photographs of victims from different American states in a row. The man's signature was staring them right in the face. Almost all the victims had long brown hair parted in the middle.

Having decided to follow this line of enquiry, investigators were soon able to link Bundy's movements with a number of murders in different American states. Bundy eventually got tired, as most of them do. He got bored with his murders, lazy, and was finally caught for good. He was caught speeding in a stolen car with incriminating murder/rape tools in the boot. Unsurprisingly, once in jail, finally for good and with no further opportunities to escape, he started receiving fan letters from hybristophiliac women with long brown hair parted in the middle. He finally married one, Carole Ann Booth, who ended up giving birth to his child by artificial insemination in a 'contact visit' and then disappeared off the map before his execution.

Having explored the weaknesses associated with relying on eyewitnesses, the limitations of geographical profiling, the overconfidence of relying on DNA as a foolproof forensic test and acknowledging the elusive nature of signature as a robust (and occasionally useful) investigative profiling tool, I realised that the only way to move forward was to go back to the hospital.

On this visit, I wanted to discuss with Brady some of the issues involved in police interrogation and courtroom dynamics in his own case. He talked in depth about his interrogation by police and the prosecution at the trial. Although I had read the court transcriptions, it was something of a revelation to hear what it was like from Brady's perspective. Concerning his police interrogation by three officers simultaneously, he explained:

> The general tone was set by the fact that we were taken in a Black Maria with a dozen plain-clothes people and taken up the iron staircase with police all down below ... I was then taken into this gymnasium ... That is when the shouting started ... On each side, one in each ear shouting questions simultaneously ... I could be answering three questions at the one time ... the interview ended with [Detective Chief Inspector] Mounsey grabbing the door and saying 'Bastard' and then banging the door shut. ... I was left for ten minutes and then the others [more police] took over.

According to Brady, he was never read his rights or offered a solicitor to represent him at the time of his police interrogation – not that this would have made much difference in retrospect, except in terms of certain statements being deemed inadmissible as evidence. He told me that DCI Mounsey and the other police involved made a number of threats, including showing him a copy of the *Manchester Evening News*, which had printed a picture of one of the victims' relatives struggling with police and making very public threats to Brady's and Hindley's lives. The police showed it to him and suggested that they could orchestrate a private visit with Brady: 'We can arrange it.'

'Mounsey was the worst. He was the "bad" cop, the worst one.'

Later in the interrogation, the police apparently threatened to have Brady and Hindley's dog killed. During the trial, Brady was asked about threats from police. He replied, *'There was one threat from Mounsey. He said, "We will destroy your dog and maybe you will realise what it is like to lose something you love."'*

A week later the dog was dead, apparently under anaesthetic during a veterinary examination to determine its age to support the accusation that one photograph of Hindley squatting on the grave of one of their victims holding the dog fitted an accurate time frame for the murder. I guess Brady was getting his first serious taste of hate and condemnation, but I doubt at that time even he could not have perceived how deep that hatred would go and how long it would last.

The police interrogation was by most accounts gruelling and, according to Brady, they bent the rules to try to scare him into making a confession. This may well be true. However, there was so much insurmountable evidence stacked up against both of them that, even if they had had

Perry Mason fighting their corner, it would not really have made much difference. They did not really stand any chance of acquittal, and Brady and Hindley knew it, although both of them were stubborn to the end, pleading not guilty in what was basically a no-win situation by claiming they had no involvement with any of the abductions and murders other than that of Evans. The jury did not believe them.

The trial lasted for 14 days. Brady was on the stand for almost three. He showed me how, while he was standing in the dock being cross-examined, he had managed to retain his composure. He said, '*I braced myself against the barrage of interrogation from the prosecution barrister Mr Heilpern and the Attorney General Frederick Elwyn Jones by gripping the wooden rail of the dock.*' He demonstrated this to me by gripping the arms of the force-feeding chair until his knuckles were white.

It was all for nothing at the trial, though. At this point, it was just a case of future damage limitation, as the damage already done could never be reversed. The best Brady managed to achieve at his trial was to get Hindley's accusation of involvement with one murder reduced to harbouring Brady afterwards and getting her cleared of being convicted of the actual killing. This got her seven years on top of two life sentences for the other two murders she was convicted of. Two and a half life sentences rather than three did not really make a lot of difference in the end. They were both going to jail for good.

CHAPTER SIX

COMMUNICATION GULAG

The following information contains further transcriptions from my interviews and the correspondence that Brady and I exchanged while he has been confined at Ashworth Hospital. Although he gave me permission to use any material he supplied to me, I have not reproduced every single letter he wrote – many of which were repetitive to the point of self-parody – or every letter I wrote to him. The material that I have included in this book therefore focuses primarily on the key issues that we discussed both in interviews and related correspondence.

Maintaining contact has been very difficult for a number of reasons, and, when this book is published, our discourse may possibly end. The authorities at the hospital scan, examine and sometimes destroy some of the things he is sent and he has forwarded me a pile of the official notifications that confirm this. The authorities also copy and examine every letter he sends out. Despite my sending all of my mail to him by recorded delivery, some of my letters seemed to just vanish. At one point, I heard, from a friend in common, that Brady had not heard from me in over a year. During this period, I had sent him long letters and even a Christmas card, none of which appears to have reached him. Of course, none of this can be proved conclusively, as always, but this was highly frustrating from a research perspective and required incredible patience on both sides; but I soon learned that there was precious little I could do about it. In order to circumvent this, there had to be a lot of reading between the lines. After a few initial exchanges of information, we developed a way of continuing, and it became possible to second-guess and bypass the always intense but seemingly random Ashworth security scrutiny which occasionally made the research so difficult.

After one of my visits, I wrote to Brady to describe to him some of my impressions of the asylum. This was his reply: '*Your traumatic experience of Ashworth "Security Dept" saves me much effort. The talents and the abilities* [of the staff] *would suit them for use as crash-test dummies*' (2004).

When it came to the next visit, Ashworth, who were by now obviously reading all of our letters, were clearly becoming fed up with me. Their initial suspicions about me had now calcified. I began to dread going to the asylum, my mouth going dry as soon as I saw the exit sign from the motorway. This time after I got through security and into the wards I felt even worse than before. The deeper you go into the complex, the more depressing the environment becomes. The atmosphere is stale and the air seems to have little oxygen; there are unpleasant smells, jarring noises, doors slamming, keys jangling, people shouting and banging on the windows or crying in their cells. This time the staff tried to get me in there as slowly as they possibly could and then out of there as fast as they possibly could. The one Ashworth employee who had been helpful and supportive of my research on my first visit had long since left the hospital and at this point I was having to deal exclusively with guards who seemed to be finding it difficult to conceal their dislike of my visits. Brady told me that most of the decent people with a shred of integrity who work there do not last very long before they resign and move on. I would, of course, be very interested to review the staff turnover rate at Ashworth.

'The more redundant [who are] *employed here the worse the conditions become. Exemplifying why decent staff are expressly retiring early to escape becoming mentally ill.'*

If the staff in the mental hospital are cracking up and walking out in despair, what hope do the patients have? Under the circumstances, it is amazing that Brady appears not to have become clinically insane or at the very least seriously depressed.

I'm fully conscious of the retrograde effect Ashworth's conversion to a camouflaged, overmanned prison has had on me. For twenty years in accepted prisons I maintained a positive attitude, daily transcribing books into Braille on my own initiative, studying, painting, etc. Ashworth halted all creativity except staff job-creativity, using euphemistic support structures to suppress and destroy inmate initiative and independence of thought – 'security', 'hospital policy', 'health and safety' and other transparent justifications to divert aggression from themselves, the initiators of pettiness for personal profit [2004].

In March 2007, I sent him a CD of some music I had recorded in reply to a music cassette tape he had sent to me. The compact disc I had sent was (eventually) returned to me by the authorities. Brady commented in his next letter:

Your reference to the CD contents were a waste of time. How does it feel? Even Dr [Harold] Shipman did not sink to joining the penal service, and doubtless 'Hannibal' [Lecter] even occasionally cured his patients before eating them.

It is helpful for people outside to know that you cannot even send a CD copy of my own tape here; that they ban computers and word processors, both of which are allowed in prisons. They don't yet burn books but limit prisoners to ten; at last week's cell search I had five over that limit, so rather than let them be buried in the main stores, where warders traditionally steal everything, and barring that it is impossible to retrieve anything that gets sent there anyway, I tore them up. All were on Zen and Chinese philosophy, obviously of no practical use in a zoo like this. Last week I learned that outside you can buy a device the size of an MP3 player which stores thousands of books. So, by contrast with outside advances, it reflects the infantile mental level of this regime of applied ignorance, the degree of paranoid fear and inferiority of the insecure individuals now running it, and is therefore a reverse form of flattery. Equally, the labels they most consistently apply to inmates being projections of their own moral and character defects provide analysis of the administrative and medical impersonators sheltering behind these walls.

I had told him that I had participated in an 'open day' at a university where I was lecturing at the time. Brady came back with: *'You won't believe this, but when this place was a hospital they used to have one here!'*

I mentioned how there seemed to be a growing number of television programmes broadcast about serial killers and their detection, *CSI*, *Cracker* and suchlike. Television is one of the few distractions he has left. Brady replied:

> *I watched 'Big Brother' once, for ten minutes, that, and other 'reality' television shows, explains why serial killers exist. Another show I don't watch is 'life on mars' [sic] which suggests that 1970s policing was more inconsiderate than today. Back then the police did not dress as Star Wars troopers, carrying machine pistols and battering rams, etc. [2007].*

We moved on to the subject of war:

> *As the staff in this mausoleum are paid 'danger money' perhaps they should be sent to supplement the Black Watch in Iraq in another attempt to help American republicans win the election. Pity I can't go myself – to assist the Iraqis . . . People will do anything as long as they are given the cover of authority, but in military action they have to be trained to kill, efficiently as well. The disgust and nausea provoked by the slaughter in the Gulf war, by western troops, has apparently been 'cured' by military psychologists and now the United States troops in particular slaughter without compunction in Iraq, with enthusiasm and no 'ill effects'. Isn't science wonderful?*

I shifted the dialogue to his thoughts on censorship. This particular question was highly revealing. This was his response:

Desensitization has been a recurring issue since the advent of mass media. In my day they banned American comics, 'Tales from the crypt' and suchlike, and now I'm in one! [The one-time clean-up-TV campaigner] *Mary Whitehouse objected to violence in 'Tom and Jerry' cartoons in the 1970s. When sex was taboo in the media, violence in the media became acceptable. If violence ever became taboo in the media, would people similarly seek it out? You only ever have isolated instances of emulated copy-cat violence. The modern 'comic-book' portrayal/ acceptance of violence must have varying peripheral influences, general and individual. The effect of sanitising war with so-called 'smart' weaponry is a designer programme to encourage slaughter and mayhem, furnishing concrete proof of influence. Join the army and get official permission to murder, torture and kill abroad! Your country needs you! Nothing new really, pilots dropping bombs on unseen victims have never shared the problems and psychological barriers of face to face killing. So, logically, the improved killing performance of US/UK troops in the middle east* [sic] *means the new training methods are designed to produce psychopaths/psychotics. In which case, provisions will have been made to keep them suitably employed, controlled or channelled when they return home. Or, if they logically extend the same criteria they apply to 'criminal' psychopaths and psychotics, institutionalise them or confine them to barracks. Or, like radioactive waste, liquidate and bury them down a mineshaft.*

This seems initially to be plausible and does have a limited logic to it, but only at first. Think it through and it becomes problematic when he tries to extend this to his own circumstances. For sure, Brady had to deal, emotionally, with the '*the problems and psychological barriers of face to face killing*'. But Brady's killings did not have any significant purpose other than his own hedonistic entertainment. He cannot even fall back on that old cop-out of 'just following orders' (although Myra Hindley tried that defence more than once while trying to rally sympathetic support for her prison circumstances). Statements like the one above obviously make it pretty much impossible for anyone to sympathise with Brady by condemning war crimes in relative terms with his murders. Furthermore, injustices that he believes he is subjected to – even if we acknowledge his veracity and their pettiness – make it even harder for anyone to galvanise any positive action to improve conditions at the 'special hospitals'; and, if any other articulate patients were to voice concerns, their names would get dragged into the equation. 'Brady's hospital? Whoever ends up there must be *really* bad.' No easy answers, then. Back to crime as Brady sees it, as it is represented on television today:

> *In my time, criminals would generally talk themselves through roadblocks and other police confrontations. Nowadays, I see police with machine-guns, battering rams and other accessories, I don't think the same consideration would generally apply now.*
>
> *Decades before these fake reality television shows I dreamed of a genuine one: Televised duels between prisoners. Now I would restrict eligibility to challenge to prisoners who have served over thirty years. I would*

also extend the applications to the general public and penal staff, the prisoner having choice of priority in selecting applicants. The restrictions might allow several duels a day. Conditions: enclosed yard, synchronised electronic doors, one-shot large-calibre target pistols, fire at will when doors open. That would definitely get an audience. Even if I lost I would win! On the other hand if I was dumped on an uninhabited desert island with the intelligent company of monkeys, parrots and other wildlife, I would die a peaceful hermit. But all you will ever hear is the 'prisoner in a box' vision clarified by total lack of hope and ambition. Once there was a situation where my dogs chased sheep and an armed shepherd suddenly appeared pointing his rifle at my dogs, not seeing me practicing [sic] with pistols below the hill. He lowered his rifle. That's real luck. His, not mine. [2008]

So *if* the shepherd had shot at Brady's dogs, Brady would have shot him dead without a second thought.

To call someone mad is an easy way of dismissing them. The minute you label someone as being 'crazy', they cease to be a human being and lose all rights associated with that status. Add the endless rumours and embellishments concerning Brady's convictions that have been broadcast as facts, and Brady's 'insanity' becomes an irrecoverable self-fulfilling prophecy. Then, according to Brady, the person can be disposed of without anyone feeling any guilt. Quite the reverse, he says, they can feel comfortably and self-righteously justified: *'isolate, diagnoses from internal staff (independent corroboration blocked or frustrated), infantilise/ drug the person until they don't know what day it is, banish them to a gulag and then finally bury them and forget them'.*

For my fifth visit, Brady did not waste any time because I was not allowed the freedom to conduct a detailed and structured interview, as I had done in the previous visits. Guards repeatedly interrupted us, opening the door and asking if we were finished and, if not, how long we were going to be. This was infuriating. Talking very fast, Brady gave me as much information as I could possibly absorb within the constraints imposed by the hospital staff. Despite the unnerving attention of the guards peering through the Perspex slot in the door, waving at me and tapping their watches, I found out a lot of useful information (as soon as I left the asylum, I jotted down notes as fast as I could and then reworked them in greater depth on the way home in the car while they were still fresh in my mind). After an hour or two, it became apparent that guards were going to break up our conversation for good whether we were finished or not and I had no choice but to shake hands with him, say goodbye and leave. After exiting his ward I had to go through the usual security rituals. Normally it takes as much time to exit the hospital as it does to enter it. The same security procedures are followed when you leave as when you arrive, but in reverse.

The information that follows consists of Brady's allegations.

Brady claims, '*The average stay of a patient* [in the hospital] *is twenty years and then an indeterminate number of years in the "discharge ward".*' (If this is true, then it seems they must have a fast-track rehabilitation schedule.)

'*There are no regular independent inspections.*' (This was a surprise. As far as I was aware, British prisons are inspected annually by independent assessors; apparently the high-security mental hospitals are exempt from such routine inconveniences.)

'*Two judicially chaired public inquiries comprised of medical experts concluded that Ashworth is criminally corrupt beyond redemption and recommended immediate closure.*'(This is true, as I explain later.)

'*The staff steal the patients' food.*' (Probably. This sort of thing happens routinely in large institutions, although I cannot see how that would affect Brady personally, since he was on hunger strike, but of course that does not make it acceptable, as some of the other patients may want to eat, no matter how horrible the hospital food is.)

'*Prison recidivism* [reoffending] *rates are 95 per cent.*' (When I looked into this, I found he was exaggerating. It was not as high as that, but it was certainly high enough. If you look at the various studies, the average reoffending rate seems to be around 70 per cent in America and approximately 50–60 per cent in the United Kingdom. Even so this is a damning indictment of penal-reform systems on both sides of the Atlantic. It seems more than *half* of the people released from prisons when they are paroled hit the streets and commit further crimes. It seems the taxpayers are not getting terribly good value for their money.)

Meanwhile back at Ashworth:

'*For over seventeen months on Lawrence Ward I was subjected to sleep deprivation with six warders directly outside my cell door day and night … [they] … stopped painkillers for my spondylitis, my cataracts remain untreated.*' (I had noticed his cataracts were getting progressively worse each time I visited.)

'*All mistreatment aims to break spirit. Ashworth has nothing to offer me except isolation.*'

When I got home after this visit, I started digging into the official reports on the hospital. There are two very important ones, both government-sponsored investigations, which are available to anyone who cares to read them. All of the important information is in the public domain from both of these reports; some of it is abridged but that does not really matter because the overall conclusions are identical. The 1992 Blom-Cooper public inquiry into violence by staff in Ashworth (then known as 'Park Lane') basically concluded that the place should have been shut down years ago. The Fallon public inquiry seven years later came up with the same thing: 'We have no confidence in the ability of Ashworth Hospital to flourish under any management. It should close ... years of corruption, abuse and failure' (Peter Fallon QC in a letter to the Secretary of State, January 1999). However, both of these thorough and professional government investigations were ignored, according to Brady, because of *applied ignorance and expediency* (2009).

It gets worse. As far as the mind-numbing routines at the hospital were concerned, Brady sent me endless anecdotes concerning the obtuse and frustrating behaviour I had myself encountered from the staff there while I was attempting to conduct my research and gain some insight into what was going on at this place. However, one incident in particular should suffice to sum up their attitude rather neatly. This is what Brady told me: *'On September 30th 1999 as I sat writing legal notes in my cell I was jumped on by twelve masked prison warders in riot gear in an hour-long, unprovoked attack which fractured my wrist ... this violence was inflicted on me despite my never having touched any of the staff during my forty-four years of imprisonment.'*

I cannot vouch for there being 12 control-and-restraint guards. That seems excessive to overpower one frail man who had been on hunger strike for a number of years. But his wrist was certainly fractured. As for his denial of ever committing any violence against prison or hospital staff, this may be true. He told me that he had once saved a guard from an assault by another inmate, although I could not confirm this.

As far as isolation and sleep deprivation are concerned, human beings require sensory stimulation when they are awake and undisturbed sleep in order to function properly and maintain a foundation of psychological equilibrium. Stare at a blank wall for a day, for a week, for a month, and you will almost certainly experience some alarming side effects. I defy anyone reading this to try this without experiencing hallucinations, cognitive malfunctions and almost certainly severe depression. Throw in sleep deprivation as well and, unless you happen to be David Blaine, you have a formula for a psychological meltdown (Blaine is an illusionist and magician who makes a living by somehow being able to bypass the psychological trauma of claustrophobia, vertigo and fear of drowning, which most people would find intolerable).

So Ashworth is not much fun for the patients, despite what you might think if you look at their holiday-brochure-style website, which rather surreally showed (at that time anyway) pseudo-patients sitting on a swinging sun-lounger apparently having a picnic, albeit an unconvincing one. Brady is not included in the images, for obvious reasons: it might not look terribly authentic if someone on hunger strike were photographed enjoying a picnic. Not that Brady would ever have agreed to this anyway.

As well as the guards, Brady also has to cope with attempts from psychiatrists and social workers to study him. '*I will never tell them anything, ever.*' This is conjecture, but I think probably the main reason the hospital authorities and his psychiatrists disliked my visits was that

Brady talked to me but refuses to talk to them. It may be the simple fact that I am operating independently, and that was all that was really needed.

A common public perception is that prison officers and guards who work in the maximum-security hospitals are in constant and terrifying danger of attacks from raving psychopaths wielding homemade weapons. Although this might happen occasionally, Brady claims that this is a lot less likely than the media would have people believe. He said that, if anyone got hurt, it would most likely be because they had harmed themselves. As far as I was concerned, I sense a lot more danger of being physically attacked when walking through a city centre at night than I ever felt visiting Ashworth.

'Over 2,000 staff here are employed to count plastic spoons and regularly search the patient's increasingly barren cells' (2004). As if the counting of plastic spoons qualified them for 'danger money'! Brady states that they now have hundreds of staff to deal with security issues *'previously accomplished by only seven. In 20 years here I have never witnessed any patient attack staff, only staff attacking patients.'*

At this point, my internal alarms went off and I had to remind myself that *of course* he would say this, whether it was true or not. Brady has considerable skills of misdirection. Such skills may not have been refined enough to significantly influence jury members at his murder trial in 1966, but since then he has had more than ample time to refine them. So I had, once again, to force myself to take a step back and reconsolidate an objective perspective. Like most serial killers, Brady is incredibly manipulative and, if you attempt to work with such people, it is essential to make sure you do not get drawn in. As I stated earlier, he might possibly have thrived as a successful politician if he had not decided to gamble his life and take the lives of others on an 'existential exercise'.

So, according to Brady, physical attack in these places on visitors or staff is not a major threat; however, psychological attack is omnipresent and I agree that in some ways it can be a lot more dangerous.

For my next visit, I was not going to take any chances with Ashworth authorities. I took a ton of identification in with me. The security searches were elaborate to the point of absurdity. Tiny metal clasps on my shoes set off the metal detectors so I had to be 'wanded'. They debated whether or not I should be allowed to continue to the wards with or without my shoes; they actually made phone calls to make risk assessments concerning my shoes! After some discussion, they finally let me keep them and I did not have to walk through the hospital barefoot (although they carefully examined my shoes on my way out later to make sure the tiny buckles were still there and I had not slipped one to Brady for him to turn into some kind of homemade 'shank' with which, realistically, it would have been tricky even to kill an ant).

Onward into the suffocating airlocks. The door hissed shut. As far as I could tell, you cannot open these from the inside. Incarceration is a horrible feeling. Most of us take it for granted that, if we are in a closed room and do not like where we are or what might be happening in that room, we can simply open a door to leave and go somewhere else. When that option is removed, the loss of control is disorientating and unnerving.

Eventually, I got to Brady's ward and was escorted to the hideous 'family room' again, while the guards went to 'extract' Brady from his cell. This time he looked extremely tired and a lot thinner. He told me, *'Psychiatric hospitals create mental illness in order to justify their existence, in very much the same way as prisons create criminality and ongoing recidivism for the same reasons.'*

During this interview, Brady talked mainly about the horrors of the prison system and the 'special hospitals' again. This was material he had discussed at length in correspondence and, to be honest, I was starting to get weary of hearing the same things over and over again.

He also elaborated on how the penal justice system *creates* criminals. Criminals are the currency. If people did not keep offending and reoffending, there would be no need for prisons, and all the prison staff would be out of work. Therefore, pretty much the entire prison system is designed to roll along as a thriving growth industry. Any attempt at rehabilitation is treated with suspicion (the Barlinnie 'progressive' prison is probably the best example: it was swiftly shut down when it started to show positive results). With the current penal systems, even the toughest convict, when/if paroled, leaves the prison psychologically shattered. They also leave with a host of new criminal skills and underworld contacts, and also a huge festering focus of resentment and a desire to get even. The convict has been brutalised, intimidated and undermined psychologically for many years; any initial level of resentment when convicted of a crime is likely to have been escalated by the process of incarceration.

This situation is pretty much the same in the high-security mental hospitals, although, on top of all their new criminal skills and resentments, the chances are that patients/prisoners will probably be addicted to a cornucopia of hardcore psychiatric drugs and, without a very controlled supervised withdrawal programme, this is highly likely to result in psychotic episodes and new crimes, which will most likely lead them back to the asylum in a revolving-door scenario. If there were no 'mental patients', there would be no need for 'mental hospitals'.

The authorities certainly do not want these places closed down, despite conclusions to that effect that are drawn in some cases from their own research. They want to keep the institutions as full as they can – a full staff being the priority, while keeping the number of patients to a large but manageable number. There is a terrific amount of money involved, so much so that even the government reports that invariably conclude that Ashworth, Broadmoor, Rampton (and others) should all have been shut down decades ago have not been enough to ensure they are closed down. With Brady at Ashworth, obviously they cannot declare him sane because, if he *were* certified sane, what is he doing being sectioned in a psychiatric hospital? Ascertaining sanity is not rocket science, although some psychiatrists will give you the impression that you could not possibly understand the process without decades of clinical training.

WHY WILL THEY NEVER CLOSE?

There are no magic answers but, from my experience, one thing that I am certain of is that I do not see anything especially creative coming out of the criminal-justice and maximum-security mental-health systems as they function in the United Kingdom at the current time. Patients do not appear to receive any significant therapeutic help. Quite the opposite: rehabilitation, if it ever happens, is almost accidental. Brady claims it is '*actively discouraged*'.

Very few individuals seem to remain viable or positive for long under the conditions I have witnessed, and that includes both patients and staff. The 'special hospital' websites boast about extensive art and education programmes; I saw precious little evidence of these in any of my visits to Ashworth. The website has pictures of happy laughing people sitting in the sunshine; all I saw was a bunch of grumpy security guards locking obviously heavily drugged men into small cells. Of course, it is usually pointless to try to explain this to people. If I tell anyone that the inmates are having a miserable time, they usually just say 'good'.

'*I am told I am the person most people want dead by popular vote on the Internet*' (Brady, 2005). But *do* they? I have come across a lot of postings on the Internet where people have basically said 'keep him alive', but, thinking this through, I wonder about their motives.

Brady is a unique case, but there are hundreds of other prisoners suffering under comparable regressive conditions, and Brady's notoriety does them few favours. Once identified as being held captive in 'Brady's hospital', they are assumed to be the perpetrators of crimes of comparable magnitude. If they are ever released from the 'discharge ward' back on to the streets and reoffend, the consensus of opinion is likely to be: 'What did you expect? They should never have been let out in the first place.' From what I have seen, there are a significant number of patients who really should not be there at all, but circumstances dictate that they really have nowhere else to go, so they remain in the hospital and get worse.

I asked Brady if he was going to write anything else. He said it would be impossible in such a repressive environment and I tend to agree.

For every exception who produces creative work in regressive captivity, how many thousands do not? How

> *many inarticulate individuals silently smoulder in cells? Those employed in the penal industry have a vested interest in failure – deform, not reform, ensuring constant expansion ... The public are paying higher taxes for ever-increasing risk when captives are released more criminally professional and motivated than when they entered. No, I could not write anything creative in this suppressive menagerie now. I would be better off in a cell down a mineshaft served by a dumb waiter. After almost forty years as a resident folk-devil and scapegoat, dying is the only rational creativity here. Naturally I knew I had no future outside, it took Ashworth to convince me there is none inside either.*

The big mental-illness machine rolls on and on. Jamieson *et al.* (2000), reporting a ten-year study of the 'United Kingdom special hospitals' concluded that referrals showed no decrease. The data did in fact show an *increase* but this was conveniently omitted. There was an increase in admissions of pre-trial and sentenced male prisoners, and of transferred patients from other hospitals. More and more people are being referred to these places, but this study shows that fewer people are being accepted, fewer women especially. A tiny step forward, I suppose, but no giant leap.

So why are these places still open? There are two reasons. The first poses the question: what do you do with the patients? There are a number of possibilities. Some could be let back into the community, but there would be a public outcry and, anyway, hardly anyone would leave. Brady has told me repeatedly that, if the patients were locked out for whatever reason, most of them, having nowhere to go, would be banging on the doors wanting to be let back in, especially when it was dinner time or medication time. Echoes of *One Flew Over the Cuckoo's Nest*. Obviously, there are some people with dangerous histories and Brady is never going to be released for political reasons. No Home Secretary would want to be named in the press as being the person who authorised his release and, anyway, he would not last very long on the street. He just wants to go to prison and die, which is probably the best he could possibly hope for. There are, however, some patients who have been there for decades for relatively minor infractions and are now institutionalised beyond redemption. Brady told me there has been one patient in there for decades for burning down a barn, another for stealing a milk float. These patients may have been disturbed to some extent at the time of their offences and possibly needed some psychiatric support (although I do not know all the details, it seems likely that these may have been simply teenage pranks or possibly dares that backfired). However, after decades in Ashworth, it is absolutely certain they *will* be in dire need of psychiatric help if they are ever going to function effectively outside.

After so many years in the asylum, these people are naturally seething with resentment and thoughts of revenge that have been percolating for decades. They may indeed *now* pose a risk if allowed back on to the streets after all this time. At this point, they will not be considering barn burning or stealing milk floats. They are more likely to be planning to blow up the hospital. According to Brady, these are just a couple of cases out of scores he has witnessed over the years.

The more serious cases might be transferred to a 'real hospital' (Brady does not consider Ashworth to be a 'real hospital' but merely a *'warehouse for storing societies* [sic] *cast-offs'*). Some could be transferred to prisons, but this is highly unlikely for a whole host of reasons that are beyond the scope of this book. So these are the highly limited options for the patients.

This brings us to the second and real reason why the hospitals have not been closed, and that is because of the staff. The patients have been institutionalised – this is pretty much unavoidable – but so have the staff. Brady says Ashworth operates as a superficial employment scheme for many people who are not qualified enough or who do not have the relevant experience to work in a 'real' hospital or even in a 'real' prison, and claims that they would have almost as much trouble surviving on the streets as the patients would.

The American Rosenhan experiments, 'On Being Sane in Insane Places' (1973), addressed the validity of psychiatric diagnosis. The study was done in two parts. The first part involved the use of healthy associates or 'pseudo-patients' who briefly reported auditory hallucinations in an attempt to gain admission to twelve different psychiatric hospitals in various cities in five different states in America. The pseudo-patients told staff that they could hear a voice in their head saying 'thud' or 'hollow'. This was the *only* symptom they presented. All were admitted and diagnosed with psychiatric disorders. After admission, the pseudo-patients acted normally and told staff that they felt fine and had not experienced any more hallucinations. Hospital staff failed to detect a *single* pseudo-patient, and instead believed that *all* of the pseudo-patients exhibited symptoms of ongoing and serious mental illness. Several were confined for months. No one would believe they had faked their mental illnesses as part of an experiment. Red faces all around when the psychiatrists found out they had all been duped. All the 'pseudo-patients' were finally forced to admit to having a mental illness if they had any chance of getting out and most had to agree to take antipsychotic drugs as a condition of their release.

The second part of the experiment involved asking staff at psychiatric hospitals to detect non-existent 'fake' patients. The staff managed to falsely identify large numbers of genuine patients as impostors. 'Thud' indeed!

The study concluded, 'It is clear that we cannot distinguish the sane from the insane in psychiatric hospitals.' Well, that's just great, isn't it! Results also illustrated the dangers of depersonalisation and labelling in psychiatric institutions. It suggested that the use of community mental-health facilities that concentrated on specific problems and behaviours rather than psychiatric labels might be a solution and recommended education to make psychiatric workers more aware of the social psychology of their facilities.

Schizophrenia is probably the easiest mental illness to fake other than depression (depression in prison does not need any special theatrical moves once a person is incarcerated: almost everyone is depressed in prison, inmates, guards *and* visitors).

Lots of criminals have tried to avoid prison by faking insanity. For example, Vincent 'the Chin' Gigante quickly rose to power during the 1960s and 1970s as an American Mafia boss. When he knew the authorities were on to him, Gigante deliberately wandered the streets of Greenwich Village in his bathrobe and slippers, mumbling incoherently and having arguments with himself. Gigante later admitted that this was an elaborate act to avoid prosecution. Half a dozen psychiatrists from Harvard, Columbia, Cornell and other esteemed American universities had already interviewed him and had all diagnosed serious mental illness (Raab 2005).

David Berkowitz, the New York 'Son of Sam' killer, blamed his killing frenzy on his neighbour's dog, which, he said, had been possessed by the spirit of an ancient demon and was telling him to kill. Years later, he admitted this was just nonsense he made up at the time to try to avoid prison.

Peter Sutcliffe, the Yorkshire Ripper, tried a similar move with stories about an ethereal voice coming out of a Polish gravestone and ended up in Broadmoor. Recent legal action ensures he will never be released from there.

As far as demonstrating mental illness is concerned, I discussed some of this research with Brady in one of my visits. He showed me how easy it was to do, so easy, in fact, that you can, alarmingly, do it by accident. He said, *'If I drop my pen when I'm writing, or my cigarette lighter and then I swear "Dammit!", just like pretty much everyone would do, then they* [the hospital staff] *immediately write a report: "Patient is delusional, has been observed talking to himself."'*

So faking insanity is easy enough to do if you know the basic symptoms, but the bad news is, as the participants in the Rosenhan study discovered, once you fake it and get sectioned, it is almost impossible to unfake it. It doesn't matter what you do or do not do, they can keep you there as long as they want, regardless of any sentence you might have been awarded for any original crimes you have been originally convicted of. The medical authorities can make up any story they like to keep you there for as long as they want to, it is a frying pan/fire scenario.

Brady sent me the following from the *Guardian* newspaper:

Prisons are required to do everything they can to

stop even their most loathsome inmates from committing suicide. Having been diagnosed as a psychopath in 1985 and sectioned under the Mental Health Act, he [Brady] was stripped of the right enjoyed by normal citizens to starve to death if they feel like it. It is only because he is officially mad that we are able to do this. We could not do it to the Irish Republican hunger strikers in the 1980s because they were sane. Whatever else may be wrong with Brady's mental health, it seems quite sane of him to want to die [Chancellor 2006].

After my most recent trip to the hospital, I could thoroughly understand why Brady had stopped all social visits many years before. The environment in the hospital is simply not conducive to any kind of positive rehabilitation at all. In fact, it seems almost deliberately set up to pre-empt and destroy anything other than just a barren experience of incarceration, for patients, visitors and staff alike. In all my visits to the hospital, I do not think I ever saw another visitor other than a single woman sobbing in the car park, and I can understand why.

In my most recent visit, Brady seemed more frail than he had done before. His skin was now almost translucent and it is quite alarming to see the reality under the harsh fluorescent lights in the hospital. They may have managed to drain him physically with their deprivations over the years, but, despite his obvious emaciation, he was more animated than I had ever seen before. Perhaps the absence of carbon monoxide from his previous chain smoking had something to do with it. He launched into a detailed description of the state of the world as he perceives it from his limited perspective within the hospital. Waves of anger and hostility towards pretty much everything were almost physically tangible in the room. We talked about war and terrorism. Brady sees everything in relative terms. *'Three thousand people killed in the Twin Towers bombing? So what? How many Iraq civilians have been killed by the Americans?'* Relativism again.

We talked for as long as they would let us. Then they said they had to close down and I had to leave. They searched Brady thoroughly, as they always do, in case I had somehow managed to slip him poison or some kind of weapon; then they marched him back to his cell. I was taken back the other way through all the airlocks, past the ruined tennis courts, past the handful of patients banging on the shatterproof windows of their wards and then finally released outside into the car park. The last door slammed and was bolted behind me as the place went into shutdown. As I waited for my lift to arrive to take me home, I watched the stream of cars entering and leaving the Ashworth complex. Lots of cars, hundreds of new expensive cars. An endless stream flowing in and out of the asylum gates.

It had been bitterly cold inside the asylum. I mentioned this to Brady in a subsequent letter. He replied:

Curious you should mention the heating here – they have now confiscated heaters that prisoners here bought to heat their cells and have had for decades. I keep my coat on and get under the blankets. This week they have also cut the prisoner's [sic] rations of cheap tea bags and coffee in case they keep warm that way. Naturally, the ward staff continue to steal all hospital food supplies and hospital meals, as they have done traditionally, daily, for the three decades this place has existed. Despite every public inquiry having exposed

190

and condemned the practice repeatedly; another example of staff psychopathologically resistant to experience. And as this place has over two thousand staff freeloading an easy living from two hundred odd vegetables prisoners, it is obvious where the bulk of supplies are going ... Most of the Christmas food will also be stolen by them as usual. The drones here receive 'danger money' for counting plastic spoons, books and tapes. Again, who is to blame for that?

CHAPTER SEVEN

GENDER PROFILING

As well as using the by now somewhat stale categorisations of serial killer as either 'organised' or 'disorganised', criminal profilers also adopt two method-ological approaches in the dynamics of their craft: inductive and deductive profiling. Inductive profiling involves the application of statistical data in order, hopefully, to draw a reasonable conclusion about the person you might be hunting.

To illustrate this very simply, say, hypothetically, the body of a Caucasian woman is found strangled in the woods and no witnesses come forward. (1) You start with simple premises, for example, 'Most serial killers are men and kill women of the same race as themselves.' (2) You look at previous unsolved cases in the local area in order to support the first premise that most women are killed by men. Are they? Yes, they are. Do most serial killers murder people of the same race as themselves? Yes, they do. (3) Then you draw conclusions: 'There is a high probability that we should be looking for a white male,' and proceed with your investigation along those lines.

This may appear somewhat obvious or simplistic, but this is usually the starting point for a forensic investigation. You use this to eliminate possible suspects.

Deductive profiling uses logic, not knowledge drawn from previous experience. Instead, you try to draw conclusions based on an interpretation of the evidence that has been found at the scene. (1) You find clues at the crime scene, say a fingerprint, a strand of hair or particles of skin under the nails of the victim as they fought their attacker. You run the print or the hair or skin DNA through your matching computer and find it belongs to someone who has been convicted of a similar offence. (2) You deduce that there is a high probability that this might be the person you are hunting. So you go and hunt them, hopefully finding further data to support the premise along the way. Who knows? You might get lucky and catch the person you are looking for really quickly.

Most profiling involves a combination of these approaches, but, whichever approach is adopted, it can easily go horribly wrong. Paul Britton's profile of the murderer of Rachel Nickell in London in 1992 was used directly to hunt, arrest and prosecute a man, Colin Stagg, who fitted Britton's profile exactly. The case was, eventually, thrown out of court when it became obvious that Stagg had nothing to do with the murder, and Britton's methodology and career were seriously compromised (Petherrick 2005). Neither approach, or a combination of the two, is infallible, even when adopted by someone with Britton's considerable experience and expertise.

Would Brady have been caught by profiling, as it was used at the time and is still being used today? Probably not. Say, for example, Brady's first victim, Pauline Reade, was the first of his victims to be discovered. A standard profile of the possible killer (UNSUB) could be developed along the following lines:

The person you are looking for is:

1. a male (here you immediately eliminate half of the population before you have even started);
2. aged between 18 and 35;
3. someone who has some history of mental illness;
4. someone with a history of minor/lesser crimes;
5. someone who is uncomfortable in social settings;
6. someone with a history of failed relationships with the opposite sex;
7. a loner, living/operating alone;
8. someone with a short temper.

All the clichés. It could apply to a lot of people and any exceptions are rather unscientifically used to prove the rule. Brady would probably have been quickly eliminated from the possible suspect pool if his data had been included in an investigation using the above criteria, as he would not have scored at all on 3, 5, 6 and 7. Hindley would have been eliminated at the very first step.

Female profiles are a little more elaborate in scope but present similar interpretative problems. There are three main categories of female killer that are used in criminal investigation: 'black widows', 'revenge/anger-retaliatory murders' and 'sadistic sex murders'. There is one additional category, 'murder as art', but this is extremely rare. Profiling of female suspects in a murder investigation along these lines has just as many problems as profiling men, and for similar reasons. The chances are that the perpetrator is likely to be operating within an overlapping and evolving motivational context that introduces additional complexities when you are trying to build a profile. These categories are once again false dichotomies, as discussed in Chapter 4. The matrix of factors may be more elaborate than those applied to the profiling of male perpetrators, but no less flawed or limiting for investigators who apply them rigidly. These are the categories and the common problems associated with them.

'BLACK WIDOWS'

Female murderers are not usually recognised as sex killers. They are more frequently represented in criminological histories as basically greedy individuals, secret predatory spiders who quietly murder their husbands or other members of their family to collect inheritance/insurance payouts, often using poisons and usually operating alone. Not always, though. There are cases of female nurses, predatory Florence Nightingales who get fed up with the chore of cleaning up their incontinent patients and decide it is easier just to hold a pillow over their faces. Sometimes, these women team up and kill their patients for fun and maybe a share of any inheritances that their senile charges may have benevolently allocated to them in their wills. Some of these women may use poison or withhold or overdose essential medication.

Poison is a stealth killer, effective in minuscule amounts, easily obtainable, usually tasteless, and simply mixed into drinks or food. While this may have been quite foolproof or at least very difficult to detect a century ago, modern murders with poison are idiotic and are almost always identified using modern toxicology analyses. In 1998, Judy Buenoano was executed in Florida for killing various people, including her husband, with poison for insurance claims. She also killed her son, who was handicapped. He could not swim and wore heavy leg braces, so, when she pushed him out of a boat into a lake, he sank very quickly. She was also involved in the attempted murder of a number of other men. Buenoano was the third woman to be executed in America since capital punishment was reinstated in 1976 (Anderson and McGehee 1992).

REVENGE/ANGER-RETALIATORY

Some murders in this category might involve women who have been pushed over the edge in abusive relationships and decide to kill in a pre-emptive strike to avoid further abuse or possibly even their own deaths, or perhaps to prevent abuse or harm to their children. This explanation is frequently used as a defence in homicide cases and, unfortunately, the cases where the evidence is fabricated throw a shadow over genuine cases. With genuine cases of retaliatory murder, there is usually just a single death. These women are rarely serial killers.

Once again, though, there are exceptions. Aileen Wournos (1956–2002) is possibly the best example of the anger-retaliatory category for multiple murders. She killed at least seven men in Florida between 1989 and 1990. She was executed after conviction on four counts of first-degree murder. Her MO involved picking up men on the Florida highways, soliciting them for sex and driving with them to secluded places where she would quickly shoot them and steal their money, cars and possessions. When captured, she lied to her friends, her lawyers, journalists, police, psychiatrists, everyone. In 2001, she announced that she would not issue any further appeals against her death sentence. She petitioned the Florida Supreme Court for the right to fire her legal counsel and stop all appeals, saying, 'I killed those men, robbed them as cold as ice. And I'd do it again, too. There's no chance in keeping me alive or anything, because I'd kill again. I have hate crawling through my system ... I am so sick of hearing this "she's crazy" stuff. I've been evaluated so many times. I'm competent, sane, and I'm trying to tell the truth. I'm one who seriously hates human life and would kill again' (Reynolds 1992).

In the Wournos case, there were two women involved. Wournos did not commit her crimes with an accomplice present at the time: she killed her victims on her own. However, she did have a partner, Tyria Moore who, while not actively participating in the deaths, certainly knew they were happening and participated in enjoying the proceeds: the cars and the money obtained from the victims. When apprehended, Moore quickly shifted all the blame to save her own neck. She turned state's evidence in exchange for immunity and testified against Wournos who was executed by lethal injection in Florida in 2002 after running out of appeals and finally admitting that her defence had been a pack of lies.

These were not sex crimes as such: they were crimes for monetary gain, although perhaps with an undercurrent of revenge against the male sex who she considered to be all potential rapists and abusers. Maybe she had good reason to think so from her own limited experience as a highway hooker in Daytona Beach, Florida, which must have brought her many experiences that were less than edifying.

SADISTIC SEX MURDERS

Many murders by women are violent, explosive and often highly sadistic. With this third category, there is usually no history of defensive violence leading up to last-resort homicide. These women kill for rather different reasons. Women can go into just as much of a psychosexual killing frenzy as men. Highly sadistic female killers can be traced back a long way. Erzsébet Báthory (1560–1614) was a Hungarian aristocrat who tortured and murdered hundreds of servants and peasants (mainly women and children) for a number of years in extremely horrible ways. She was protected by her influential family until her crimes reached such extremes that even her most powerful protectors within the Hungarian aristocracy could no longer shelter her from the consequences of her terrible crimes.

She was eventually prosecuted and convicted and finally bricked up in a chamber in her castle where she died a few years later (Newton 2000). Báthory is something of a mythic character now. Brady was familiar with her history and mentioned her to me in a letter: 'I had photos of the ruined castle of Countess Bathory, taken in frost and mist' (2005).

Jeanne Weber is another extreme case. She was a multiple child-strangler operating in Paris in the early nineteenth century. After strangling her own offspring and a number of other children, she was finally caught in the act of murder. She was surprised while strangling one of her charges and apparently was unable to voluntarily release her grip on the child's throat while a number of rescuers were trying to pull her off. She was locked in a killing frenzy which she appeared to have no conscious control over.

She was committed to an asylum where, two years later

and with no more children available to kill, she strangled herself with her own hands (Davis 2001). The homicidal rage associated with the capacity to do something like that takes her even beyond the scope of this category and into the realms of serious psychopathological illness. While her murders were not obviously hedonistic 'sex crimes', they certainly have elements of the same kind of out-of-control ferocity that puts them in a similar league motivationally. This is an unusual case but it is by no means unique.

We cannot be sure of all the facts and evidence in these cases after so much time, but there are a number of more recent incidents concerning women who kill purely for thrills. In Chicago in 1980, Yvonne Kleinfelder, who called herself 'Satan's voodoo dancer', tied her naked boyfriend to her kitchen table and then took six days to boil him alive with pans of water heated on the stove. She was caught, bizarrely claimed that the murder had been 'an accident', and was convicted and sentenced to 25 years in prison (Baumann and O'Brien 1991).

One case does have elements of the 'black widow' scenario but finally evolved into a farcical catalogue of ineptitude and escalating violence. This occurred in San Diego in the 1970s. Carole Hargis lived with her marine-instructor husband, David Hargis, and her two sons from a previous marriage in a house overlooking San Diego Bay. Unfortunately she made friends with her next-door neighbour, Teri Depew, who lived alone, and their friendship developed into a passionate romantic relationship. Both of them wanted David out of the way so they could claim on a substantial insurance policy on his life and presumably live happily ever after.

Together they decided to kill him, although this did not turn out as easy as they thought. Carole Hargis's first attempt, which had apparently been inspired by an episode of *Alfred Hitchcock Presents* on television, involved throwing her electric hair dryer into the shower stall while he was using it. As her husband was standing on a rubber mat he did not even get a shock. The two women plotted again. This time the idea was to poison him. They contemplated switching his martini for household lye but realised he would be highly unlikely to swallow such a foul-tasting corrosive liquid. Hargis had a pet tarantula spider. She removed the spider's venom sac and baked it in a blueberry pie. David Hargis ate the pie, but pushed the poisonous sac to the side of his plate saying, 'I don't know what the hell that is, but it sure isn't a blueberry!'

Next they bought a large quantity of LSD and mixed it into an egg mixture, which was cooked and served to him on toast for breakfast, but they had not realised that the cooking process had evaporated any serious toxic effects the drug might have had. David Hargis just developed a stomach ache. Next they mixed sleeping pills into his beer to knock him out and then tried to inject him with a large air bubble, hoping to give him a heart attack, but the needle broke off in his arm. He woke up thinking he had been stung by some kind of insect. They decided to abandon that method.

David Hargis must have thought he was going mad with all these horrible accidents happening on a daily basis, as he apparently seemed to have had no idea that his wife and the neighbour were trying to kill him.

Next the two women contemplated putting bullets in the carburettor of his car to make the engine explode, but realised that even if it worked it would be certain to leave incriminating forensic evidence. Beginning to despair, the women realised they were going to have to get their hands bloody. They drugged him again and when he was asleep in bed Teri Depew beat him over the head with a lead weight. Not much finesse, but finally it had worked and the man was dead. But the bed, walls, curtains, floor and Depew were now covered with blood. Carole Hargis scrubbed at the stains, which would not come off completely, and then quickly painted the walls, hastily redecorating the room while Depew drove the body to a canyon and threw it over a bridge. The body was found within hours and when the police visited the house and saw blood seeping out of the newly painted bedroom the truth immediately came out. Their attempts to hide the evidence completely sank them legally and they were both sent to jail, each blaming the other one for committing the murder (Rule 2001).

The reason I have included this case (and the Michael Alig case in Chapter 5) is that, while neither of these cases was committed by a serial killer, they both illustrate four critical mistakes that Brady and Hindley made that ultimately resulted in their capture.

- Two of their victims were people that Brady and/or Hindley knew. If they had just stuck to strangers they would have been much more likely to have remained undetected.
- There was an independent witness at the scene of their last murder (a big mistake).
- They committed their final murder in their own house (an even bigger forensic mistake, as it is almost impossible to remove every shred of evidence from an indoor murder).
- A blunt instrument was used (in Brady's last murder). This saturates a crime scene with forensic evidence: blood, body tissue, hair fibres. These are virtually

impossible to remove completely from detection if modern methods of forensic analysis are employed.

Brady and Hindley, like very many serial killers before them, had become lazy, overconfident and arrogant. After five murders without apprehension, they assumed they were untouchable, invincible.

This happened with Colin Ireland, the London 'gay slayer' who, after reading FBI texts and with considerable forensic awareness, stupidly left a fingerprint in the apartment of one of his victims. Dennis Nilsen also got sloppy by blocking the drains with the body parts of his victims while he was attempting to flush their remains down the toilet. Brady and Hindley certainly made a ridiculous number of mistakes with their last murder. It was almost inevitable they would be caught at that stage, even if the witness to the killing had not telephoned the police. Maybe, at that stage at least, one of them, possibly both, *wanted* to get caught?

I suggested this to Brady once in an interview but he immediately changed the subject. Maybe I had hit on a home truth that was simply too painful to discuss. While I was talking to him about his crimes I felt I was walking on extremely thin ice. There was no telling what question might anger him and cause him to terminate the interview, so I had to resort to just being a non-judgemental, objective presence and let him tell me what he wanted to tell me. I had to be incredibly patient. If he ever got the impression I was digging for sensitive information, he would usually switch the subject to something else. This happened occasionally and, when it did, I could not and would not push things, since he might have simply yelled for the guard and got taken back to his cell, leaving me with a four-hour drive home and nothing to show for it. Yes, he wanted to talk, but he wanted to talk only about what *he* wanted to talk about, when and if *he* felt like it.

The man is not stupid. People have been trying to get him to elaborate on his murders for decades with limited success. I had, for reasons I still do not quite understand, somehow found myself in a unique position. I wanted to learn and I was determined not to ruin the opportunity. Decades of psychiatrists and psychologists fumbling at his head and attempting to get him to talk about his crimes have made him highly defensive and, unlike those of most people, his defences are not usually transparent. His emotional barriers are as opaque as the cataracts in his eyes. Talking to him could be occasionally almost like talking to smoke if the thread of our conversation started to move towards a context he was uncomfortable discussing.

Of course, this changed from interview to interview (multiple personae again – see Chapter 2). Sometimes Brady was totally open and I believe honest with me; other times he was guarded and paranoid. This is perfectly understandable. As far as either of us knew, Ashworth may well have been recording our conversations and then immediately racing to the telephone to sell the information to tabloid newspapers. This had happened before, not with my visits, but with various observations the Ashworth staff had made about him in the past and then sold to the gutter press.

FEMALE PREDATORS AND THE 'ABUSE EXCUSE'

At the time of their murders, most of the women I have discussed so far were acting independently as predators in every sense of the word. In these cases, while things might have eventually got out of their control, it seems quite obvious that during their murder cycles they *enjoyed* killing and could be just as cruel and sadistic as men, sometimes even more so.

Men do not have a monopoly on recreational murder and hedonistic killing. In 1982, Judith Neelley committed her first confirmed kill, which evolved into a catalogue of crimes including murders, firebombing, mugging and rape. At age 18, she was the youngest woman ever to be sentenced to death in America. Her first killing was of a 13-year-old girl picked up in an amusement arcade in Georgia. The girl was kidnapped, sexually attacked by Neelley and her husband Alvin in a four-day ordeal in a motel, then Judith Neelley killed her. The murder was horribly sadistic. Judith Neelley drove the girl to a remote canyon, tied her to a tree and injected her repeatedly in the throat with syringes of caustic drain cleaner before shooting her in the head with a pistol and pushing her over a cliff (Davis 2001). In court she claimed she was carrying out Alvin Neelley's orders because she was so scared of his violence, but the jury did not fall for this. Neelley's death sentence was eventually commuted to life imprisonment and she will become eligible for parole in 2014.

Unfortunately, such cases are not exceptional. Rose West was another who played the 'battered wife' card in her trial and very nearly got away with her crimes (Masters 1996). Carol Bundy, Martha Anne Johnson, Catherine Burney, Karla Homolka, Charlene Gallego, Gertrude Baniszewski – and on and on. Crimes committed by predatory females are increasing in frequency. There are many female serial killers operating and they can equal or surpass the intensity of violence exhibited by many of their male counterparts, and these are only the ones we know about. Statistically it usually takes a lot longer for female serial killers to be apprehended and many never get caught at all.

Once bodies start being found and without any glaringly obvious evidence to the contrary, police investigators almost always start with the assumption that they are looking for a male perpetrator. A female serial killer therefore is likely to remain undetected for much longer. Apart from some exceptions, 'The male serial killer is statistically caught after approximately four years, his female equivalent after eight' (Davis 2001). As far as the death penalty in America is concerned, apart from some rare cases such as Buenoano, Wournos and Neelley, who were all sentenced to execution, for the most part women who *are* convicted of capital crimes are very unlikely to receive a death penalty.

As of 30 June 2009, there were 53 women on death row in America. This constitutes a very small percentage of the total death-row population, approximately 3,297 persons at that time. In most cases, women manage to avoid the death sentence for murder and even if they are found guilty, convicted and sentenced to death, they usually win their appeals and get out of jail a lot sooner than their male counterparts. Killing women is not politically expedient for government officials who are campaigning for the public's support. In the past hundred years, approximately forty women have been executed in America, eleven since 1976, when the death penalty was reinstated after a period when it was declared unconstitutional.

Female murderers usually kill men. More than 90 per cent of their victims are men but very few are executed for these crimes. If the death penalty had been still active in the United Kingdom at the time when Brady and Hindley

were convicted, it would have been extremely unlikely
that Hindley would have been hanged but Brady almost
certainly would. In fact, it was the public outcry
concerning the execution of Ruth Ellis in 1955 for a single
murder that was largely responsible for the abolition of the
death penalty in the UK. (See Appendix B for advice on
how best to avoid being executed in America. Being female
certainly seems to give some convicted murderers a
significant advantage in the United States, a situation that
campaigners for equal rights for women understandably
tend to overlook.)

I had asked Brady specifically about gender differences in
serial-killer cases. I suppose I was trying to get him to talk
more about the dynamics of his relationship with Hindley
while circumventing the scrutiny of the Ashworth
authorities who pretty much monitor *all* of his
communications. *Anything* he says about Hindley, no
matter how trivial, is likely to be sold to the gutter press, so
we had to rely on analysis by hypothesis again and both of
us had to read between the lines. This was his reply:

*As for the gender/choice question. A shortcut would be
to study the crimes of male/female concentration camp
guards condemned at Nuremberg. Ten years ago the
home office sent me an envelope containing background
information from our trial. The home office, and others,
have made a luxurious living from the crimes. It
revealed that the judge had secretly recommended forty
years – a political decision to impress the world
journalists [sic] with the phoney show of English
humanity. I had hoped for an honest 'natural life' or
one hundred years, knowing full well that I was going
to die in prison [2008].*

Taking Brady's cue, I did a little research along these lines. Brown (2002) and others suggest that female guards in German World War II prisoner-of-war and concentration camps were often a lot more sadistic and murderous than the men, especially towards female prisoners. But that line of enquiry does not really go anywhere because those women were operating under an entirely different set of influences, right in the middle of a world war where the usual modes of human interaction are temporarily distorted. There is no direct comparison with Hindley that I could see other than that of any other woman who might have found herself in such circumstances. From what Brady has told me, I doubt very much that Hindley would have ended up in the same league as an Ilsa Koch or Irma Grese, the infamous concentration-camp guards who took brutality to unprecedented levels. Hindley *did* choose a female victim for her first murder, but that is the only comparison I noted.

COUPLES WHO KILL

As we saw in Chapter 2, when two people of like-minded criminal potential and ambition link up, the resulting killing cycle is sometimes activated, fertilised even, and then accentuated by their union. However, when everything goes wrong and they get apprehended it is almost invariably the case that one will turn on their partner and turn Queen's or state's evidence in order to try to wriggle out of the mess they have made and the consequences they face. It is very rare for a couple who kill together to remain supportive of each other when they have been captured. When they are caught and imprisoned separately, it is not usually very long before they realise that the glue that had bonded their relationship so solidly has quickly evaporated. It is normally the case that partners who murder together, but who are tried separately, end up testifying in court as the main prosecution witness against their co-accused. When the story breaks and everyone now knows what was previously highly confidential information, the secret pact that they had kept with each other usually bursts like a soap bubble.

Brady and Hindley, however, were a very unusual couple and they were not tried separately. They sat next to each other in the dock throughout the whole procedure, during which they remained fiercely loyal. Brady tried repeatedly to shoulder the blame and cover for Hindley. Afterwards, they remained faithful and loyal for a number of years, writing letters to each other, learning German together, even applying to get married, saying that if their relationship was a common-law one of husband and wife then they should be allowed to be formally married so that they could visit each other (predictably, the Home Office rejected this request). Although this degree of devotion continued for a number of years, eventually they had to accept that in both their cases life imprisonment meant exactly that and they would never see each other again. They dealt with it in different ways. Brady with almost a stoic resolve to make the most of his situation. He became almost totally insular, refusing to cooperate with anyone in authority and participate in any pantomime of regret, remorse or rehabilitation, which would be the normal route that a convicted murderer who is hoping for parole in the future would have to follow.

Hindley finally succumbed to a very serious case of gate fever. She made a big tactical mistake by applying for parole too soon. As soon as the public became aware that she was trying, people threw their arms up in horror, wrote to their Members of Parliament, signed petitions and – somewhat ironically – made death threats. Brady told me that if Hindley had just kept her head down for another five or ten years before applying for parole, a whole generation would have evolved and, while people might still remember the Moors Murders, the time lapse might have diluted some of the anger and outrage that the crimes had instilled in the public consciousness in the 1960s. But Hindley could not wait and only succeeded in stirring up the whole hornets' nest again in the public consciousness. Now a new generation of people got to read all the details of the crimes and once again the heat of public condemnation was turned right back up to boiling point.

With a heterosexual couple who kill together, it is usually the male who initially conceives of the first murder that they commit; but, with certain types of female, it does not take long for them to join in the planning and they may perhaps elaborate the killing cycle further than it might have been originally conceived by either of them. Once captured though, most women almost immediately shift into victim mode and lay the blame squarely on the shoulders of their partner.

Here are some examples of couples who kill that show some of the same patterns that occurred with Brady and Hindley.

Charlene and Gerald Gallego murdered a total of ten (confirmed) young women between 1978 and 1980 in California. They kidnapped, raped and then killed to avoid identification and capture. Their method of operation was almost identical to Brady and Hindley's. The victim is identified and selected. Then the female initiates the abduction (a potential victim in most cases is much more likely to climb into a vehicle when invited by a woman than by a man). This is especially the case with child victims. Most children have been warned never to get into a car when invited to by a strange man, but, if it is a woman who is doing the inviting, they usually will not anticipate danger or threat. This is the trap that the Gallegos used and was also Brady and Hindley's standard method of operation.

Once the victim has been successfully kidnapped, they are then taken to a place of isolation, killed, then buried or hidden in some way. Then the crime scene is tidied up, hopefully unobserved by any witnesses. Taking the victim to a place of isolation is quite common. It introduces an element of control.

In the Gallego case, while it may have been Gerald Gallego's fantasy to commit the crimes, it was Charlene who tricked the victims into climbing into their van where Gerald was hiding with a gun. The victims were then taken to remote spots in the desert, where they were raped, murdered and buried. Charlene explained their motivation in simple terms: 'We had this sexual fantasy, see, and we just did it because it was so easy.' The couple were arrested when Charlene 'confessed' in a fit of jealous rage in order to get even with her husband over some domestic eruption in their violent relationship. In 1984, Gerald Gallego was tried for murder in both California and Nevada. In both instances, Charlene testified against him. In exchange for her testimony, Charlene was not charged in California and she agreed to plead guilty to murder and received a sentence of 16 years and 8 months in the Nevada trial. Gerald was convicted in both states and was sentenced to death in both trials (Hoffman 1992). Charlene was released from prison in 1997 and is now free. Gerald Gallego died of cancer in prison in 2002 before he could be executed by the state. As we saw in Chapter 1, you have to be healthy before they will execute you.

Karla Homolka met Paul Bernardo in 1987 in a hotel in Toronto. Homolka was a vivacious, high-dominance female, extremely self-confident and reckless. Bernardo was a highly sexed, high-dominance male. Unfortunately, by that time, he was also a serial rapist. They slept together only hours after meeting each other and embarked on a tempestuous relationship that almost immediately went out of control.

Their first kill together, in 1990, was something of an accident. Bernardo, who had ingratiated himself into the Homolka household, where Karla lived with her parents and sisters, had decided he wanted to have sex with Karla's 15-year-old sister Tammy. Karla arranged to offer her sister's virginity as a Christmas present to Bernardo. Karla Homolka had obtained drugs from the veterinarian hospital where she worked and together they drugged Tammy on Christmas Eve and both had sex with her while she was unconscious. Tammy choked on her own vomit and died. The couple quickly got rid of the evidence as best they could and, despite some forensic anomalies that were hard to explain, the death was finally ruled to be accidental. After all, Tammy was Karla's baby sister. What possible motive was there for any kind of foul play? No one suspected that it was a brutal premeditated sex attack. This was not even considered at the time. Nor could many people really believe it until the facts finally arose in the courtroom when the videotape Bernardo had made of the attack was shown to the jury.

Tammy's death had not been part of the plan but it set their *modus operandi* for their future killings, where death was definitely part of their plans. The next murder they committed together occurred in 1991. Bernardo, operating alone, abducted a 15-year-old Canadian girl, Leslie Mahaffy, from the street. Mahaffy was streetwise and cautious but Bernardo (like Ted Bundy and Ian Brady before him) could be incredibly charming when he wanted to be in order to spring his trap. Mahaffy was captured and taken back to Bernardo and Homolka's house. After raping her for a few days, Bernardo had had enough; like many serial killers, he had got bored, and so he strangled her. Then he cut her body into a number of pieces, which he then encased in cement blocks. Homolka joined in with the sexual assaults and later helped him attempt to dispose of the body parts by throwing the concrete blocks into Ontario's Lake Gibson. It did not take long before the parts were discovered by fishermen.

Here we can see an almost identical pattern as with Brady and Hindley. The female is initially unsure about the idea of killing, but once it has happened and been accepted as something that is irreversible, and she has realised that she is basically just as guilty in the eyes of the law as her partner, the couple become inextricably bound together by their shared secret. At this point, some females, but by no means all, can take to killing with even more enthusiasm than their male partner. With the next Bernardo–Homolka murder in 1992, Karla Homolka was an active accomplice in the abduction of 16-year-old Kristen French on a Toronto street in broad daylight. When they got the terrified girl back to their house, Homolka participated in prolonged sexual attacks, which Bernardo videotaped over a number of days.

Videotape recordings of all the murders were found hidden in their house after their arrest and were screened at their trial to a horrified jury. These included the Tammy murder/rape tape. Homolka also participated in the disposal of Kristen French's body. Although Bernardo and Homolka had married not long after the Mahaffy murder, their commitment to each other immediately and typically evaporated when they were both arrested following routine police enquiries. Karla Homolka became the chief prosecution witness, blaming everything on Bernardo in order to attempt to secure full immunity for herself from prosecution. However, when the tapes were played in court, they clearly showed the jury that Homolka was as much an active participant in the rape/murders as Bernardo. She claimed she was a 'battered wife', and did indeed have hospital evidence of injuries to support this assertion. However, the tapes were just too damning. Although she was denied full immunity, she did manage to orchestrate a plea bargain for manslaughter and ended up with a conviction and a comparatively lenient 12-year sentence. She is now free.

Bernardo received a full life sentence, which he is currently serving at Kingston Penitentiary in Canada. There is no death sentence in Canada, but Bernardo may perhaps by now be wishing there were, as he spends his life in a specially constructed Plexiglas cage, hated by everyone who has anything to do with him, prison officers and fellow prisoners alike who queue up to flick nasal mucus and probably much worse into his food (Burnside and Cairns 1995).

Most child murderers are subjected to similar treatment in jail. It goes with the territory. In March 2010, Ian Huntley, the United Kingdom sex killer of two ten-year-old girls, Holly Wells and Jessica Chapman, in Soham in 2002, had his throat slashed by another prisoner. Child killers almost always have a horrendous time after they have been captured, convicted and incarcerated. It is not really a surprise that Brady remains on hunger strike. Prison food is bad enough as it is without additional substances that child killers and rapists find mixed into their meals. Many killers, after being convicted of such crimes, attempt suicide. Huntley has tried to kill himself three times, each time unsuccessfully, and now resides in the Suicide Crisis Suite at Frankland high-security prison, which by all accounts has echoes of the 'discharge ward' at Ashworth.

Fred West, another killer of teenage girls and children, managed to hang himself in prison, if you can believe the official reports, and I am not sure that I do. West could easily have been strangled or hanged by other prisoners or even the guards there, and, because of the nature of his crimes, anyone suspected of doing it would have probably received a round of applause. Gloucester serial sex killer partners Fred and Rose West have had so many books written about their case that it seems pointless to repeat the whole sordid saga again, but, as an aside, there is one interesting psychological aspect that is worth mentioning. Rose West was convicted of the murder of 10 of the 12 young women whom the couple killed over many years. These included two of their own children: Fred killed one, Heather, and buried her under the patio; Rose killed the other, Charmaine, and buried her under the coal in a cellar in a different house while Fred was in jail for earlier but slightly less serious crimes.

Not long after he was finally arrested for murder, Fred West was found dead in his prison cell on 1 January 1995. This was before he could be convicted and we will probably never know for sure what actually happened. Some psychologists believe that people who attempt suicide in many cases really want to kill someone else (Davis 2001).

However, the West case shows a curious reversal. Fred West had left a suicide note saying he had killed himself for Rose. However, Rose herself had a different analysis, which she explained in a conversation with Sandra Gregory (2003), a convicted drug smuggler who ended up at Durham Prison on the same wing after she had been extradited from Thailand:

> 'Sandra,' she would say, her voice lifting. 'He [Fred] was a fucking psychopath. Do you know what a psychopath is?'
>
> 'No, Rose,' I replied, 'I don't think I do but I think you are going to tell me.'
>
> 'Do you know why he fucking hung himself?'
>
> 'No. To protect you, I suppose. Or he wanted to take the easy way out?'
>
> She was foaming at the mouth by now. This is what she did when she was excited.
>
> 'No, no, no,' she screamed, 'none of those. I'll tell you why, because all their lives they are planning the ultimate fucking murder. Do you know what the ultimate murder is?'
>
> 'No, Rose,' I replied, nervously, 'I don't.'
>
> 'Their own. Their own murder. That's the ultimate murder for a fucking psychopath. He planned all his life to kill himself. When it came down to it, he carried out the ultimate murder and hung himself. Not for me. For himself.'

So the compulsion to murder continues, even after incarceration. If there are no more victims readily available, serial killers carry on killing any way they can, up to and including themselves.

To conclude, there are plenty of female killers out there (although only approximately 2 per cent of serial-killer cases result in the conviction of female perpetrators). With cases of couples who kill, the female when captured will almost inevitably switch loyalties in order to save herself, or at least get a lighter sentence. In lots of murder cases, obviously, guilty women are acquitted. This undermines the statistics. Interestingly, the Brady–Hindley case is one of the very rare instances where the female did *not* sell out her partner when captured in order to negotiate the possible option of a plea bargain with the prosecution during the trial. Hindley could so easily have blamed everything on Brady and he would have backed her up, at that time, anyway. A few years after conviction, though, her loyalties shifted elsewhere.

With couples who kill, researchers often cite the French term '*folie à deux*', which loosely translates as a folly or madness shared by two. It is a rare psychological occurrence in which symptoms of psychosis are transmitted from one individual to another. Psychiatric classifications refer to this syndrome as a shared psychotic disorder (*DSM IV* 2000). Two perhaps lonely or alienated people meet and link up, and then their criminal career is fertilised, quickly gathers momentum and begins to grow out of control. On their own, neither of them might ever kill, but together their mutual support and encouragement may work as the catalyst that starts a cycle. They become each other's nemesis.

This explanation is often cited in the case of Brady and Hindley. True-crime writer Colin Wilson believes this to be the core explanation for their crimes: 'The answer, I believe, lies in his [Brady's] relationship with Myra and in that strange psychological riddle known as "*folie à deux*"' (Wilson, cited in Brady 2001).

I think Wilson is either ignoring or is unaware of the synthesis of many other factors. Brady and Hindley's case goes far beyond such a simplistic explanatory diagnosis. 'Psychological riddles' as explanations, for me anyway, do not stand up as credible empirical foundations for any kind of robust analytic certainty.

After they had both been captured and sent to prison for life, Hindley – although, as we have seen, loyal to Brady for a number of years – finally realised that her desire for freedom was more important to her than her commitment to him, and she started her repeated, and doomed, attempts to get parole. Blaming Brady for the murders to pretty much anyone who would listen, including Peter Topping (one of the police investigators), social reformer Lord Longford, Peter Timms (the religious adviser who attempted to get Hindley to talk about her crimes in a series of interviews until the prison authorities stopped him from visiting her), as well as various journalists and friends. She was wasting her time. Brady knew that neither he nor Hindley would ever have any chance of release, and so has never applied for parole. What would be the point? Brady has said this in print on a number of occasions, and has told me so himself.

At their trial, Brady took most of the blame for the crimes, and even now remains protective of Hindley's memory, although earlier, at one point before her death in 2002, he did lose his temper over her press releases and apportioned blame to her concerning one of the murders that they had both been convicted of, that of the ten-year-old girl they had kidnapped in 1964, Lesley Ann Downey: '*She* [Hindley] *insisted on killing* [Downey] *with her own hands, using a two-foot length of silk cord, which she later used to enjoy toying with in public, in the secret knowledge of what it had been used for*' (Brady, *Independent*, 29 January 1995).

I noticed a connection here with the Homolka–Bernardo murders. After *their* second murder, while cleaning up the crime scene Karla Homolka suggested they should throw away the electrical cable that Paul Bernardo had used to strangle Leslie Mahaffey. He refused; he wanted to keep it. Homolka stated in court that she 'did not think it was a good idea to have the murder weapon in the house', but Bernardo dismissed this and kept it anyway (Burnside and Cairns 1995). A souvenir of the killing, I suppose. This is not uncommon. Most serial killers keep souvenirs of their crimes and their victims: jewellery, photographs, hair, maybe, like Nilsen or Bundy, the entire body if they have somewhere they can conceal it. Schaefer (Chapter 2) kept teeth.

PART III
VANISHING POINTS

CHAPTER EIGHT

THE 'SPECIAL' HOSPITALS

'*They will sell your organs for a percentage bonus.*'

When Brady made this statement in an early letter to me (2004), I thought it was a joke. When he said the same thing in my second interview and then again in a letter the following year, my research antenna clicked on and started to vibrate. I went home, got on the Internet and started doing some research. Brady had sent me some rather unnerving material. Although he frequently sent me such things – news clippings about killers he knew I was interested in and suchlike – this particular letter seemed unusually disturbing, although I was not sure at first quite why, because superficially it seemed like just another repetitive tirade of ranting about how horrible the conditions were at the hospital. I quote:

> *It is seriously comic that raving lunatics walk free while 'patients' in this place have been kept locked up for decades for stealing a milk float, setting fire to a*

haystack, or for no crime at all. Even more farcical is the fact that many of the staff here are more mentally ill than the patients, exhibiting obsessive/compulsive disorders and other pathologies they project onto patients along with their other moral and character defects, thus providing a psychological profile of themselves unwittingly.

The same story? Or was it? I had to treat material like this with some caution. It could just be the delusional repetition of someone who was becoming senile and institutionalised. Also I had to bear in mind that Brady was not in there for stealing a milk float or setting a barn on fire. His crimes were rather different. Despite the tone and raw anger that came across in many of his letters and in interviews, which I was starting to get used to, this particular comment did not sound like ravings to me. It sounded like a dare. A lot of my interactions with him had that aspect, almost as if he would wait until I was getting bored then would flip me some bait, some hint, implying, Yes this *is* outrageous, and whatever you have heard is absolutely true and, guess what, there is lots more besides. Do you believe me? Have you got the calibre of nerve to find out? Face to face with evil – the real thing, not some Hollywood representation?

I imagine many people reading this might think it was stupid for me to continue with my work at this point, but, then again, maybe I could take it even further and, with my research background, if I did not follow up any and all leads, I would always be wondering whether I had missed something critical.

Brady taunted and goaded me. I mentioned once I had been paintballing. He came back with: '*Paintballing? No substitute for the real thing. Are you strong enough?*' What was

I going to do? Walk away? (My research drives cannot be put on the shelf and forgotten once they are ignited. I needed to find out as much as I could and take things as close to conclusion as possible.)

Then there was more. He explained why he did not want people visiting him there (other than his solicitor and me, at this time anyway).

> *I am now in my 71st year, the 44th of perpetual incarceration and 10th of being force-fed by nasal-tube. When this place became a regressive prison I wouldn't want any decent people contaminated* [by the environment.] *I have five stacks of prison officers, approximately half a ton, sitting at the apex of the corridors jabbering about holidays, overtime and what to take next from prisoners, what is on the menu to steal etc. They only become animated by free food, cell and body searches of those they leech a living from. I halted all visits from relatives and friends in 1998. They then had the temerity to bombard me with their self-seeking 'social-workers', after my social life was finished! I had to threaten one with a restraining order through my solicitors. Their only function now, apart from freeloading, is as informers for the 'doctors'* [2009].

I can vouch for the size of the guards: they are not terribly tall but they are quite seriously wide. Having read through the Blom-Cooper Report and the Fallon Inquiry (see Chapter 6), both of which concluded that Ashworth should have been shut down years ago, I came across a third report, the Tilt Inquiry (2000). This was apparently compiled by a single Prison Service bureaucrat after the other two research reports had unequivocally declared that

Ashworth should have been closed. Here is a representative synopsis of what was essentially an internal inquiry.

The Tilt review team made 50 general recommendations: three-quarters related to procedural security issues and a quarter to physical security. Recommendations to increase the physical security at the high-security hospitals included enhancing perimeter security, changing to a magnetic locking system and examining the feasibility of locking the rooms at night of all patients on the admission and intensive-care wards, and those of all 'high-risk' patients. Recommendations for procedural security included enhancing the profile accorded to security itself within the hospitals: increasing the staffing levels in the security departments, developing 'an effective security intelligence system' at each hospital and having dedicated search teams.

So, basically, more guards, more bars, more fences, more cell shakedowns, more alarms, more walls. This is the usual story in the penal industry. This seems to me to be a waste of taxpayers' money. No one has ever escaped from Ashworth as far as I am aware. It is difficult enough to escape when you are there as a visitor as we have seen. If you are a prisoner there, then you might as well be on the moon.

Brady told me he had had a judicial review in February 2000. This was before I had contacted him for the first time. Although this was held in a closed court, he claims he was surrounded by six security guards. He even states that his solicitor had a brief mental breakdown while trying to represent him under such conditions. Next, Brady later alleged they took away his pens, *'although I daily use pens in captivity, Ashworth restricted me to blunt pencil stubs for writing legal instructions'*.

Danny Rolling (see Chapter 2) described similar restrictions. Apparently, the reason they allow prisoners only tiny pencil stubs is that, if they were to be supplied with normal-length pencils, they could be used as stabbing weapons, whereas tiny pencil stubs would be pretty much useless in a violent situation.

> The politically chosen establishment judge for the judicial review was the one who, weeks prior, allowed [former Chilean dictator] General Pinochet to flee the UK and escape charges of war crimes, outstanding at the Hague by finding him 'not fit to stand trial'. He found Pinochet unfit to stand trial for the torture and murder of 4,000 political prisoners, and me not fit to die by voluntary starvation, refusing to halt Ashworth force-feeding me [2009].

Moral relativism yet again. Yes, Pinochet seems to have been responsible for a large number of deaths, but that does not make Brady's crimes any less excusable. I can see no comparison other than that lives were taken unfairly and that punishments were inflicted unequally. Killing five innocent people or killing four thousand innocent people? To me, both crimes seem equally wrong. Maybe I am missing something here.

> A year of sleep deprivation having failed [Ashworth] resorted to the customary method of perverting the course of justice, forcible drugging by violence ... this eventually resulted in me collapsing unconscious in the shower.
>
> Never have so many leeched off so few for so long and for so much. Additionally irony being that I have served almost half a century for my crimes, while Ashworth daily commit major crimes without fear of penalty, and

still do. This inhuman criminal abuse which the law serves and protects allows Ashworth to solve every problem by violence and forcible drugging [2009].

Brady told me that his appeals to be transferred back to prison have been systematically turned down by internal hearings and gave me some references:

... concerning the reports exposing patient's [sic] *deaths in Ashworth's 'sister' hospital, Broadmoor, I have been informing/updating MPs/media of such facts for the past ten years, without result. I have not exercised in the open air since 1975 and my social visits and phone calls ended in 1998. I detail these matters to illustrate what I am force-fed to endure and to dispense with Ashworth's medical/altruistic pretensions, exemplifying that after over 44 years of prehistoric captivity I expect and ask for nothing except to return to prison ... In the meantime, to deprive of a voice is to deprive of humanity* [2009].

The final sentence in this statement had a very hollow ring to it, coming, as it did, from someone who was convicted in a court of law of *permanently* depriving at least five people of their voices and their lives. Unfortunately for Brady, the authorities seem to be determined to keep him alive until his last possible breath. His notoriety means they *can't* kill him or even let him die by his own hand. It would be all over the news internationally. Unlike those of some of the other unknown people who have died in the 'special hospitals', Brady's death would not be an easy one to cover up. Every news outlet in the world would want the story. They are stuck with him for as long as he is alive, and he is very much stuck with them.

So, what to make of all this? Well, it *is* a tragedy, a horrible tragedy for pretty much everyone concerned. Brady is poked and prodded like a particularly dangerous endangered species that is kept in a special high-security cage but is too valuable to euthanize. It seems he forfeited all of his human rights half a century ago. Nobody is ever going to let him forget his crimes, and I suppose that includes me to a certain extent, because I wanted to learn from him. I began to understand why he is in favour of capital punishment. Initially, that did not make much sense to me, but, after I had experienced the suffocating confinement of the airlocks of Ashworth Hospital, it gradually began to become clear. Whenever the guards would come to collect me from my interviews, although I might be angry at all the waiting around, I cannot deny the sense of relief that I felt when I was finally able to walk out into the car park and drive away. Having that place as a home would be one of the worst possible fates I could imagine.

At my first visit, we had been talking for over three hours and the interview had been fast-paced, productive and interesting. I noticed the time; Brady saw me looking at my watch. The look of weary resignation on his almost translucent face as he contemplated going back to his cell is not easy to forget. Despite all his criminal bravado and mental chess games, there was a very tired man looking at me as I shook his hand before leaving. The guards grabbed him, frisked him and marched him down the corridor back to his cell. I asked if I could see his cell, but they said no, that it was 'impossible', and marched me out the other way. I asked him about his cell in a letter and he described it to me. Apparently it is about 12 feet by 8. He has a bed, a small chair, a small desk/table and a window that looks on to a brick wall. '*Ashworth will probably object to me attending my own funeral*' (2008).

229

CHAPTER NINE

MOTIVELESS MURDER

American schoolchildren take automatic weapons to school and use them. In Columbine High School, Colorado, in April 1999, two teenage students, Eric Harris and Dylan Klebold, shot dead twelve of their classmates and one teacher. They seriously wounded many other people and then shot themselves dead. Did no one notice the depth of resentment those two young men had? Maybe no one cared. Blame it on violent video games, then? I don't think so. They give violent video games to prisoners awaiting execution on death row in American prisons in order to placate them. Apparently, it works better than television to keep them calm.

With Columbine, I think perhaps the mechanics involved in shooting up a building may have been learned from endless games of *Doom* or *World of Warcraft*, but not the motivation. Blame it on violent films, blame it on the parents, blame it on social workers, etc., *ad nauseam*. What people have to realise is that there is not one single scapegoat factor that is responsible and can be isolated and addressed. There are multiple factors.

In some British schools now, the children have to walk through metal detectors to be admitted to their classes. British children take knives to school in their lunchboxes. Gun culture in the United Kingdom will probably escalate as things predictably catch up with American culture. Youngsters make bombs in their kitchens using Internet recipes and then detonate them for reasons that even they do not fully understand. Arson is commonplace. 'I just hated to see them buildings standing there' (Toole, cited in Newton 2000). What psychologists need to focus on now is not how but why these things are happening.

The violent crime rate continued to rise dramatically towards the end of the last century (Erzinclioglu 2000). Additionally, the motives for many of the crimes being committed became more and more superficial. People, many of them children themselves, were choosing violence as a recreational activity.

Even before the horrific James Bulger case in Liverpool in 1993, when a two-year-old child was abducted and killed by two ten-year-old boys for no particular reason, murderers seemed to be getting younger and younger (Morrison 1997). Look back even further and you can see that, around the time of Brady and Hindley's crimes, some very alarming precedents were being set. Graham Young at 15, for example, was convicted in 1962 of poisoning members of his family and possibly killing his stepmother (she had been cremated so there was no forensic evidence to work with). Young was found guilty but insane and was sent to Broadmoor. At the trial, the judge had said, 'Such people are always dangerous and are adept at concealing the mad compulsion which may never be wholly cured.' Nine years later, Young was released, even after telling one psychiatrist, 'When I get out I am going to kill one person for every year I have spent in this place.'

On his release, just like Henry Lee Lucas (see Chapter 2), he was true to his word and quickly started poisoning people he worked with at a photographic-equipment factory. He poisoned pretty much everyone there with thallium and antimony, but managed to kill only two before he was captured. A dismayed psychiatrist at his trial stated that 'most of his victims were not especially disliked, they were simply the nearest people he had for his purpose'. Young kept a diary, meticulously detailing doses of poison he had put in his colleagues' tea and food. When his victims ended up in hospital, he would visit them with gifts of poisoned food in order to ensure they ended up dead (Robins and Arnold 1993). I asked Brady about Graham Young, as I knew he had met him in Parkhurst. Brady shrugged. He said, *He was nothing remarkable. He just killed anyone who got in his way'* (2008).

What is perplexing here is the absence of recognition of focused hostility. The victim is eliminated because their presence is inconvenient or annoying, not because of any brooding resentment or revenge motive. The police found Young's illustrated diary, decorated with skull-and-crossbones motifs. Young might as well have been swatting flies. At his trial, he stated that his 'death diary' was a rough outline for a novel he was developing. The jury were not exactly convinced by this rather lame assertion. Young seemed to have no conception or empathy regarding the pain and suffering he was causing. That was all totally irrelevant to him. The killing itself *was* the motive.

Brady claims that he does not read newspapers any more. Possibly, but I know he tracks the news on Teletext from within his cell at Ashworth instead. He predicted the escalating momentum of violent crime many years ago. Now he watches his predictions coming true with each new update. As far as serial killers are concerned, Brady uses analysis by hypothesis again. So it is pointless in most cases, according to Brady, to look for motive. The murder *is* the motive; it exists as a self-explanatory '*creative*' act, which requires no explanation. If this is the case, how can people possibly defend themselves against such individuals? The first line of defence (as well as possibly being the last) is, as always, practical.

Colin Wilson has been predicting a steadily increasing trend of serious crimes, including murder, since the 1960s and his predictions have been accurate. For example, take the Tylenol murders in Chicago in 1982. Pain-relief pills were laced with potassium cyanide and sold to the public. Seven people died. The killer did not even know their victims. They were strangers, and whoever was doing it was never apprehended. This caused a nationwide panic in America and copycat crimes appeared in Colorado and Florida, where corrosive acids were substituted for eye drops and mouthwash (Newton 2000).

Crime not for gain but enacted out of an almost blind hatred is alarmingly commonplace now and, sadly, it is often the most vulnerable who become the victims: old people, women, children. Just pick up a newspaper, the chances are there will have been a horrible violent crime conducted in your area today, and there will be others by tomorrow. Erzinclioglu (2000) states that this phenomenon is relatively new and places the blame squarely on a tangible malignancy within the soul of contemporary society. When discussing the criminal mind, he concludes that such acts are not committed out of a great sense of injustice, or even for monetary gain. The crimes are an end in themselves.

There have always been murders and other violent crimes throughout history, but until recently there was nearly always a clear motive and usually a great sense of remorse and tragedy for everyone concerned. Many modern murderers do not seem to possess the inclination or even the ability to experience guilt or remorse or empathy. Wilton Earle (see Chapter 2), when discussing multiple murderer Donald Gaskins, draws the following conclusion: 'In that space where usually dwell the traits of conscience and compassion that make us human, Gaskins had only a lacuna – a void of darkness – a vacuum where morality, probity and virtue do not exist' (Wilton Earle, in Gaskins 1993).

Gaskins is now dead, killed in the electric chair, so we cannot learn anything more about him. I would imagine his executioners sleep quite peacefully in their beds, but one thing we can be certain of is that there are plenty more people out there to replace him, and many more others coming along to replace *them* – unless we can find ways to identify and stop them.

But how can you do this if you cannot trust your babysitter (Jeanne Weber), postman (John Merlin Taylor and others; lots of these, the 'killer postmen', have become a category all to themselves), dentist (Rajesh Talwar), doctor (Harold Shipman), landlord/lady (Fred and Rose West), pharmacist (Frank DeLuca), police (Gerard John Schaefer, David Gore, Dennis Nilsen)? Or the polite young couple who live next door (Brady and Hindley), your psychiatrist (Nidal Hasan), rape counsellor, psychologist and lawyer (Ted Bundy), school caretaker (Ian Huntley), tea boy (Graham Young) – and possibly even yourself?

Just who *can* you trust?

There are scores of reasons and mitigating circumstances and examples of situations that may be *accountable* for murders, but ultimately such events are not *responsible*. Big difference. And this is where most people who are not potential serial killers draw a line: whatever a person's motivation and whatever has happened to them, they either kill someone or they do not. Nobody ever does anything they do not choose to do, even with a gun to their head. So apportioning blame can go only so far. It may be possible to make a few tentative predictions. For example, anyone reviewing Gaskins's and Brady's early lives (see Chapter 2), while probably not being able to predict accurately that they would become murderers, could almost certainly make a safe bet that these men would be unlikely to grow up into psychologically positive and altruistic members of any community. But, on the whole, explanatory theories are very limited.

As far as the teenage Brady was concerned, the impact of being thrown into the penal system for relatively minor offences and taken on a guided tour of a functioning gallows is unlikely to have instilled in him a positive regard for human life. Standing on the trap of the gallows in some kind of misguided negative-reinforcement object lesson at Hull Prison would not have done him any favours psychologically (he makes this very clear: his response was '*Get guns*'), but on the whole you cannot reduce the complexity of human behaviour so neatly to a set of influences, no matter how negative they might have been. Negative life events should be taken into account, but it is important that they be viewed as flexible indicators not *a priori* determinants or self-fulfilling prophecies. There are too many factors at work and this is the Achilles' heel of the criminal-profiling rationale. Human nature is far too complex to be neatly boxed into convenient pigeonholes of motivating factors and predeterminable precedents. Arriving at the truth involves tackling the issues from many different perspectives. If the conclusions you can draw are supported by *multiple* evidential links, the chances are you might have reached some kind of valid analysis or at least made some progress. This is why profiling must be a multidisciplinary set of converging procedures if we are going to take it beyond the realm of creative guesswork.

The killers themselves are usually at a loss to explain their behaviour, even when they have been captured and condemned and have had plenty of time to think about it. The game is finally up, for good, and they have nothing left to lose or live for, and yet a few of them want to understand what happened just as much as everyone else does. Unfortunately, when their crimes have been actualised, many of them seem to get to a point where they really do not care any more. Danny Rolling (see Chapter 2) was an exception. For most convicts sitting on death row in America waiting for their final appeals to be rejected, they often reach a point where they give up both the hope and desire for any kind of explanation. Rolling, after the rape/murder of eight people, was executed in October 2006. Before his death, he was asked to explain his murders. He blamed the killings on revenge: 'Revenge against society, revenge for a lousy childhood ... revenge for years of abuse by the prison system, revenge for a failed marriage. I know ... it sounds like a cop-out. Well, I'm sorry. That's just the way it is' (Rolling and London 1996).

He certainly had a rotten childhood. His father was a very brutal man who made life for his entire family a frightening and violent nightmare. This apparently reached a crescendo and Rolling shot his father in the head (the father survived, just). However, his later serial murders cannot be explained by a simplistic anger-retaliatory explanation. His later crimes were rape murders. There was a strong sexual element, which comes through very clearly when you read his analysis of his crimes, in which he tries but ultimately fails to conceal their gleeful and predatory nature. Rolling was a serial rapist long before he ever killed any of his victims, but sexual frenzy is not a simple explanation for most of these people. As we have seen, for many serial killers, the sexual element can be almost like an afterthought; it is peripheral to the act of killing. The killing itself is the motive.

As I have attempted to explain, murder can be either a complex plan, based on fantasy that has been rehearsed and refined over many months or years, or a kinetic reaction made in a second. Yes, Rolling's homicidal attacks may have been sparked off by lust combined with anger concerning negative events that had happened in his life, but, whatever the motivation involved, he made the *decision* to rape and then kill to eliminate the only witness. It is significant to note that once he had killed a few times he began to enjoy it as much as, if not more than, raping his victims. This is illustrated when you consider how his crimes rapidly escalated from brutal rapes to outright overkill involving mutilation and decapitation. He did one marginally admirable thing before his execution: he had the belated and almost insulting courtesy to come up with a checklist of useful tips to avoid being killed by someone like him (see Appendix A).

I believe everyone is capable of killing under certain circumstances, perhaps to save a loved one, to save themselves or to save their colleagues in a war situation, or even as an act of furious revenge. But only very few would want to repeat the event. Jeffrey Dahmer's first sex murder haunted him for years. He did everything to try to forget it, going to university (he failed in the first term), joining the army (he was discharged), becoming alcoholic, dating women, dating men, anything he could think of to exorcise the experience. It was constantly on his mind for many years until he finally decided that, in order to try to put the ghost of his first victim to rest, he needed to try the only thing that he had not attempted: another killing, almost as if this would make some kind of sense of the first. But, predictably, it did not. It just started him off on a whole series of killings. Finally, he was caught, convicted of 15 murders and sentenced to 957 years in prison, but he still had not found the answer and he never would, since he himself was killed in prison.

So-called 'crimes of passion' usually do have a motive, which is often the result of a horrible emotional betrayal or the sudden confirmation of something that has been brooding under the surface for some time and suddenly and unexpectedly escalates beyond fear and desire or prediction. For the tiny minority who would instigate violence, a crime of this nature would be very unlikely to be repeated. However, for a very small number of people, such an event seems to become a catalyst.

Even carefully planned, rehearsed lust murders based on sexual avarice or emotional greed are usually isolated incidents. Once the rape and murder have been committed, the horror at what has happened and why it has happened is usually enough to ensure the perpetrator will feel no need or desire to repeat the event – in most cases, anyway. But for certain individuals even unpremeditated killings can sometimes evolve into a cycle. The enormity of the first murder throws things out of control; the perpetrator crosses a line that might lead to a second killing to cover up the first, then a third, and on and on. Or, worse, having killed, the murderer finds out that they actually enjoyed it and wants to do it again for aesthetic and hedonistic reasons (see Chapter 2). The momentum of circumstances rationalises the truth into a distortion that is psychologically acceptable to the murderer. They *have* to live with it; they do not have any choice; they cannot turn back time.

When working with serial killers, it is hard not to draw the conclusion that most of them enjoyed their murders. People do not generally repeat behaviour that they do not enjoy psychologically. Why would they? So, after one murder, a second is perhaps going to be a little easier, a little more psychologically satisfying and conducted with a little more confidence and with less trepidation.

> I probably did enjoy these acts of killing. It was intense and all-consuming ... How the hell do I know what motivated me to kill someone I had nothing against at that particular time! I needed to do what I did at that time. I had no control over it then. It was a powder keg waiting for a match. I was the match [Nilsen, cited in Masters 1985].

However, there are different types of multiple murder. Some of the dynamics appear in fictional representations, which effectively show how fast everything can get out of control when a premeditated murder is conducted. I discussed a few fictional representations of the psychology of murder with Brady. Dostoyevsky's *Crime and Punishment* is the usual benchmark scenario cited. In Dostoyevsky's book, the perpetrator of a murder, Raskolnikov, a penniless student, kills an old lady to steal her valuables. He is unexpectedly interrupted at the crime scene and has no choice but to commit another killing, which he had not planned, in order to cover up the first. The situation escalates out of control as soon as it starts.

This is not uncommon in crime fiction. It is a standard plot device. In Graham Greene's novel *Brighton Rock*, the main character Pinkie Brown, has to cover up a whole chain of murders by doing more and more. The situation spirals out of control. Each killing is carried out to cover up the previous one, which just makes things worse and generates more clues, as well as more pressure for the perpetrator, until ultimately the only person who can be killed in order to stop the chain of events is himself. I discussed this with Brady, who is fond of the book and the film that was made from it. Brady identified certain parallels with his own criminal career from Greene's narrative.

This was, of course, a discussion of fiction. Crimes to eliminate witnesses or reinforce alibis, or scare people into keeping their mouths shut, occur frequently in literature and film but are very rare in real-life criminological history. In any real-life courtroom, any façade and glamour quickly evaporates and the perpetrators are almost inevitably destined to face consequences that are likely to be considerably more dire than they might have anticipated. With multiple murders, as the incidents of killing escalate, more and more evidence becomes available for investigators to use in a prosecution and the killer becomes trapped in a web of lies and duplicities, which ultimately cannot be rationalised and are easily demolished in a law court. Real-life murder is not like that portrayed in fiction.

With serial sex murders, the dynamics are rather different from what people might have seen in gangster films, where

FACE TO FACE WITH EVIL

a clear motive is almost always presented. Sometimes with these crimes, the first death can be almost as much of a surprise to the killer as it is to the victim. It certainly was for Schaefer (see Chapter 2), assuming you take his word for it. He claimed that that his first murder was an accident, that he was just messing about with a girl he had met on a Florida beach, just playing, pulling at her scarf. But then, suddenly, he pulled a little too hard and it closed the carotid artery and cut off the oxygen to her brain. This can quite easily happen:

> ... the inhibition of the vagus nerve (because of the pressure applied to it) during strangulation may cause death suddenly and quickly, before the usual symptoms of asphyxia appear. In such cases the natural tendency to struggle to breathe does not happen [Erzinclioglu 2000].

So Schaefer may well be telling to truth and the woman just suddenly dropped dead, which apparently was as much of a surprise to Schaefer as it was to his victim.

According to Schaefer, she died almost instantly and he thought she was just pretending, playing possum, and he was completely shocked by what had happened. Of course, we have only his word for this. It is just as likely that he brutally strangled her while raping her, and anyone who reads his *Killer Fiction* (1989), written while he was in jail for a whole string of hanging/strangling murders, is likely to draw the same conclusion. However, the fact remains that, if a complete stranger is the victim, and there is no evidence to link the murderer to them and no one sees the actual killing or the disposal of the victim, it is highly unlikely that the killer will be apprehended.

Whether a first murder was accidental or not does not really make a lot of difference. It has still happened. Once that reality has sunk in, there is usually no going back whether they get caught or not, so they carry on, making more and more mistakes, until they really do not care any more about being captured and may even have started looking forward to it.

For Brady and Hindley, as with all murderers, freedom evaporated the second of their very first killing, as did any sympathy they might have gained regarding any explanations for their motive. As the law stood at that time, they knew that, if captured, they would both be hanged. I am not offering this as any excuse for the momentum of their murder cycle, but it is relevant. As far as the death penalty is concerned, it certainly did not act as any kind of deterrent for them. Brady, after being captured and realising that there was absolutely nothing he could do to change events that were now outside his control, spent his time on remand apparently reading Joseph Heller's novel *Catch-22*. Then, just before they were tried, the death penalty in the United Kingdom was suddenly abolished. Now, both Brady and Hindley had to anticipate and consider the ramifications of a different type of death penalty, the 'whole-life tariff', which Brady, having experienced it, now believes is actually worse than being hanged.

Myra Hindley could not cope. After numerous futile failed attempts at parole and one bungled escape plot, she just gave up hope and chain-smoked her way to an early death. American research has clearly shown that the murder rate rises there when people are executed. It almost kick-starts serial-killing cycles: why just stop at one murder when they are going to kill you anyway? Meta-analyses indicate the death penalty is no deterrent and actually significantly *increases* the murder rate (Donahue and Wolfers 2006).

As we have seen, people who have tried to understand Brady have made various suggestions to account for what happened: *folie à deux*, revenge, even the occult (see Chapter 2). Here, for what they are worth, are my suggestions as to why Brady killed and as to why he was a lot more lethal than killers who were acting alone.

1. BRADY WAS BORED

His early crimes – small-scale robberies and deceptions – did not give him a terrific amount of satisfaction. '*After borstal, I resolved never again to be involved in anything trivial*' (2008). In prison, before he had been branded a 'nonce' for killing children and permanently lost all respect within the criminal fraternity he aspired to be a member of, he had hardcore gangsters as mentors, people to look up to within the limited context of the penal environment: bank robbers, stereotypical 'hard' men who had embraced a life of crime as a full-time career.

I think this is a critical point, but why murders? Some psychologists assume that sex crimes are initiated by sexual frustration, rape being the predominant motive and the murder of the victim being a practical solution to eliminate the only witness. But this explanation does not really apply here. Brady, in his early twenties, would have had no trouble finding partners for sex and he certainly found a very willing partner in Myra Hindley, who seemed to have very little reluctance in exploring fetishist/fantasy sexual acts with him, including being photographed in the process.

But it was not enough, even with a willing partner who was quite happy to experiment and try anything. He wanted to take things to a higher level and she wanted to go with him. So, sexually driven attacks of the type committed by Danny Rolling or Donald Gaskins or Gerard Schaefer are not really in the same dimension as Brady's murders. For Brady, it was the murders that were the primary motivational force. Any sexual acts associated with these events were almost peripheral.

2. MUTUAL SUPPORT

He had a partner to cover for him; they were 'natural born killers' who supported each other, provided alibis and, just by their presence in each other's life, encouraged each other to continue with the murders, even when they started to understand how their actions would change both of their lives for ever and with no way of going back.

She drove the victims to the kill sites, Brady did the killing (usually, not always), he buried their victims and then Hindley drove him home. He could not, and most likely would not, have committed the murders without her driving his victims to the moors and covering for him.

3. HE HAD A PHILOSOPHY

Most serial killers rarely have one, or, if they do, they are not consciously aware of it. He designed his murders as an architect might design a building. Death seen as a construction rather than a destruction: *'my existential exercise'*. Using analysis by hypothesis, he describes serial killers as *'creative architects of wrack and ruin ... [the killers] feel neither the desire nor the need to justify their "crimes" but rather regard them meritorious in themselves'* (2001). Here he is discussing Ted Bundy but he might as well be talking about himself.

4. HE HAD PLENTY OF RESENTMENT

And he certainly still does. There is no doubt about that. It is a smouldering anger that may well have ignited his fuse. He also had the ability effectively to disguise this, which is what made him so dangerous. His furious contempt for most aspects of human hypocrisy leads me to believe that his killings were initially anger-retaliatory, but, as he could not blow up the entire criminal-justice system, he struck out laterally and randomly.

5. HE PLANNED EVERYTHING METICULOUSLY

He was an archetypically 'organised' serial killer, so organised, in fact, that this is what ultimately got him convicted. This level of precision eventually worked against him in court by making him appear incredibly cold and calculating. His complex planning and recording of all the details of the murders gave the prosecutors more evidence than they needed to convict him. When this all came out in court, it was really just a desperate case of damage limitation which he realised would be highly limited in face of the overwhelming evidence against them.

Having been found guilty of the Moors Murders and been sentenced to life without parole, he was asked if he had anything to say before he was 'taken down'. But at this point there was really no point in saying anything. All he could think of was to mention a minor detail in the prosecution's documentation of the evidence chronology: 'Do you have anything to say, Mr Brady?'

'No, only that the revolvers were bought in July 1964.'

The guilty verdict had been passed, the murders having spoken for themselves, and his entire life was about to change for ever; it was all over bar the shouting (which has never really stopped since).

When Brady had been taken down into the court cells to await his transfer to jail, it was Hindley's turn to speak. She could not think of anything she wanted to say at all. At that point, neither of them was going to give anything away.

WOULD BRADY KILL AGAIN?

Is it likely that Brady would, given the chance, kill again? Probably. He has told me as much. I do not think that he would kill with the same MO used in the murders he was convicted of, or even with the same signature. But, if I visualise him behind the telescopic sites of a high-powered automatic rifle with some hated politician or despised Ashworth authority figure in the crosshairs, I do not think he would have much trouble pulling the trigger: *'Paintballing? No substitute for the real thing'* (2003); *'One (real) bullet can change history'* (2004); *'At least Columbine demonstrates that there is some spine left in America'* (2004).

One early reference to the power of a gun to change history came from a statement he made in the 1980s concerning former Prime Minister Margret Thatcher:

My favourite image of what her 'new spirit of Britain' opportunistic drivel inspires in me: I imagine her 'royal' waves on the steps of No. 10 – her scalp suddenly disintegrates like a rotten turnip, ending up on the pavement, resembling the fur of a newly skinned rabbit and her blood-spouting trunk buckles backward to join it in its rightful place – the gutter. That would be 'the new spirit of Britain' – an 'enterprising' individual with some initiative and a magazine of hollow-nosed, high-velocity bullets [Brady, quoted in Harrison 1986].

Negativity is paramount; it is omnipresent. Brady's life is something of a barren void. No future, a virtually hopeless present and a past that can never be undone. Brady had his proverbial 15 minutes back in the 1960s; now he is a dweller in a world that, according to his perspective, is immutable, irrevocable, irredeemable and basically rotten. Perhaps focusing on the grotesque aspects of the world *outside* of the hospital makes it possible to make the miserable conditions *inside* the hospital marginally less difficult to live with. A kind of psychological rebalancing, which is unlikely to work terribly well. If the life force is something more than words, he endures with no life.

Two years ago, I mentioned in a letter that I had been on a short trip to the North Pole on the *QE2* and described a storm crisis that had occurred where the crew had entered all of the cabins to lock the portholes when we hit rough weather. Brady replied, '*Impressed that they still have portholes you can open in the cabins, a perfect way of eliminating unwanted baggage.*' Then, later in the same letter, '*No offence, but pity it did not hit an iceberg.*' In my most recent interview with Brady, after discussing various atrocities he had seen in the media, he lowered his glasses and looked me straight in the eye through his cataracts and said, very clearly, '*I wish this place and this country and this world ill*' (2009). The words kind of hung in the air. On every single occasion where I tried to introduce anything positive in correspondence or during interviews, Brady would come back with a negative and bleak interpretation.

Having experienced the Ashworth environment repeatedly for myself, I did not find this hard to understand. '*Why should I care about anything in this penal pit?*' (2005). I have never met anyone so overwhelmingly cynical before. When he was talking along these lines, his comments echoed those of Wournos (see Chapter 7). The human spirit is not indestructible. 'The most powerful human appetite is a craving for meaning, if this is denied, it may turn sour or violent' (Wilson 2005).

It certainly did in Brady's life. We talked about sex and violence. Were his and Myra's crimes 'sex crimes'? There was a sexual element, yes, but that was not the primary motivation at the time. He is 71 years old as I write, so I doubt he has a raging sexual appetite, and I was certainly not going to ask him anything along those lines. However, he *does* retain a secondary fascination with weapons that came up over and over in his letters.

As with a lot of Brady's comments and conclusions about the world, it took me a little while to appreciate the irony. As I discussed in Chapter 2, most people seem to think that under the right circumstances they would be capable of serious crimes, including murder. Brady is contemptuous of people who overestimate their own callousness, even though he himself has admitted that he did so. He thinks it is somewhat ironic that people get upset when he suggests to them that they might *not* be capable of killing: *'There is no great gulf between the criminal and others except the will to enact.'* In one conversation, I remarked that I was having irritating problems with a petty bureaucrat I was currently trying to work with. Brady smiled and replied, *'Well, I've told you what to do.'* I blinked in surprise. Was he really suggesting what I thought he was suggesting? Yes, I do believe he was.

In 2004, he wrote,

> *At age sixteen I conversed with a Glaswegian serving in Cyprus during the EOKA* [national organisation of Cypriot fighters] *troubles there. I asked him if he*

would kill a member of EOKA if ordered to and why? Probing and demolishing every conditioned response, I finally had to offer the answer myself: He would kill rather than spend a few months in the glasshouse as a disobedient conscript. So his price being that cheap, he needn't feel morally superior to 'criminals'. A documentary last week had a soldier in Iraq reassuring his UK comrades: 'Don't worry, We've got permission to kill anything we want here'. This also excuses torture in Iraq prisons. 'Just following orders' which was rejected as a defence in the Nuremberg trials.

Is Brady an evil man? Good question. Define evil. Brady defines evil in relative and political terms: '*State-delegated authority is the natural refuge of the obscurely evil. The delusion of non-accountability/immunity nurtures or reinforces a collective psychosis. A form of grandiose mental illness of artificial power intoxicates spiritual and intellectual dwarves.*'

Here he is talking about Ashworth and the criminal-justice system: '*Awareness that the captives comprehend the self-serving corrupt charade naturally exacerbates the official psychosis, resulting in additional compensatory deprivations and restrictions being imposed to inculcate spiritual degradation and obfuscate reality*' (2004).

Assuming that you equate evil acts with conclusive proof of an evil person, then, yes, I think you can say Brady was an evil man at the time of his murders. As to whether he is an evil man now, nearly half a century later, I leave that to you, the reader, to make up your own mind. I have tried to describe to you why I think he has developed such a refined sense of nihilistic velocity over the years, but people change and I think it is amazing that the prison authorities have not managed to crush *all* humanitarian instincts out of him. After all, they have had almost half a century to do this.

'Good and evil might be presented simply as a matter of what we can get away with without sacrificing reputation. To all intents and purposes, the majority regard themselves as law-abiding, decent, god-fearing people, right up until the moment they are caught.'

Is Brady a psychopath?

> Psychopath; without heart, conscience, or remorse. Psychopaths think nothing of lying, cheating and stealing. We are aware of the extreme cases, psychopaths who commit serious crimes such as serial rapists and serial killers. However, we are less educated about psychopaths in the political arena [Smith 2006].

Basically, this term refers to individuals who are capable of recognising the harmful consequences of their actions but incapable of feeling any remorse. They see no reason why they should stop doing whatever they feel like doing whenever they want. When asked why they commit antisocial acts, a psychopathic response might be to say, 'Why not?' The term 'psychopath' is closely related to 'sociopath' but implies rather obliquely that there are some unspecified pathological undercurrents.

> *I am aware that the word 'psychopath' strikes harshly in the layman's ear, and that it conjures up all manner of horrors, such as lunatic asylums and the like. By way of explanation I should like to state that only a small fraction of so-called psychopaths land in the asylum. The overwhelming majority of them constitute*

that part of the population which is alleged to be 'normal' [quoting Jung, 2009].

Certainly, the Ashworth authorities have a vested interest in making sure the patients are insane. After all, there would not be a lunatic asylum if there were no lunatics. Brady has to be classified as an insane psychopath from their perspective, so throughout his incarceration this is how they see and treat him.

When anti-psychotic drugs are used on non-psychotic patients it results in drug-induced psychotic effects which can be conveniently interpreted as genuine psychotic symptoms to justify the original false diagnostics. In the mid-1980s I was wrongly prescribed an anti-psychotic, Mellaril. It resulted in the following weeks being a complete blank except for flashbacks of continually falling down [2009].

Mellaril, a proprietary name for thioridazine, is a piperidine antipsychotic drug belonging to the phenothiazine drug group and was previously used in the treatment of extremely overt cases of schizophrenia and psychosis. It has major central-nervous-system side effects, some of which the subject might never recover from. It can permanently damage brain functioning. With even mild doses, it results in drowsiness, dizziness, fatigue and vertigo. I will not go into any more detail here. All of this information is available in pharmacological textbooks and on the Internet. Suffice to say this is a hardcore drug for extremely serious cases who are totally out of control. It is almost never prescribed these days – well, as far as we know.

Whatever the possible effects that thoridazine may have

had on Brady, this would be impossible to test without doing a thorough medical examination using ECG, EEG, CAT and MRI scans and suchlike. These are outside of my authority and expertise. I am a cognitive psychologist, not a medical doctor, and, as I have only visited the man in hospital, I offer no claims of any kind of medical diagnosis or prognosis. Perhaps the best way I can tentatively comment is to run down Brent Turvey's (2002) checklist of what determines the makeup of a psychopath and relate each one to behavioural characteristics that I have observed and recorded from my interactions with Brady. Here is Turvey's definitive list with my related comments beneath each one.

1. *Lack of empathy, and inability to understand the situation, feelings or motives of others.*

No, I have not noticed this. While Brady is somewhat indifferent to other people's circumstances and almost always relates them to his own personal misfortunes, as in 'you think *you're* having a tough time? What about *me*?', that is not to say he does not understand other people's feelings or motives. He responds to acts of kindness, he expressed condolences when I mentioned to him my mother had passed on and suchlike. Someone with no empathy would not care less.

2. *Conning/manipulative. Behaviour intentionally deceptive for personal gain. This characteristic can be inferred when an offender uses deception or a 'con' method of approach to get close to a victim.*

When you consider his MO for the crimes he was convicted of, he scores 10 out of 10 on this one.

3. *Criminal versatility. This is inferred when an offender evidences MO behaviour that is suggestive of competency with criminal activity other than that typically necessary for a given type of offence.*

Yes, Brady would score highly on this one, too, although it seems reasonable to suggest that he might not have had this characteristic if he had not been sent to jail as a teenager, where he had all the time in the world to learn about criminal activity and a literally captive population of hundreds of convicted criminals to teach him.

4. *Failure to accept responsibility for actions.*

Brady, in court, being examined about the axe murder of his last-known victim (the following is directly from the trial transcription):

HOOSON (Brady's defence lawyer): Do you know how many times you hit him?

BRADY: No, the point was when I had hit him, I thought he would shut up. I hit him again and it wasn't having any effect. There was blood appearing. Then, after that, it was just a question of ... I don't know how many times I hit him. I just kept hitting him until he shut up.

Then, the next day on cross-examination:

HEILPERN (prosecution lawyer): You killed Evans. There is no qualifying that, is there?

BRADY: I hit Evans with the axe. If he died from axe blows, I killed him.

This clearly shows that Brady knew, accepted and admitted he was responsible for his actions.

5.*Glib and superficial. Terms that refer to behaviours that are done with little concern or thought, with intent to be evasive or conceal a lack of emotional depth ... The offender exudes an insincere and superficial charm as part of a con that is used to acquire a victim's trust in their method of approach.*

Yes, he would score highly on this one. If this makes Brady a psychopath, then it is hard not to agree with Brady's assertion that we are rubbing shoulders with psychopaths pretty much every day of our lives.

6.*Grandiose sense of self-worth. An offender's inflated view of themselves and their abilities.*

Yes, I guess so. Brady repeatedly told me that '*Intelligence-wise, I am in the top five per cent of the United Kingdom population*' (2009). And '*The peer group report compiled by over twenty Ashworth executive/medical administration unanimously conclude* [I am of] *superior intelligence*' (2009).
    Grandiose, certainly, but that does not mean he is not telling the truth. If Brady was not repeating these conclusions in order to get himself certified as sane and cognitively competent, the temptation would to be regard such statements as unnecessary and unflatteringly pompous.
7.*Impulsivity. Reactionary behaviour with little or no thought of the consequences.*

Here he would score 0 out of 10. Brady knew exactly what he was doing and exactly what the consequences might be every step of the way. He was, and tries to remain, very much in control to the point that it can be a little unnerving. If he was to score highly on this factor, it would put him very clearly into the category of disorganised offender. The fact that he would score zero on this one makes him an organised offender in every sense of the term.

8. *Lack of remorse or guilt.*

Remorse, yes, but who is the remorse for? Brady does feel remorse, but he is honest enough to state that '*the line between remorse for the victims and remorse for being captured can be somewhat blurred*'. He certainly feels remorse for what happened to Hindley, even after she shifted all of the blame for the murders on to him, but he does not necessarily agree and finds it hard to accept that she tried to throw him to the wolves in order to gain an advantage in her ceaseless and hopeless quests for parole. He still carries a torch for her memory to a certain extent.

Remorse for himself? Well, yes, but it is more like attrition, regretting crimes because of the consequences that have to be endured because of them, not because they were truly wrong in themselves from any kind of moral perspective.

Brady expresses remorse through actions. Most of his are derailed, refused or belittled by the Ashworth authorities. A number of years ago, he attempted to donate a kidney to someone, anyone who needed one; this was refused by the authorities. He spent over 20 years transcribing classical texts into Braille for blind people until the authorities removed his transcription machine, claiming it might be a dangerous weapon. He gives what little money he gets (and is not allowed to keep) to charity. The Ashworth authorities block this every step of the way and confiscate simple thank-you gifts that are sent from the charities he has tried to contribute to. It is ironic that people expect Brady to express remorse and then put him in a position where any altruistic action, no matter how small, is immediately stamped on and extinguished. As far as any public expression of remorse is concerned, Brady remains pragmatic and logical. He just does not see the point: *'It is just bringing up ancient history and revives, openly, old wounds and sores. Nobody is going to gain by it, nobody.'*

9.*Poor behavioural controls. Violent damaging or reactionary behaviour that is not controlled even when the consequences may be harmful for the offender. This may be inferred when the offender is easily angered or frustrated.*

He would score zero here, too. From what I can conclude, it is somewhat surprising that Brady manages to retain control given his circumstances. Within the ambience of Ashworth Hospital, it is incredible that he manages to retain even a modicum of polite decorum; but, incredibly, he does.

So, from Turvey's list of factors Brady scores very low on most of them. Such psychological checklists should be considered with a healthy degree of scepticism, though, as I am sure Mr Turvey would agree. Furthermore, results and conclusions are likely to fluctuate significantly as life events unfold. Nearly half a century ago, Brady might well have exhibited a different pattern of characteristics. People change, and I can present my thoughts based only on my experiences of visiting the man over the past six years. I make no claims to any medical conclusions.

The forensic psychologist Dr R. P. Brittain, having researched many cases of serial murder, discusses the expression of regret:

> He [the killer] will frequently express regret if asked, but he does not feel it, or, if he does, his feeling is only transiently sincere, is shallow, and is quite insufficient to prevent him from killing again. Such expressions of regret are commonly to create what he hopes is the right impression and one designed to achieve some advantage for himself ...
> He knows he is responsible for his offence but regrets only its legal consequences [1970].

I moved the conversation towards regret for what has happened in his own life and how it might have been different for both him and Hindley if they had taken a different path. He said,

> *The past being prologue it's difficult to know how the future would have evolved had we not been interrupted. We certainly intended to retire young or die in the attempt. Observing the steady deterioration of the UK, we would have moved abroad, returning only to slum and be reminded occasionally. However, had we stayed, it would have not been as passive observers. Enforced endurance and observation these past four decades confirms we would have known exactly what was required in many specific instances [2008].*

Ironically, Henry Lee Lucas – convicted of ten murders in 1985, although suspected of many more (and who confessed to literally hundreds of murders he had nothing to do with) – was covertly overheard describing both the motivation and solution with a rare flash of lucidity when discussing his compulsion to kill with another convicted murderer, Otis Toole:

> It is ... something forced on us that we cannot change. There is no reason denying what we have become we know what we are. There is no way of changing what we have done, but we can stop it and not allow other people to become what we have, and the only way to do that is by honesty [Lucas 1983].

Lucas died in prison in Texas in 2001.

People who have worked in hospitals and mortuaries washing and otherwise preparing bodies for internment or cremation invariably tell me that what is frightening is not the smells or the wounds or the decomposition or the rigor mortis, not even when the body suddenly opens its eyes, groans, expels gases or moves and sits half up. Such occurrences quickly become routine. What frightens them most is not the mechanics of death but the absence of life. Most serial killers have no such fears. Extinguishing life is part of their plan and in many cases it becomes their dominant driving force, at least while they are undertaking their murder cycle. The penal system and the secure hospitals do not help much, if at all. In fact, they tend to make things worse for everyone involved, convicts, patients and staff alike. Their concern is with warehousing, not rehabilitation. Plenty of individuals are following in the footsteps of the people I have documented here, and there are more now than ever before. The number of active UNSUB serial-killing cases is constantly rising and identifying and understanding them more accurately is essential. If just one single person can recognise someone they care about as being either a potential victim or indeed planning a murder, then my work will be worthwhile.

Freedom is a precious commodity these days. With serial killing, freedom is quickly and irrevocably evaporated. No one here gets out alive, as Brady himself finally admitted to me. The termination of life along with the possibility of positive advancement for everyone concerned (victims, relatives, killer, everyone) overshadows everything. As far as murderers are concerned, the people who commit crimes such as I have documented in this book can never be really free again whether they are captured or not. If we fail even to *attempt* to understand them, perhaps neither can we.

I guess it is only fair to conclude this work with some words from Brady. Regret came through clearly and frequently in nostalgic asides in his letters. I asked him what he dreamed about and he replied '*journeys mainly*'. This is understandable as the longest journey he can take now is three paces across his cell and back and two trips a day down the corridor to the force-feeding room. Travelling scenarios came up nostalgically in a number of letters:

> *Probably steam engines have given way to electric and diesel by now, the solid upholstered carriages replaced with sterile open-plan coffins. I liked staring towards the chugging engine, luxuriating in the back draft of smoke and soot and greeting the passing farmhands and animals looking up at our frivolous train in their quiet territory. On night journeys far off solitary farm*

lights always fascinated, inviting speculative reverie on who was sharing being alive and alert while the rest of the world slumbered, stealing an extra slice of life with me [2005].

When I left the 1960s the streets were deserted after midnight in the United Kingdom when people had real jobs and needed real sleep. Only an occasional copper on the beat or nightshift worker would pass by in the empty city canyon. I prefer those days to what I see now. I wonder if future old age pensioners will look back nostalgically to today? I always favoured secondary routes as more scenic at home and abroad. Particularly the old Great North rather than the motorways which we used only for speed. Always preferred after-midnight journeys from Manchester to Glasgow, road or rail: the trains entirely empty of course back then. Learned scenes of perfect content and well-being stick in the mind for no reason. Empty carriages with two-dimensional windows. The night outside and the reflected interior travelling together, nightscapes speeding past in constant juxtaposition, with comfortable reflection of whiskey and cigarettes on the seat beside. Or stopping at a country petrol station, strolling the gravel in mild night air, no jacket, .38 under waistcoat, gazing across dark fields to the black outline of distant hedges and trees, not a care in the world, just the freedom and anticipation of travel. A mood rather than anything else, the cliché of cosmic awareness, if you like, ubiquitous sentience.

Felt an earthquake last night after midnight, confirmed on radio this morning. Pleasant experience, only marred by its mildness. Lay hoping for an earthquake of apocalyptic proportions, knowing there would be no such luck. Such is the luxury of hopelessness when the worst is the best and what other people fear is welcome. [2008]

I suppose virtual journeys are better than none at all.

CHAPTER TEN

AFTERTHOUGHTS

The nature and gravity of Brady and Hindley's crimes has made both of them permanently unforgivable in most people's eyes, no matter what they might have managed to achieve after being convicted and sentenced to life imprisonment. In both of their cases, the sentence of life incarceration with no possibility of reprieve meant exactly that.

As I have mentioned, when discussing other serial killers Brady defines them as: ' ...*vengeful beings ... beyond the intellectual scope, imagination and experience of most ordinary people*' (2001).

Serial killers are highly skilled manipulators who are adept at assessing and interpreting essential aspects of other people's psychological framework which they then comply with in order to achieve their own goals. They have no compassion and they sneer at notions of morality. In our discussions Brady usually branded any suggestion of morality as being either hypocritical, self-delusional or simply evidence of blatant deception. Yet again, he elevates his perception to levels beyond which he believes the normal population are too dim-witted to even comprehend, let alone adopt.

While I have attempted to explain biographical elements that may well have influenced his development into a perpetrator of such serious crimes, as I have stated, Brady himself has no time for deep-rooted explanatory theories. It seems that enjoying killing was a good enough reason as far as he was concerned. Having the power to choose whether or not someone lives or dies can be something of a heady experience. An experience that the serial killer wants to repeat again, but each time *better* because it was not quite as good as had been anticipated.

Earlier, I mentioned the possibility that killers can delude themselves that, by killing, they somehow become *more free*. They have transcended the petty workaday drudgery of the 'borings' and 'normals' and have transported themselves into an elite realm on a heightened plane of existence. Brady and a number of other killers I have already discussed certainly seem to attempt to hang on to this crumbling shred of self-delusion.

Such a perspective does not stand up to serious analysis. Once a potential serial killer has murdered for the first time, they have more or less murdered themselves, whether they are apprehended or not. Any lofty ideals of superhuman choice/power are effectively destroyed once the murders start. The killer becomes just as trapped by their actions as any of their victims ever were. Then, when it finally dawns on them that they have destroyed their own lives just as effectively as they have destroyed the lives of the people they have killed, they realise that they have essentially marked out and dug their own grave 'Serial killers are deeply sad people who can take no joy whatsoever in anything they derive from life, seeing only unhappiness that reflects their own miserable state, both before and after they are apprehended' (Norris 1990). Shortly before his execution, Ted Bundy stated that his murders never really achieved what he wanted them to. His killings left him unsatisfied and depressed. Brady, when he discusses Bundy, mentions the same thing.

Some people – but I would not say *most* – believe it is possible to understand the causes and motivations of those whose behaviour might seem alien and frightening to us without identifying with such behaviour on a personal level. Attempts to try to understand the growing serial-killer phenomenon as I have tried to do with this research is preferable to me than choosing ignorance and hoping that these types of crimes will somehow magically disappear if we execute the perpetrators or lock them away and throw away the key. Recreational killing is a growing phenomenon that is simply not going to cease unless we try to understand the causes and effects.

Of course, there are emotional elements that can influence our perception and interpretation of the types of criminal events that I have described and psychologists are no less immune to these than anyone else, no matter how objectively they attempt to conduct their research. For the most part, people can usually see where the best interest lies in the situations they deal with in life but what people perceive is often inseparable from what people feel. This can be a stumbling block and I have come across this time and time again while conducting my research. Emotional reactions often seem to make more sense to people at a gut level than logical explanations can. I have lost count of the times I have mentioned to people that I have been visiting

Brady in an asylum for the criminally insane and that conditions are really bad there and they invariably say 'good' and then without even drawing another breath they say, 'What is he *like*?' This is not terribly surprising; people have always been fascinated with murder and mayhem and probably always will be – that's entertainment. People were brutalised and killed in Roman gladiatorial events in front of huge crowds; public hangings in England used to be very popular in the Middle Ages. A fascination with the darker side of human nature is as strong now as it ever has been. Lots of people head off to the cinema whenever a new Hannibal Lecter film, *Hostel* or *Saw* movie is released and vicariously enjoy depictions of extreme violence. The public gets what the public wants. But this is not to say that the millions who enjoy these types of films are budding serial killers – there is a fundamental difference between watching fictionalised violence and instigating actual violence in real life.

So what good might possibly come out of my research? My answer to that question is: perception, comprehension and understanding which hopefully might enhance prediction and prevention. If we can understand the criminal behaviour and more specifically the dynamics involved in serial murders, then maybe we can do something about the phenomena. What I have attempted with this book is to offer a multidisciplinary approach, converging operations. I had one big advantage here in that most of the analyses and theories concerning serial killing in the literature are based entirely on court and newspaper reports and are written by authors who have no access to the actual subjects they are writing about.

'Too often, research into the career and motivations of criminals is conducted by individuals who have never seen

prisons and asylums for the criminally insane make them terrible places to be. Being sectioned and then incarcerated in one of the 'special hospitals' is very much a one-way ticket. Many of the patients are never going to be released, and in a number of cases it seems that eventually the authorities concerned may perhaps not even remember why certain patients were ever admitted in the first place. However, I am a pragmatic realist and I am fully aware that Brady cannot fall into that category because nobody is likely to ever forget the crimes he was convicted of.

I do not believe that Brady and Hindley (and most of the other people who committed crimes of comparable magnitude) were 'mad' in the conventional sense when they were committing their crimes. To call somebody insane is an easy way of dismissing them. The minute you say that someone is 'crazy', they stop being human and lose all entitlement to the human rights that most of us take for granted. The structure and process of the criminal justice system which Brady endured as a young man almost certainly had an influence on his behaviour but this offers no conclusive explanation or mitigation. Brady was extremely angry and maybe he had good reason to be so enraged, but, almost without exception, both Brady and Hindley were in conscious control of their actions, at first anyway. When they first started killing they knew exactly what they were doing. They took their chances knowing full well what could happen if they were apprehended. We can endorse their incarceration and/or their execution and then rant about how much better off the world is without them, but that does not really take us anywhere useful. Alternatively, once we have developed successful strategies to identify people who might be heading down a similar route, then perhaps we will be better equipped to track them down and catch them *as fast as we possibly can* and hopefully before they start to get into a killing cycle (*which is critical*), then maybe we can talk to them and gain an understanding of why they might be planning to murder. Then we should be able to get more efficient at effective forensic detection when the next pattern of murders starts somewhere else. Unless we get smart or get lucky, and I prefer to rely on the former, there are going to be a lot more deaths. The retrospective juggling of theories and behavioural constructs certainly has a place but posthumous understanding of murder motivations is not much compensation for the victims. We are not likely to get terribly far if we limit our research to working backwards *after* the event. We need a focused, multidisciplinary *pre-emptive* strike if we want to save lives.

There are plenty of serial killers actively operating at this time. We cannot be sure of exactly how many but there are approximately 50–100 in America and perhaps around 15–30 in the United Kingdom, with plenty of others in different parts of the world – but these figures are *very* conservative estimates. Since 1980, approximately 25 per cent of all murders were 'stranger homicides' in which the killer has no obvious rational motive and no apparent connection with the victim. Many of these may never be apprehended. The other 75 per cent of homicide cases are likely to conclude with a fairly quick capture of the perpetrator. You do not need experts to solve these crimes; the killers usually give themselves up.

What I have tried to do within the limits of my ability and opportunity is to learn as much as I possibly could about that 25 per cent by using information that I have discussed with Brady, as well as from related sources which appeared to highlight similar patterns. It has not been easy material to work with. On more than one occasion, even with my objective researcher firewall set high, I have found myself being drawn in by material that can both repel and attract at the same time and there is no doubt that I have been influenced by the psychological manipulation that most serial killers can switch on and off so effortlessly. The whole project has been fraught with dangers that I never could have anticipated when I started. I was initially working with the belief that it is only by examining what we fear the most that we can learn to defuse those fears and the negative energy they generate. What I perhaps underestimated is the power of that negative energy. Of course, any mention of negative effects that my research might have had on my own life is usually treated with indifference or a reaction of 'What did you expect?' But please do not forget that I am not the one in jail for life for killing strangers. I am just trying to find out why it happened and why it is still happening in order to help to try to stop further tragedy in the future.

THE FUTURE

In this book I have perhaps given the impression that serial killers are devoid of all compassion and human feeling. This is not strictly true. Human beings require attention and loathe rejection. Ian Brady had no legitimate family he could be sure of while he was a child and Myra Hindley had unstable family cohesion in her early years. This may perhaps be important in that when they met, they finally achieved the attention they needed from each other. It is a tragedy that it all went so horribly wrong. Despite the indifference Brady claims to have felt for

Hindley and her fate, he cannot quite totally conceal the fact that in some respects he still cares. Even now, years after her death, she is still special to him. Other than the emotions of constant anger and bitterness he demonstrated when raging about the horrible conditions he has been living in for so many years, if Myra's name ever came up in our conversations, I saw different emotional flickers in his eyes. Guilt? Remorse? It is hard to say which and to whom it actually applies. Yes, he must blame himself as being the main protagonist in the destruction of lots of lives (including both of theirs) and, yes, she failed him after they were imprisoned and she turned her back on him and betrayed him. Although he is far too stubborn to admit this, I think he still carries a torch for her. Whenever her name was mentioned during my visits, this was one of the few times that I saw glimmers of human feelings, emotions that were in sharp contrast to the tough-guy persona he consistently attempted to project. Despite Brady's projected loathing and anger at the world, the prisons, Ashworth and pretty much everything, I found it impossible not to have some empathy myself. Technically, he has done his 'time' in terms of the amount of years he has been locked up.

Brady endured terrible things happening to him in his youth, but rather than trying to resolve them in a positive manner he responded by making terrible things happen to other people. But his crimes did not and could not cancel anything out. As with most serial killers, each of Brady's murders turned out to be disappointing and simply acted as a catalyst which resulted in the next one having to be even more violent and outrageous, and *still* he could not find peace. It is a tragedy; there is no other way to view it.

I am not offering any excuses for Brady's crimes and I never will, but the whole thing is over now. If I have possibly been able to offer some insight with my work, then this surely cannot be anything other than a good thing.

Dr Chris Cowley, January 2011

APPENDIX A

HOW TO AVOID GETTING KILLED

Danny Rolling was executed in Florida in 2006 by lethal injection. This was for the multiple rape/murder of five students. He left some useful tips on how not to get murdered by people like him.

Rolling specialised in home invasions. He would spy through windows on nighttime 'hunting expeditions', carefully locating the apartments where vulnerable women were staying. He would meticulously track the movements and routine of women who caught his eye for many nights before finally embarking on a rape attack. His usual MO was to enter the house while the occupant was elsewhere and then hide in a darkened room until they arrived home alone and locked themselves into their apartment.

Then he would take control and rape and kill them. Rolling was a huge, powerful, well-armed man who carried all the tools he needed for his killing with him (duct tape, knives, handcuffs, etc.). Before his execution, however, he came up with a checklist designed to advise potential female victims on what to do to protect themselves from anyone like him with a similar agenda. These guidelines might possibly be useful for students (Rolling's victims were students living on university campuses, frequently preferred hunting grounds for serial killers).

1. Park your car in the light.
2. Buy yourself a revolver, carry it on your person, put it in your handbag.
3. Buy some Mace on a key chain and have it ready when you get out of your car.
4. If your bedroom window does not have a screen, get one and nail it to the windowsill. Always make sure your windows are locked, preferably bolted shut.
5. Place a bunch of empty glass bottles on your windowsill.
6. Get some curtains and make sure you close them before undressing (as this can act as a trigger for an assailant).
7. Buy a deadbolt and put it on your bedroom door so you can lock yourself into the room. You cannot rely on the front door and the attacker is probably waiting in your bedroom if it is not bolted (make sure you have a telephone in your bedroom, preferably a mobile phone in case the attacker has cut your landline connection or could be listening in).
8. Sleep with your gun under your pillow; it won't go off by accident.
9. If someone bothers you, don't ever let the attacker get control. Fight for your life. Scream as loud as you can. Spray Mace in his face, kick him in the balls, scratch at his eyes.
10. Pull out your gun and blow him away.

'Take it from one who knows,' he says. 'It pays to be paranoid!' (Rolling and London 1996).

Some of these suggestions maybe seem a little obvious, but if everyone followed them they might well save themselves from a horrible attack or rape or even murder (a gun under the pillow may not be possible in some countries, of course, depending on firearms laws in force there). When Rolling was stalking neighbourhoods looking for victims, the little details such as the glass bottles or wind chimes in the window could be enough for him to change his mind about a particular victim and select the next one on his list.

Richard Chase (mentioned in Chapter 2) simply walked along the streets of Sacramento in broad daylight trying the doors of houses (most murders happen in the daytime). If the door was locked, Chase would move on; if the door was unlocked, he would enter the house and kill everyone there.

'If the door was unlocked, it meant I was welcome.'

So, something as simple as remembering to lock and or bolt the door can make all the difference. There are various other useful basics to follow. In rape-prevention exercises, women are taught not to yell 'Rape!' People are unlikely to intervene. Yell 'Fire!' and you will have everyone within earshot running to check it out.

APPENDIX B

HOW TO AVOID BEING EXECUTED

Bobby Lewis on death row suggested some simple tips on how to avoid getting executed if convicted of a capital crime in America (Lewis, cited in London 1993). I paraphrase:

1. *DON'T* do the crime. Although this is not always foolproof, Lewis estimates from his experience that approximately one in twelve people executed in America is innocent of the murder they were convicted of. Other statistics hover around one in eight, but, as we saw in the first chapter, it is very hard to verify facts from people mixed up in capital-punishment dynamics.

2. *DO* accept a plea bargain, even if you are innocent. This must be an incredibly hard thing to live with, but if your life is on the line and that is the only choice you have ...

3. *DO* commit your murder in the North of America. More than 90 per cent of executions are in the South.

4. *DO* have friends in high places.

5. *DON'T* be poor. Rich people are very rarely executed. 'If you have the capital, you don't get the punishment.'

6. *DON'T* kill anyone important. Lewis claims it is open season on ethnic minorities and in many cases there may not even be a police investigation if a black man kills another black man. The Alig murder mentioned in Chapter 5 was not even properly investigated for many months, even after the body had been recovered from the Hudson River in New York, because the victim was a Hispanic drug dealer. The police were simply not interested until the press got hold of the case.

7. *DO* be a woman. As discussed in Chapter 7, only a tiny handful of women get executed; hundreds of men do.

REFERENCES

Anderson, C., and McGehee, S. (1992), *Bodies of Evidence*, St Martin's True Crime.

Apter, M., and McDermott, M. (1987), 'Social Reactivity Scale'. (The Social Reactivity Scale (SRS) is a psychometric test developed by Apter and McDermott in 1987. It has been discussed in many psychology journals. One specific reference to it is as follows: Apter, M. J., Kerr, J. H. and Cowles, M. P. (1988), *Progress in Reversal Theory*, Elsevier Science Publications B. V. (North Holland).)

Baron, R. A., and Byrne, D. (1994), *Social Psychology*, Simon and Schuster.

Baumann, E., and O'Brien, J. (1991), *Murder Next Door*, Bonus Books.

Berry-Dee, C., and Morris, S. (2008), *Murder.com*, John Blake Publishing.

Bernard, T., and Vold, G. (1986), *Theoretical Criminology*, Oxford University Press.

Blom-Cooper, L. (1992), 'Report of the Committee of Inquiry into Complaints about Ashworth Hospital', Vol. 1, London: HMSO.

Brady, I. (2001), *The Gates of Janus*, Feral House.

Brittain, R. P. (1970), 'The Sadistic Murderer', *Medicine, Science and the Law*, Vol. 10.

Britton, P. (1998), *The Jigsaw Man*, Corgi Books.

Brown, D. P. (2002), *The Camp Women*, Schiffer Publishing.

Burnside, S., and Cairns, A. (1995), *Deadly Innocence*, Warner Books.

Canter, C., and Young, D. (2008), *Applications of Offender Profiling*, Ashgate Publishing Ltd.

Chancellor, A. (2006), 'Let Ian Brady Die', editorial, *Guardian*, 4 February.

Chisum, W. J., and Turvey, B. (2000), 'Evidence Dynamics: Locard's Exchange Principle & Crime Reconstruction', *Journal of Behavioural Profiling*, Vol. 1(1).

Davis, C. A. (2001), *Women Who Kill*, Allison and Busby.

REFERENCES

Davis, C. A. (2005), *Couples Who Kill*, Allison and Busby.

Darley, J. M. (1991), 'Altruism and Pro-Social Behaviour Research: Reflections and Prospects', in M. S. Clark, *Prosocial Behavior*, Sage Publications.

Donahue, J., and Wolfers, J. J. (2006), 'The Death Penalty: No Evidence for Deterrence', *Economists' Voice*.

Douglas, J. (2003), *Anyone You Want Me to Be*, Pocket Books.

Douglas, J., and Olshaker, M. (1998), *Obsession*, Simon and Schuster.

DSM IV (2000), *Diagnostic and Statistical Manual of Mental Disorders*, 4th edn, American Psychiatric Association.

Du Clos, B. (1993), *Fair Game*, Titan Books.

Erzinclioglu, Z. (2000), *Forensics*, Carlton Books.

Fallon, P. (1999), 'Report of the Committee of Inquiry into the Personality Disorder Unit, Ashworth Special Hospital', HM Stationery Office.

Fuselier, G. D. (1999), 'Placing the Stockholm Syndrome in Perspective', FBI law-enforcement bulletin, July, pp. 22–5.

Gaskins, D. (1993), *Final Truth*, Titan Books.

Gekoski, A. (1998), *Murder by Numbers*, André Deutsch, London.

Gore (1983), taken from
http://serialkillercalendar.com/Serial-Kilelr-quotes.html

Gregory, J. (2003), *Sickened*, Arrow Books.

Gregory, S. (2003), *Forget You Ever Had a Daughter*,
Vision Paperbacks.

Harrison. F. (1987), *Brady and Hindley*, Grafton Books.

Hoffman, E. V. (1992), *A Venom in the Blood*,
Warner Books.

Jamieson, E., *et al.* (2000), *The British Journal of Psychiatry*,
Royal College of Psychiatrists.

Jung, C. G. (1928), *Two Essays on Analytical Psychology*,
Routledge, London.

Keppel, R. and Birnes, W. J. (1995), *The Riverman*, Simon
and Schuster.

Keppel, R., and Birnes, W. J. (1997), *Signature Killers*,
Arrow Books.

Kirk, P. L. (1953), *Crime Investigation: Physical Evidence
and the Police Laboratory*, Interscience Publishers Inc,
New York.

Leyton, E. (2001), *Hunting Humans*, John Blake
Publishing Ltd.

REFERENCES

London, S. (1993), *Knockin' on Joe*, Nemesis Books (this volume contains contributions from Gerard Schaefer, Danny Rolling, Robert Lewis and Mark Defreist).

Lucas, H. (1983), in Newton, *Encyclopedia of Serial Killers*, Checkmark, Library of Congress.

Masters, B. (1985), *Killing for Company*, Jonathan Cape.

Masters, B. (1996), *'She Must Have Known': The Trial of Rosemary West*, Doubleday.

McGuire, C. and Norton, C. (1989), *Perfect Victim*, Barnes and Noble.

Morrison, B. (1997), *As If*, Granta Books.

Moss, J. with Kottler, J. PhD (1999), *The Last Victim*, Warner Books, New York.

Newton, M. (2000), *Encyclopedia of Serial Killers*, Checkmark, Library of Congress.

Norris, J. (1997), *Serial Killers: The Growing Menace*, Senate, an imprint of Random House UK.

Norris, J. (1993), *Henry Lee Lucas*, Shadow Lawn Press.

Owen, M. (2006), *A Miscellany of Abduction Cases*, Felicity Press.

Petherrick, W. (2005), *Criminal Profile*, Modern Books.

Pincus, J. H. (2001), *Base Instincts*, Norton.

Raab, S. (2005), 'Vincent Gigante, Mafia leader who faked insanity, dies at 77', *New York Times*.

Reynolds, M. (1992), *Dead Ends*, Warner Books.

Ressler, K., and Schactman, T. (1992), *Whoever Fights Monsters*, Simon and Schuster.

Robins, J., and Arnold, P. (1993), *Serial Killers and Mass Murderers*, Bounty Books.

Rolling, D., and London, S. (1996), *The Making of a Serial Killer*, Feral House.

Rosenhan, D. L. (1973). 'On Being Sane in Insane Places', *Science*, January.

Rossi, M. R. (2001), *Waiting to Die*, Fayard Publishing.

Rufus, A. (2003), *Party of One: The Loner's Manifesto*, Metro Publishing.

Rule, A. (2000), *The Stranger Beside Me*, Warner Books.

Rule, A. (2001), *Empty Promises*, Pocket Books.

Schaefer, G. J. (1989), *Killer Fiction*, Media Queen; 2nd edn (1995), Feral House.

Smith, W. L. (2006), 'Psychopathic Personality: The Absence of Conscience', online at

REFERENCES

http://ezinearticles.com/?Psychopathic-Personality:-The-Absence-of-Conscience&id = 348219 (2009).

Soering, J. (2004), *An Expensive Way to Make People Worse*, Lantern Books.

St James, J. (1999), *Party Monster*, Simon and Schuster.

Tilt, R., *et al*. (2000), 'Report of the Review of Security at the High Security Hospitals', Department of Health.

Turvey, B. (2002), *Criminal Profiling*, Elsevier Press.

Williams, E. (1968), *Beyond Belief*, Pan Books.

Wilson, C. (2005), *A Criminal History of Mankind*, Mercury Books.

Wilson, C., and Pitman, P. (1961), *An Encyclopaedia of Murder*, Arthur Barker.

Whittle, B., and Ritchie, J. (2000), *Prescription for Murder*, Warner Books.

Zimbardo, P. G. (1971), 'The Power and Pathology of Imprisonment', *Congressional Record* (Serial No. 15, 1971-10-25), hearings before Subcommittee No. 3 of the Committee on the Judiciary, House of Representatives, 92nd Congress, First Session on Corrections, Part II, Prisons, Prison Reform and Prisoner's Rights: California, Washington, DC.

BIBLIOGRAPHY

NON-FICTION

Berry-Dee, C. (2003), *Talking with Serial Killers*,
John Blake Publishing.

Blake, L. (1992), *The Encyclopedia of Forensic Science*,
Headline Book Publishing.

Canter, D. C. (1994), *Criminal Shadows*, Harper Collins.

Canter, D. C. (2003), *Mapping Murder: The Secrets of
Geographical Profiling*, Virgin Publishing, London.

Davidson, G. C., and Neale, J. M. (1986), *Abnormal
Psychology*, John Wiley and Sons.

Ford, M. R., and Widiger, T. A. (1989), 'Sex Bias in the
Diagnosis of Histrionic and Antisocial Personality
Disorder', *Journal of Consulting and Clinical Psychology*, 57,
pp. 301–05.

Goodman, J. (1994), *The Moors Murders*,
Robinson Publishing.

Hare, R. (1993), *Without Conscience: The Disturbing World
of the Psychopaths Among Us*, Simon and Schuster.

Jones, L. (2005), *Cannibal*, Berkeley Publishing Group.

Leyton, E. (2001), *Hunting Humans*,
John Blake Publishing.

Sereny, G. (1998), *Cries Unheard*, Macmillan.

Trombley, S. (1993), *The Execution Protocol*, Anchor Books.

Wilson, C. (1972), *Order of Assassins. The Psychology of
Murder*, Granada Publishing.

Wilson, C. (2004), *The History of Murder*, Castle Books.

Wilson, C. (2005), *A Criminal History of Mankind*,
Mercury Books.

Wilson, C., and Pitman, P (1961), *An Encyclopaedia of
Murder*, Arthur Barker.

FICTION

Some novels that I have found useful while conducting
this research contain some acute insights and relevant
quotations, which illustrate some of the psychological
tangles I have attempted to unravel in this book.

BIBLIOGRAPHY

Burgess, A. (1962), *A Clockwork Orange*, Penguin Books. Arguably one of the best novels written on the state of corruption in British prisons and in the National Health Service's 'special hospitals': 'Prison taught him the false smile, the rubbed hand of hypocrisy, the fawning greased obsequious leer. Other vices it taught him, as well as confirming him in those he had long practised before.'

Dostoyevsky, F. (1865), *Crime and Punishment*, Wordsworth Edition (2000).

Ellis, B. E. (1991), *American Psycho*, Random House, New York. 'There are no more barriers to cross. All I have in common with the uncontrollable and the insane, the vicious and the evil, all the mayhem I have caused and my utter indifference towards it I have now surpassed. My pain is constant and sharp and I do not hope for a better world for anyone, in fact, I want my pain to be inflicted on others, I want no one to escape, but even after admitting this there is no catharsis my punishment continues to elude me and I gain no deeper knowledge of myself. No new knowledge can be extracted from my telling, this confession has meant . . . nothing.'

Greene, G. (1938), *Brighton Rock*, William Heinemann.

Harris, T. (1981), *Red Dragon*, Dell Publishing.

Harris, T. (1988), *The Silence of the Lambs*, William Heinemann.

Heller, J. (1961), *Catch-22*, Simon and Schuster.

Kesey, K. (1962), *One Flew Over the Cuckoo's Nest*, Methuen & Co.

Zola, E. (1867), *Therese Raquin*, France. See www.SerenityPublishers.com

INTERNET

Be aware that Internet addresses are constantly changing. These were accurate at the time of writing:

Boyd, P. J., and Davis, R. (2010), http://realcostofprisons.org/blog/archives/alternatives/index.html.

This next site presents a multimedia presentation of the procedures and main conclusions of the Zimbardo prison experiments: http://www.prisonexp.org.